Take Two

Film Europa: German Cinema in an International Context
Series Editors: **Hans-Michael Bock** (CineGraph Hamburg);
Tim Bergfelder (University of Southampton); **Sabine Hake**
(University of Texas, Austin)

German cinema is normally seen as a distinct form, but this new series emphasizes connections, influences, and exchanges of German cinema across national borders, as well as its links with other media and art forms. Individual titles present traditional historical research (archival work, industry studies) as well as new critical approaches in film and media studies (theories of the transnational), with a special emphasis on the continuities associated with popular traditions and local perspectives.

Volume 1
Concise Cinegraph: An Encyclopedia of German Cinema
General Editor: Hans-Michael Bock
Associate Editor: Tim Bergfelder

Volume 2
International Adventures: German Popular Cinema and European Co-Productions in the 1960's
Tim Bergfelder

Volume 3
Between Two Worlds: The Jewish Presence in German and Austrian Film, 1910–1933
S. S. Prawer

Volume 4
Take Two: Fifties Cinema in Divided Germany
Edited by John E. Davidson and Sabine Hake

TAKE TWO

Fifties Cinema in Divided Germany

Edited By

John E. Davidson and Sabine Hake

Berghahn Books
New York • Oxford

First published in 2007 by
Berghahn Books
www.berghahnbooks.com

©2007 John E. Davidson and Sabine Hake

Library of Congress Cataloging-in-Publication Data

Take two : fifties cinema in divided Germany / edited by John E. Davidson
and Sabine Hake.
   p. cm. -- (Film Europa: German cinema in an international context ; v. 4)
Includes bibliographical references and index.
   1. Motion pictures--Germany (West)--History. 2. Motion pictures--
Germany (East)--History. I. Davidson, John E. II. Hake, Sabine, 1956-
PN1993.5.G3T35 2007
791.430943--dc22   2006100458

British Library Cataloguing in Publication Data

A catalogue record for this book is available from
the British Library

Cover Images:
Wilfried Seyferth and Elfi e Fiegert in Toxi (1952). Courtesy Filmmuseum Berlin.
Anita Gutwell and Rudolf Lenz in Echo der Berge (1954). Courtesy of the
Filmarchiv Austria.
Günther Simon in Ernst Thälmann‹Führer seiner Klasse (1955). Courtesy DEFA
Archive.
Peter van Eyck and Nadja Tiller in Das Mädchen Rosemarie (1958). Courtesy BFI
Film Stills Archive.
Debra Paget in Der Tiger von Eschnapur (1959). Courtesy of the Modern Museum
of Modern Art, New York (MoMA).

Printed in the United States on acid-free paper

ISBN-13: 978-1-84545-204-9   hardback

CONTENTS

oks Ltd

1
56

e think will be of interest to your journal.

; the Fifties
n a Divided Germany
vidson and Sabine Hake
07
Europa
4545-204-9
ck
/ £45.00 (hb)

pies to our Oxford office addressed to
w to publicityuk@berghahnbooks.com

REVIEW
REQUEST

Berghaḥ

3 Newtec Place
Magdalen Roaḍ
Oxford OX4 1ℝ
United Kingdoⱨ

Tel: +44 (0)18₄
Fax: +44 (0)18

Please find enclosed one of our recent titles

TITLE:
SUBTITLE:
EDITOR:
PUBLISHED:
SERIES:
ISBN:
BINDING:
PRICE:

On publication of the review please seⁿ
David Crabtree, Publicity UK or email

INTRODUCTION

Sabine Hake

The fall of the Berlin Wall in 1989 has profoundly changed our critical perspectives on the postwar years, and on the 1950s in particular. In the same
way that historians have begun to revisit and rethink the Adenauer era,
the Ulbricht era, and the Cold War, film scholars in Germany and in the
English-speaking world are now turning their attention to what must be
considered the last terra incognita of German film history. Until recently,
little was known about a popular cinema denounced by the signatories of
the 1962 Oberhausen Manifesto as shallow, mediocre, and utterly conventional. Their battle cry of "Daddy's Cinema Is Dead!" allowed subsequent
generations of film scholars either to ignore the period altogether or to
dismiss its films and directors as unworthy of closer analysis. Such indifference is no longer possible, or necessary.

German unification and the return of an unabashedly popular genre
cinema during the 1990s have brought renewed interest in the 1950s as a
cultural paradigm that contributed to the German-German division during the Cold War and that gave rise to the competing projects of nation-
building under socialism and capitalism in the mutually dependent
public spheres and political cultures in the German Democratic Republic
(GDR) and the Federal Republic of Germany (FRG). Whereas the ideological divisions of the Cold War are now a thing of the past, the 1950s seem to
resonate deeply with our own concerns about the place of the nation-state,
and of national identity, in a postnational world dominated by transnational actors and international events; about the role of national history
and high culture in a mass-produced global entertainment culture; and
about the promises and dangers of a multiethnic and multicultural society.
All of these concerns find surprising historical precedents in the ways in
which 1950s culture completed the larger project of postwar reconstruction by formulating its modernized visions of Germanness against the
legacies of the Third Reich and the threat of Americanization and by
seeking new sites of positive identification in the discourses of history,

memory, and nostalgia. The cinema played a key role in these transformations, confrontations, and negotiations.

At a time when the opposition of art versus entertainment has lost
much of its cultural capital, it would be counterproductive for a scholarly
project such as this one to present new critical perspectives on the popular genre cinema of the 1950s by setting up an artificial opposition to the
later art film movements of the 1960s. It would be equally misguided to
project our own concerns about the 1990s "cinema of consensus" (Rentschler 2000) on a period of German film history characterized by seemingly similar artistic and ideological constraints. However, in light of
many references to, and affinities with, 1950s culture in contemporary
film and television, it is indeed high time to take a closer look at that contradictory, heterogeneous, and multifaceted body of work and to examine
the overlapping trajectories of popular cinema, art cinema, and political
cinema that informed filmic practices during the long 1950s between
the founding of the two German states in 1949 and the building of the
Berlin Wall in 1961. Participating in the competing projects of political,
social, and economic restoration, postwar cinema must be described as
one of modernist experimentation as well as generic convention, of political propaganda as well as educational zeal, and of artistic ambition as
well as escapist diversion. A closer look at both the extraordinary and
ordinary films from the period reveals a film culture that deals with the
central issues of the period in much more complex and complicated ways
that previously assumed or acknowledged: the legacies of anti-Semitism,
Nazism, and antifascism; the consequences of war, genocide, exile, and
displacement; the promises of social mobility and mass consumption in
the West and the dreams of social justice and economic equality in the
East; and last, but not least, their competing visions of nation, society,
community, and *Heimat* (homeland).

It is as part of these revisionist tendencies in German cultural studies
and film studies that our anthology pursues two main goals. First, we
hope to familiarize English-language readers with a little-known period of
German film history by presenting some of its most successful films, popular genres, talented actors, innovative directors, and influential debates.
Second, we wish to expand the standard treatments of the period in significant ways: toward more contextual readings and historical analyses
(including institutional perspectives); toward lesser known genres and
stars (especially those with a transnational appeal); and toward greater
critical awareness of the role of popular cinema in consumer culture,
musical styles, educational life as well as social movements and political
ideologies. The format of the anthology allows us both to be selective in
our choice of topics and issues and to be suggestive in our presentation

of the broader implications for film history and historiography. There is no doubt that some of the readings and contributions are colored by contemporary concerns, and it is precisely with acute awareness of our own research interest in the period that we are offering a first road map for the surprisingly complex topographies of postwar cinema.

Since German unification, the scholarly interest in the postwar period, and the early Federal Republic in particular, has been propelled by the search for historical models adaptable to what might be called yet another moment of national reconstruction and restoration. The events surrounding German unification provided the historical backdrop for several early West German publications, including two exhibition catalogues by the Deutsche Filmmuseum in Frankfurt am Main (Berger, Reichmann, Worschech 1989; Reichmann and Schobert 1991). Most of the first monographs on the cinema of the Adenauer era maintained the divisions between art film and genre cinema, escapist entertainment and the kind of politicized film culture that had given the film movements of the 1960s and 1970s a sense of identity and direction. Written from an unabashed fan perspective and with an undeniable tone of nostalgia, some early publications presented the 1950s as the golden era of German film (Bliersbach 1985; Jary 1993; Seidl 1987). At the same time, much of the criticism of *Papas Kino* (Daddy's cinema) by the Oberhausen generation was confirmed in several studies about early film production and the role of film in (not) coming to terms with the past (Becker and Schöll 1995; Bessen 1989). Meanwhile, in the Anglo-American context, the growing interest in the postwar culture of reconstruction and restoration has coincided with a proliferation of cultural studies approaches that focus on popular culture as a privileged site of ideological inscription and identity construction. From such perspectives, the historians Robert Moeller, Uta Poiger, Hanna Schissler, and others, have challenged the prevailing accounts of the conservative Adenauer era and the conformist society of the *Wirtschaftswunder* (Economic Miracle). Heide Fehrenbach's *Cinema in Democratizing Germany* (1995) and Erica Carter's *How German Is She?* (1997) in particular have expanded our understanding of the mechanisms of fantasy production by situating West German film culture within postwar discourses of consumerism, gender, and public morality. In reconstructing the difficult relationship of the New German Cinema to the 1950s, John Davidson in *Deterritorializing the New German Cinema* (1999) has drawn attention to the discourses of legitimization and delegitimization that constituted German cinema in an international context. And Robert Shandley's book on *Rubble Films: German Cinema in the Shadows of the Third Reich* (2001) has allowed us to assess the great significance of 1945, the so-called Zero Hour, and to analyze the resultant myths of a new beginning within the broader concerns of postwar European cinema and its unequal and highly ambivalent relationship to Hollywood. The first studies on the history of the cinema of the Adenauer era have also had the (perhaps) unintended effect of drawing attention to the many real and imaginary border crossings between East and West in the decade before the Berlin Wall. With the collapse of the Cold War divisions, which affected film production and reception as well as film criticism and scholarship, many earlier assumptions about a divided postwar cinema can no longer be maintained. Consequently, the history of the East German film studio DEFA (Deutsche Film Aktiengesellschaft), which has often been treated as a separate entity, has now been integrated into the larger developments of German mass culture and modernity.

The rediscovery of 1950s cinema also coincides with, and is informed by, a reassessment of popular traditions and their contribution to the making of a national cinema. These tendencies are already fully in evidence in two recent survey texts, *German Cinema Book* (2002), a compendium of case studies edited by Tim Bergfelder, Erica Carter, and Deniz Göktürk; and *German National Cinema* (2002), Sabine Hake's comprehensive history of German film, which has been translated as *Film in Deutschland* (2004). A strong emphasis on the place of the popular between the national and the international can also be found in *Light Motives* (2003), an anthology edited by Margaret McCarthy and Randall Halle, as well as in the numerous articles by Marc Silberman and Stefan Soldovieri on genre traditions in 1950s DEFA film. The recent publication of Tim Bergfelder's *International Adventures* (2004) and Johannes von Moltke's *No Place like Home* (2005) and the ongoing research projects of many contributors to this anthology confirm the significance of the 1950s to the rewriting of German film history as both a German-German and a European narrative; the same can be said about the bifurcated film histories constructed by Detlef Kannapin for the 1950s, Katie Trumpener for the 1950s and 1960s, and Hans Jürgen Meurer for the 1970s (Kannapin 2005; Meurer 2000; Trumpener forthcoming). Working with such an extended definition of national film culture, this anthology is not only interested in film historical questions but also hopes to contribute to the theoretical debates on the transnational inspired by, among other things, the production models promoted under the heading of Film Europe during the 1920s and early 1930s (see the numerous Cine-Graph books on the period) and the expanded topographies of a hybridized European cinema (e.g., in the work of German-Turkish filmmakers).

Our first discussions about editing an anthology on 1950s German cinema go back to the 2002 German Film Institute on the topic, "After the War, Before the Wall: The Cinema of the Adenauer Era" organized by Eric Rentschler and Anton Kaes at Dartmouth College. Inspired by the screenings of rarely seen films and encouraged by the lively discussions during this workshop, we decided to seize the moment and put together an anthology on what we at that point alternatively called "postwar German cinema" and "1950s German cinema." In light of the concurrent advances in the historiography of DEFA cinema, we were particularly interested in including the East German perspective in the critical reassessment of an otherwise predominantly West German phenomenon. In response to our call for papers in the usual venues for historians, film scholars, and Germanists, we received more than thirty submissions and found ourselves in a difficult position to reduce the number of contributors to thirteen. They consist of senior and junior scholars, scholars from Europe and North America, and historians, film scholars, and German studies scholars, and they are representative of a wide range of critical theories and methodologies. This anthology appears in a film book series edited by Hans-Michael Bock, Tim Bergfelder, and Sabine Hake under the programmatic title "Film Europa"— a more than appropriate framework for the intellectual project undertaken on the subsequent pages.

The individual contributions reflect the anthology's overall orientation toward cultural studies approaches and historically contextualized readings. Arguing for the continuing relevance of the immediate postwar years for the diverging projects of nation-building, Jaimey Fisher discusses the central role of the discourse on youth and education by looking at two films directed by re-émigrés, the West German production *Der Ruf* (The Last Illusion, 1949) by Fritz Kortner and the DEFA film *Und wieder 48!* ('48 All Over Again!, 1948) by Gustav von Wangenheim. Continuing this line of argumentation, the next two pieces offer case studies of remigration, the first in the terms of film authorship, the second through the star phenomenon. Barbara Mennel uses a famous re-émigré, Fritz Lang, to shed light on two rarely examined connections: the close affinities between modernism and orientalism in Lang's status as auteur and the unique contribution of two of his later films, *Der Tiger von Eschnapur* (The Tiger of Eschnapur, 1959) and *Das indische Grabmal* (The Indian Tomb, 1959), to the self-presentation of West German cinema as an integral part of German film history. Tim Bergfelder examines the contradictory star persona of Peter van Eyck and what he describes as the actor's liminality vis-à-vis nationhood and gender to challenge two widespread assumptions about West German cinema: its parochialism and provincialism and its conservative identity politics. The next two contributors deal with two surprisingly adaptive genres, the detective film and the *Heimatfilm* (homeland film), to reconstruct the postwar strategies of remembering and forgetting. Thus Yogini Joglekar offers a close reading of Helmut Käutner's *Epilog: Das Geheimnis der Orplid* (Epilogue: The Orplid Mystery, 1950) to show in what ways a marginalized genre such as the detective film made possible a complicated reflection on knowledge and guilt. And Johannes von Moltke uses the contested topographies of the *Heimatfilm* on both sides of the German-German border to connect the seemingly retrograde fantasies of *Heimat* to the experience of refuges and expellees and their subsequent inclusion in the competing postwar projects of modernization and collectivization.

The experience of displacement and the desire for belonging also provide a thematic focus for the next two articles on DEFA cinema and on its own founding myths and patterns of identity. Moving from West to East Germany, the anthology continues with two contributions that show the repeated efforts by the DEFA studio to reconcile popular tastes and preferences with the political objectives of the Cold War. In his analysis of two fairy-tale films, Paul Verhoeven's *Das kalte Herz* (The Cold Heart, 1950) and Wolfgang Staudte's *Die Geschichte vom kleinen Muck* (The Story of Little Mook, 1953), Marc Silberman discusses in what ways the uniquely German tradition of the fairy tale was utilized both to articulate questions of social renewal and national identity and to mobilize these desires for the ideological divisions of the Cold War. Russel Lemmons reconstructs the production history of the famous Ernst Thälmann films of 1954 and 1955 in order to shed new light on the complicated connection between antifascism and socialist hagiography during the freezes and thaws of the 1950s. The interrelatedness of cinema in East and West is even more apparent in the only contribution dealing with a nonnarrative genre Matthias Steinle's overview of the representation of the "other" Germany in the documentaries of the Federal Republic and the German Democratic Republic confirms the important and often problematic role of nonnarrative forms (e.g., newsreels and cultural films) in the making of German national identity.

Returning to the nexus of politics and entertainment that sustained cinema culture in the West, Jennifer Kapczynski's close reading of Geza von Radvanyi's *Der Arzt von Stalingrad* (The Doctor of Stalingrad, 1958) connects the reassertion of traditional masculinity in the war film to the remilitarization of postwar society. Confirming the centrality of gender and sexuality to this process, Hester Baer's discussion of the influential women's magazine *Film und Frau* illuminates the close ties between film culture and consumer culture by looking at typical women's issues such as balancing career and family, organizing the postwar household, and reconciling old and new definitions of femininity. Carrying the political divisions of the 1950s into decidedly popular forms, the next two contributions share an acute awareness both of the overdetermined function of genre cinema in negotiating conflicting needs and desires, and of the importance of genre analysis in uncovering the deeper contradictions of postwar culture and society. Thus, in her Lacanian reading of R. A. Stemmle's *Toxi*, Angelica Fenner uses the filmic representation of an Afro-German child to uncover the libidinal investments required in coming to terms with the past and mastering the present. In his analysis of Rolf Thiele's *Das Mädchen Rosemarie* (The Girl Rosemarie, 1958) Larson Powell turns attention to the sound track and its self-reflexive play with modernist influences, thus also connecting the generic conventions of "Daddy's Cinema" to the artistic ambitions identified with Oberhausen. Finally, an overview of the West German film industry by Knut Hickethier shows the difficulties of restarting film production, distribution, and exhibition during the period of postwar reconstruction and adjusting economic practices and policies to the changing role of cinema in the public sphere. Our account of postwar cinema in East and West would not be complete without some recognition of the fluid boundaries that have defined German-language cinema since the introduction of film sound. Accordingly, Mary Wauchope's overview of the Austrian cinema of the 1950s not only confirms the close ties between the West German and Austrian film industries, but also complicates the divisions of the Cold War through her triangulation of what could be called a German-language cinema with particular regional traditions and perspectives.

This sequencing of individual contributions in a vaguely chronological fashion represents only one way of establishing connections around key issues and debates. Postwar cinema has always been, and continues to be, linked to the difficult project of *Vergangenheitsbewältigung* ("coming to terms with the past"). Not surprisingly, much has been written about the contribution of film to the narratives of humanism and antifascism in the East and of moral and economic reconstruction in the West. The significance of these questions is most obvious in the contributions by Fisher (on the question of German guilt), Kapczynski (on the representation of World War II), Joglekar (on seeking the truth after World War II), and von Moltke (on the depiction of refugees and expellees). At the same time, the instrumentalization of cinema in larger political projects is most apparent in relation to the Cold War, as shown by Steinle on the politics of FRG and GDR documentaries, by Silberman on the didacticism of the DEFA fairy tale films, and by Kapczynski in her comments on war films and remilitarization. Yet a similar ideological investment in the projects of postwar reconstruction and restoration can also be found in the cultural area, as confirmed by Baer's comments on cinema, consumerism, and the question of modern femininity. The discussions by Silberman and Lemmons position DEFA firmly within German film history while linking the approach to genre cinema (i.e., the biopic and the fairy tale film) to the specific objectives of humanist socialism and socialist realism. Questioning the category of national cinema, Bergfelder's case study of Peter van Eyck effectively dissolves the distinction between German and European film production. And as the contributions by Fisher, Wauchope, von Moltke, and Steinle suggest, the differences suggested by political borders were much less pronounced and the similarities much more developed than often assumed; it is the changed perspective of a unified Germany and unified Europe that has made possible these crucial insights.

Throughout, this anthology confirms genre as a key category in German film studies. Its centrality can be seen in the discussion of the *Heimatfilm* (von Moltke), the fairy tale film (Silberman), the war film (Kapczynski), and the detective film (Joglekar). The centrality of genre has always been recognized in the study of postwar cinema, though until recently only in apologetic or dismissive terms. Here Fenner's reading of *Toxi* and Joglekar's analysis of *Epilog* offer instructive case studies on how the complexities and contradictions of genre provide a space for hegemonic positions as well as for marginal voices. But genre criticism provides access not only to social problems and cultural crises; it also sheds new light on film historical influences and traditions. The remarkable continuities of genre are particularly obvious in the case of the Thälmann films (Lemmons), which carry the tradition of the Nazi genius films into the project of socialist mythmaking, and the DEFA fairy tale films (Silberman), which return to the cultural and pedagogical ambitions of Wilhelmine cinema. But as the contributions by Wauchope and von Moltke suggest, even a typical "German" genre such as the *Heimatfilm* defies conventional categories of national through its regional orientation and migratory trajectories and brings into relief the complicated relationships among the Austrian, West German, and East German film industries and their equally ambivalent relationship to Hollywood. Similarly, the West German war films responded to the wave of World War II films produced by Hollywood but, as suggested by Kapczynski, also followed unique German traditions in the representation of male subjectivity, a point confirmed by Lemmon's discussion of one particular political hagiography. And as argued by Mennel, even the postwar versions of orientalism cannot be understood outside the long history of a fascination with the Other reaching back to the Weimar films and their versions of Americanism and Film Europe.

Dependent on submissions, anthologies always create their own omissions and blind spots. Topics we would have wanted to address in this anthology include the institutional and aesthetic continuities between the Ufa (Universum Film-AG) before 1945 and the DEFA after 1945; the rise of new distribution companies like Gloria and Constantin; the restructuring of the exhibition sector in East and West; the history of smaller production companies like Herzog and Berolina-Film; the influence of Catholic and Protestant media initiatives; the function of film subsidies as a part of cultural policy and regional development; the impact of the 1950s freezes and thaws on the emergence of a DEFA-specific genre cinema; the appeal of popular 1950s genres like the medical dramas or the hooligan films; the arrival of a young generation of actors, stars, and celebrities; and so forth. Now this list of desiderata represents an invitation to others to continue the process of historical discovery and critical revision—a process that is bound to increase our knowledge of 1950s German cinema and confirm that period's pivotal role in the ongoing reconfiguration of German film studies and cultural studies.

Chapter 1

THE QUESTION OF GERMAN GUILT AND THE "GERMAN STUDENT": POLITICIZING THE POSTWAR UNIVERSITY IN KORTNER'S *DER RUF* AND VON WANGENHIEM'S *UND WIEDER 48!*

Jaimey Fisher

Early Postwar Germany and the "German Student"

The date 22 January 1946 was a day that would live on in early postwar infamy. In the Neustädter Church in Erlangen, Pastor Martin Niemöller, a former inmate of the Sachsenhausen and Dachau concentration camps (KZs), gave a guest sermon to two thousand students (according to initial reports) entitled, harmlessly, perhaps deceptively, "Lecture without a Topic" (*Vortrag ohne Thema*). In retrospect, the title seems either modest or misleading because Niemöller used his time in front of the students to deliver one of the most important postwar addresses on the question of German guilt (Glaser 1986: 95). The address, however, became infamous not so much for Niemöller's controversial calls for acknowledging the guilt of all Germans but for contentiously including an open admission of guilt before the victims of Germany between 1933 and 1945. In the early postwar period, the sermon was described, discussed, and debated much more often and much more passionately in terms of Niemöller's chosen audience—the students.

Both newspapers and Allied intelligence underscored how the students violently rejected the pious, pleading sermon. According to their reports, as Niemöller asserted that all Germans must acknowledge their guilt, he was interrupted multiple times by angry protests from the students (audible murmuring, then shouting and foot stomping); he was able to continue his address only because hosting officials appealed to the sanctity of the church venue (*Die Neue Zeitung*, 15 February 1946). Newspapers reported thereafter that an anti-Niemöller pamphlet espousing Nazi beliefs was found pinned to the bulletin board of the university: though the newspapers were (most likely due to preemptive self-censoring) elusive about the details of its contents, U.S. intelligence reported that it labeled Niemöller a "tool of the Allies." Indeed, Niemöller's argument, like that of the famous *Stuttgarter Erklärung* (Stuttgart Declaration) cited above, did seem very close to the Allies' official policy of collective guilt.

Irrespective of the sermon's controversial negotiation of the labyrinthine questions of German guilt, the focus of the ubiquitous press reports remained on the behavior of the students. One revealing report in the *Mittelbayerische Zeitung* segued quickly from a report about the address and its "admission of guilt" to a lengthy castigation of the students ("Sieht so die neue akademische Jugend aus? Störungen eines Vortrages von Pastor Niemöller," *Mittelbayerische Zeitung*, 25 June 1946). Particularly telling, in this title and the subsequent article, is the conceptual slippage from student to youth, a common tendency in this context on which I shall elaborate. After upbraiding the students, the report revealingly linked their behavior to Germany's problematic past: the students' protest and rejection of Niemöller was not a surprise, given how many former Nazi officers had infiltrated the ranks of those students. Another report, this one in the *Frankenpost* and entitled "Militaristic Student Body," was statistically more specific than that in the *Mittelbayerische Zeitung* and criticized the militarism of the students, at least 50 percent, but "more likely 90 percent," of whom were war veterans ("Militaristische Studentenschaft: Die Hochschule ist kein Unterschlupf für arbeitslose Offiziere," *Frankenpost*, 13 February 1946). The hand-wringing response was not limited to Bavaria: the *Frankfurter Rundschau* published a letter to Niemöller from the director of the Educational and Cultural Department of the Jewish community in Marburg—the indignant official likened the "events in Erlangen" to Marburg, where Niemöller was also scheduled to speak. He suggested that Niemöller's reception among students was not so surprising given the students' unrepentant attitude, and invited Niemöller, a "fellow sufferer" of the camps as the author put it, to speak not to the students, but instead to the Jewish community (Israel Blumenfeld, "An Pfarrer Niemöller," *Frankfurter Rundschau*, 12 February 1946). Thus, in a remarkable rhetorical move, a Jewish survivor proclaimed unlikely solidarity with the Evangelical pastor by casting them both as victims, first, of the Nazis and, more recently, of the Nazi-inclined students.

The considerable fallout from, and afterlife of, Niemöller's Erlangen sermon seems particularly surprising given a lengthy correction that appeared in the *Süddeutsche Zeitung*, among other newspapers, a few weeks later ("Von der Kollektivschuld: Zur Ansprache Pastor Niemöllers in Erlangen," *Süddeutsche Zeitung*, 22 February 1946). There were probably twelve hundred students present at the sermon, only about twenty of whom actively protested Niemöller's sermon. Even Niemöller himself disputed the initial news reports and rejected their vociferous emphasis on "Nazi" attitudes and persisting militarism among the students.[1] Why would this episode, then, draw such attention, evoke such hand-wringing, and enjoy such an afterlife? Because, I would argue, it executes a revealing and repeated discursive displacement, exculpatingly obscuring the central challenges of postwar Germany—guilt, Nazism, and militarism—to focus instead on one social group—the youth with whom the students were associated.

The reaction to Niemöller's sermon was so pronounced because, in the first years after the war, discourse about youth played a subtle but nonetheless central role in Germany's coming to terms with the past. The constructed discourse about postwar "German youth" became an essential means for Germany to stage and to narrate its transition from its own, suddenly dubious history; it served as a means that would propel and progress the culture out of the now tainted Wilhelmine, Weimar, and Nazi periods. Like that of the youth with whom they were deliberately associated, the crisis of Germany's postwar students became a cipher for representing a general crisis in German culture and society; more precisely, students as a site for a wider crisis served repeatedly to displace and to divert attention from the ubiquitous ruins of Germany society. By focusing on the young students, these reports about the students as the "new academic youth" shift the site of postwar contestation from difficult questions of guilt to manageable challenges of generational discipline, a discipline that would then also serve as a cornerstone for postwar national identity. Such discursive displacements and diversions became a crucial mechanism within the wider processes of *Vergangenheitsbewältigung* and, as I shall also argue, the production of German national identity.

In German studies and in cultural studies in general, a growing number of analyses have foregrounded the importance of youth and youth culture in the twentieth century. Recent studies, such as those by Ute Poiger, Kaspar Maase, and Heide Fehrenbach, investigate the role and significance of youth culture in the early FRG (Federal Republic of Germany) and (in Poiger's case) the GDR (German Democratic Republic) (Fehrenbach 1998, 2001; Maase 2000, 2001; Poiger 2000). Other works, such as those by Susan Wiener and Kristin Ross, have highlighted the importance of youth and youth culture in other Western European societies (Ross 1995; Wiener 2001). Almost all of these studies, however, focus on the importance of youth in the emergent consumer culture of the 1950s as young Germans were becoming an essential, if not the central, node for the translocation of such globalizing, often Americanizing, cultures to Western Europe.[2] Surprisingly, none of these studies considers at length the transition from the war—largely fought, at least in the cultural imaginary, by young people—to the postwar period. In this way these studies risk reproducing the myth of a radical break with 1945 and its alleged *Stunde Null* (zero hour).[3] A careful study of early postwar discourse about youth can augment these studies because it helps explain why the 1950s reactions to the *Mischlinge* (mixed race) children of American GIs, to global youth culture, and to phenomena like the *Halbstarken* (hooligans) became so virulent.

In this essay, I shall show how students and reeducation, particularly in the context of the debate about the university, became key ciphers for wider discourses about Nazism, guilt, exile, and, subsequently, Cold War politics. School and education constitute an indispensable yet frequently ignored aspect of cultural and social discourse: as theorists like Michel Foucault, Jacques Donzelot, and George Mosse have argued, it is precisely at the intersection of family and education that ideological battles about the young are often waged, battles that resonate constitutively with (adult) subjectivities, society, and nation.[4] In the postwar period, the discursive sparks at this nexus became all the more intensified because of the widespread social dissolution and the heated debate about reeducation in postwar Germany.

Although their studies attend to the function of youth within adult society and culture, Poiger, Maase, and Fehrenbach, for instance, overlook the ubiquity and depth of the discussion about German reeducation. Reeducation became a catchall term, a synecdoche for the occupation in general, so it is impossible to analyze the role of youth in Germany's 1940s and 1950s without attending adequately to the widespread and wide-ranging debates about it. At a time when the Allies subverted German sovereignty on nearly everything—government and society as well as economy and culture—reeducation became a site at which Germans could make a last stand in defense of traditional German culture. Youth and education thus also became crucial building blocks in postwar German national identity, which had to reconstitute itself on the ruins of tainted cultural categories. Discussions about youth, students, and education served not only to help Germans come to terms with the past but also, at a more general level, to reconstitute German national identity. In fact, coming to terms with the past via the discourse about reeducation simultaneously helped select and emphasize elements of German culture around which national identity could be constituted in the future. Discourse about youth, students, and education afforded postwar projects and preoccupations that conveniently looked back to look forward.

One crucial arena for these symbolically central discourses about youth and reeducation was the postwar university. As I noted above in the segue from students to the "new academic youth," universities count as only one aspect among many that together constituted the postwar youth problem (*Jugendproblem*, a term that encompasses, as well, orphans, family crises, delinquency and criminality, and elementary and secondary schools). But the university was an area that was particularly polarized and politicized, in large part because of the notorious coordination of the academy by the Nazis, the large number of students who had just returned from the war, as well as the participation of many professors and students in the public sphere. Two, almost concurrent high-profile films from the late 1940s deploy German universities and students as key ciphers through which to come to terms with the criminal past, the anarchic present, and the reconstructive future. Both *Der Ruf* (The Last Illusion, 1949) and *Und wieder 48!* ('48 All Over Again! 1948) provided stars of the Weimar theater—Fritz Kortner and Gustav von Wangenheim—marquee entrées to the postwar public sphere, and both of these well-known figures revealingly chose the university as the cultural core and battlefield for postwar Germany.

Both films demonstrate how students and the university offered postwar Germans a politically permissible arena in which to unfold both anxieties about, and an agenda for, coming to terms with the past as well as a future German national identity. The films are also revealing for their markedly divergent approaches: Kortner had been in exile in Hollywood and von Wangenheim in the Soviet Union, and Kortner's film foregrounds its links to American reeducation, while von Wangenheim's film claims the historical tradition of classical German culture and, more specifically, the teaching of that tradition for the emerging GDR. With the opening of the Free University in West Berlin and the subsequent protest by the Soviets, tensions around the university were rampant, and the high-profile storm of protest around the (more) open politicization of education in *Und wieder 48!* initiated the open antagonisms of the Cold War, which was also, as Poiger has shown later in the 1950s, certainly fought on a juvenile front.

Rebuilding the University after the "Catastrophe"

Even before Germany's unconditional surrender on 8 May 1945, the Allies' policy of *Umerziehung* or "reeducation" had become a catchall term for their attempt to control all "information" in Germany (Glaser 1986; Hermand 1986; Tent 1982). The expression thus included but also transcended what was normally understood as *Erziehung* or "education," such that it included the press and the mass media. In the American sector—whose policies eventually dominated the British and French sectors, particularly after the creation of Bizonia, the Western zone, in 1947 and after the currency reform of 1948 (Fehrenbach 1995)—the Information Control Division (ICD) oversaw the schools as well as all the press and media (Tent 1982). In the Soviet sector reeducation was similarly expansive, perhaps even more so than in the U.S. sector (Dietrich 1993; Pike 1992). In a manner probably even more pronounced than primary and secondary schools, however, the university became, as the Niemöller sermon implies, an important node for a wide variety of postwar discourses about the past as well as the future of German identity.

In a subjugated country reduced to *Kulturnation* ("cultural nation")—and, after the war, peddling a highly compromised *Kultur* (culture)—many intellectuals opining on reconstruction came to regard the university as the core of German national identity, as one of the great, if not the greatest, contribution of Germany to the wider community of nations. For instance, in a radio address published later in *Neue Auslese*, Karl Mannheim called the German university—in its national function—"the highest expression of the ideal life of the nation" (1945: 50). Mannheim compared the nation's universities to the accomplishments of "German composers," "German authors," and "German philosophy." Karl Jaspers, Germany's most famous living philosopher besides the highly compromised Martin Heidegger, celebrated the university's central role in Germany's past and future as *Kulturnation*. For Jaspers, the university could come to constitute Germany's unique contribution to the wider community of nations, where the university would simultaneously reestablish Germany as a national presence ("Die Verantwortlichkeit der Universitäten," *Die Neue Zeitung*, 16 May 1947). In a decidedly more pessimistic mode, Hannah Arendt remarked in a letter to Jaspers that the university "[is] the only thing Germany has left" (Arendt and Jaspers 1992). Despite the obviously problematic link between nation and university in the wake of the Nazi regime, Mannheim even argued that the universities should grow more "national" because the task of the universities now entailed vetting, even more carefully and deliberately than before, the national tradition for good and bad culture (1945: 50). For these and for other intellectuals, the university thus served as a key means for coming to terms with a complicated past as well as a cornerstone for postwar identity—one that would require, however, the compliance of students and faculty.

Kortner's *Der Ruf*:
The High-Profile Exile as Cinematic Professor

When Fritz Kortner, one of the biggest stars of Weimar theater and film, decided to return to Germany to shoot his first postwar film, the press reports were ecstatic that someone who so personified the "better" Germany would return to help rebuild after the catastrophe (*Film Illustrierte*, 12 January 1949). Vilified very early in the regime by the Nazis for his Jewish ancestry as well as for his theatrical and film work, Kortner left Germany in the early 1930s for England and then for the United States, where he worked from 1933 to 1949 with considerable success. The publicity materials on the film make it clear that Kortner orchestrated *Der Ruf* as a deliberately high profile homecoming for an exiled son.[5] Despite the overtly autobiographical overtones, however, Kortner chose for this triumphant return, in a work that would garner much attention as well as critical praise, to cast himself as a professor returning to his students.

Although *Der Ruf*, as the modest scholarship on the film tends to point out (Becker and Schöll 1995: 43, 81; Shandley 2001: 108–14), purports to engage anti-Semitism and issues of exile, its student thematic serves to dilute and, ultimately, defuse both. A film about a Jewish exile, more so than many films of this period, must raise issues of anti-Semitism, but discourse about students serves, as in the Niemöller episode, to displace and obscure difficult issues of anti-Semitism and guilt for anti-Semitism's crimes. In its attempt to negotiate exile and return, *Der Ruf* interweaves exile and anti-Semitism with pedagogical relationships that obstruct Mauther's resumption of his position in the academy and, more generally, in his home nation. In the following section, I aim to demonstrate how important discourse about students proved to be for Kortner's orchestrated return to Germany, to the film's subtle exploration of anti-Semitism, and to its tortured confrontation of the Nazi past in general. The parallel importance of two kinds of relationship—teacher and Jewish exile—demonstrates what I have argued about here: the importance of intergenerational and pedagogical relations to stable subjectivities, looking back as well as forward, in the postwar period.

More so than Mauthner's ex-wife, Lina, or his academic colleagues— that is, key characters in *Der Ruf* who remained in Germany throughout the regime—the film's male German students come to represent persisting Nazism, its aggression, violence, and especially its anti-Semitism. Like much of the Niemöller debate, the film establishes a close link between male German students and the Nazi nation, one that threatens the adult male protagonist as well as disrupts the link between him and the nation. These young males, here and in their later attempts to oust

Mauthner from his resumed position, provide the film's key continuity from the Third Reich to the present postwar moment. They are almost invariably veterans of the war, as I indicated in the Niemöller episode. Also similar to the Niemöller episode, there is a self-serving tendency to treat the students as the German youth, which has to be disciplined and redomesticated after the Nazi's indoctrination and wars. Even if these students were not biologically young, the emphasis on intergenerational relations—that is, on professor-student relations as father-son ones—confirms how the films and context emphatically cast them as young. The young men in *Der Ruf* are thereby rendered passive carriers rather than active perpetrators of nationalist and racist evils, because casting the youth in this dubiously central role dilutes their status as racist or nationalist criminals. The young also suggest an element of passivity, of victimhood, conveniently built right into the discourse about youth. When *Der Ruf* associates "young" students with the Nazi nation, it deflects guilt from adults and dilutes German guilt altogether, because it cannot fully be the young men's fault. A system emerges in which guilt and responsibility end up, like agency generally, highly opaque. In the suspect logic of the film, the students become Hitler's willing, but innocent, executioners.

Specific scenes reinforce this sense of simultaneous Nazi guilt and innocence placed primarily on students coded as recalcitrant children. After trying and failing to reconcile with Lina in Berlin, Mauthner takes a train on the final leg of his trip from exile to his home university (probably Göttingen). Two German students stare in at him aggressively from the car's corridor, and Mauthner comments sadly to Mary, his U.S. research assistant, "Do you see these two faces? They are exactly as they were fifteen years ago," referring to the time when he was driven out of Germany by anti-Semitic hatreds. One of the students, as viewers will later learn, is Walter, his own son raised as an Aryan, who fails to recognize his biological father. With Walter, as with many young people in other films at the time, crises of traditional paternity and pedagogy lead the young, especially young men, to a life of crime (see Fisher 2001). Thus, though these male students embody the persistence of Nazi anti-Semitism, *Der Ruf* depicts these students as the misled, the infantilized, and the victimized perpetrators of crimes. In this vein of exculpatory representations, *Der Ruf* is careful to stage moments that redeem Walter and that demonstrate that he has been led astray by his mother (who hid his true father from him), by his adoptive father (a Nazi general), and by Fechner (a teacher and kind of false father throughout the film)—not to mention by Hitler.[6] He may be the film's most important Nazi, but viewers also empathize with his complicated childhood.

(Re)Inaugurating the Professor,
or the Teacher Who Could not Teach

Climactic generational conflicts transpire when Mauthner finally arrives at his home university, the final destination for his return to Germany, where the film directly engages reeducation and anti-Semitism. In the first confrontation, Mauthner delivers the lecture about the "teachability of virtue" on which he has been working for most of the film. That topic and the lecture form the film's single greatest articulation of reeducation. In the lecture, Mauthner exhorts the German students to forget war and to embrace reeducational cleansing of their studies. The film's director, Josef von Baky, lets the lecture go on for five minutes, underscoring the film's heavy-handed emphasis on reeducation. Though the scene might seem extraordinarily long and wordy to viewers today, critics at the time—perhaps attuned to the pedagogical context—praised it ("Tragödie einer Heimkehr, Fritz Kortners *Der Ruf* im Marmorhaus," *Der Morgen*, 21 April 1949). This generational duel, however, concludes not in youthful submission to its elders, the lecture ends not in a rousing reception by Germany's students but rather in their silent protest and exit from the hall. The pedagogical break between the German classical tradition embodied in Mauthner and Germany's students seems complete. Critics at the time connected this sequence to the students' infamous reaction to Niemöller's sermon in Erlangen, a link made even three years after the Niemöller episode.[7]

The next generational confrontation pits Mauthner against an even more unruly student mob. This second confrontation that seals Mauthner's paternal and pedagogical fate—and that puts an end to any hope the film held out for *Vergangenheitsbewältigung* by reeducation—comes in a pub brawl. At the beer-hall reception for Mauthner's (re)inaugural lecture, Fechner incites a debate among the students by first speculating on the nature of Mauthner's "mysterious" relationship with his research assistant Mary, and then suggesting that it would have been better if Hitler had finished the genocidal job he had started. When Elliot informs Mauthner of Fechner's anti-Semitic provocations, Mauthner leads a wedge of the older academics into the mass rumble and berates the students for defending what Fechner said. But Mauthner never attacks Fechner himself: revealingly, the expected showdown between Jewish Mauthner and racist Fechner is displaced on to a generational duel instead. In this second public confrontation between teacher and students, Mauthner's pedagogical efforts fail utterly: when he wades into the melee to castigate the students, to reeducate them, he is confronted by his own, unrecognized and unrecognizing son Walter. When Mauthner thunders that Walter should

"Go home or else," Walter retorts inches from his face, "Or else what? Or else what?" In a moment of a supreme generational conflict at the center of the film, the viewer witnesses a stunning overthrow of Mauthner's paternal and pedagogical aspirations, a subversion of the protagonist's usually effective agency. Mauthner steps down, a final defeat of the journey started back in his exile home, a journey started on behalf of those very students who act to defeat him here. Elliot grabs Walter; Mary and Emma wrap Mauthner in a coat and spirit him home. The next time we see Mauthner, he is lying sick and immobile in the bed where he will die. The double defeat in this climactic generational duel—as would-be father and teacher—has effectively ended him, his optimistic return from exile, and his reeducational efforts that stand in for all the challenges facing the celebrated (diegetically and extradiegetically) Jewish exile.

Und wieder 48! The Postwar University as Cold War Front

Der Ruf echoes the kind of discourse about students developed in the Niemöller episode: the film displaces central challenges of the postwar context—including persistent Nazism, anti-Semitism, and guilt—on to reeducation and to other conflicts between the generations. In *Der Ruf*, as in the Niemöller episode, a pedagogical subjectivity becomes normative for this context in which the operable subject positions available to Germans were radically curtailed by the war and by the occupation. In addressing questions begged so obviously by the recent past, both authors and filmmakers turned to discourse about youth, students, and education to represent and negotiate issues that had become nearly unworkable. The fate of Mauthner's U.S.-based reeducational optimism, once on German ground, reflects the prevailing German skepticism and uncertainty about both reeducational ambitions and any other efforts at navigating the perils of the postwar period.

By 1948, however, reeducation in general and the universities in particular were becoming sites contested not so much between Allied occupiers and Germans occupied as between the Soviets and the Western forces. The year 1948 was a watershed in which "Trizonia," as the loose alliance among the U.S., British, and French zones was informally called, congealed around the June 1948 currency reform; the subsequent blockade of Berlin hardened polarized positions and provoked open aggressions between "East" and "West." Given the prominent role that reeducation and the university in particular had played in early postwar discourse, it is not surprising that the university became, in this context as well, a political, social, and cultural flash point for these variegated tensions. If the Niemöller sermon and a film like *Der Ruf* confirm the centrality of the university and students for Germany's coming to terms with the past, then the 1948 controversy about Berlin universities and a film like *Und wieder 48!* demonstrate how important the university and students would continue to be within wider German culture as they became important fronts in the coalescing Cold War.

Wandering Students and the Vagaries of German History

As Gustav von Wangenheim's first film after the war, *Und wieder 48!* was, like Kortner's *Der Ruf*, taken to be a major statement by an important cultural figure bringing all his exile experience and insight to bear on Germany's postwar plight (Walter Lenning, "Über ein Jahrhundert hinweg:. . . . *und wieder 48* im Babylon uraufgeführt," *Berliner Zeitung*, 7 November 1948). Remarkably, von Wangenheim also chose to negotiate problems of the recent past and to present reconstruction via discourse about education, students, and youth. The precise terms of this film's deployment of students in the academy is, in many ways, surprisingly similar to that of *Der Ruf*: both Kortner and von Wangenheim focus on the "problem of the young," in this context usually meaning the lack of trust between the disillusioned youth and their elders. More precisely, the relationship between the generations in *Und wieder 48!* serves, as it did in *Der Ruf*, as a synecdoche for Germany's relationship to its history, both near and distant.

In *Der Ruf*, Mauthner remarks that the students' aggressive posturing toward him is the "same as it was fifteen years ago," suggesting a mangled relationship on the part of the students to Germany's recent history. *Und wieder 48!* also foregrounds the relationship between students and history, a relationship that provides the film with its overarching conceit. *Und wieder 48!* follows a group of students that has been hired—at a time of radical un- and underemployment—to serve as extras on a film about the 1848 revolution. The film opens with the shooting of this film within a film, which treats the events of the famously aborted revolution as comic absurdity. *Und wieder 48!* subsequently proceeds on dual temporal tracks, cutting (occasionally panning) between 1848 sets and those of the postwar ruins of Germany in a fashion that was heralded as "dialectical" by critics in the Soviet zone ("Hundert Jahre wie ein Tag: Wie Wangenheims Film *Und wieder 48* entsteht," *Berliner Zeitung*, 28 March 1948). For both films, such engagement with German classical culture, as characters look back to the past to come to terms with the present, helps select and celebrate certain elements of Germany's traditions for the constitution of future German national identity.

During the shooting of the 1848 comedy, one of the student extras, Else Weber (played by von Wangenheim's wife, Inge), disagrees vociferously about the nature of the 1848 events, taking to task both the film's director and apathetic students blithely happy to supplement their incomes by appearing in the film. One medical student, Heinz (played by Ernst Wilhelm Borchert, of Mertens fame in *Die Mörder sind unter uns* [The Murderers Are among Us, 1946]), resists Else's "progressive" interpretation of the 1848 events, agreeing with the director that the events were absurd. *Und wieder 48!* thereafter tracks not only the students' performance in the film within a film, but also stages an historical debate between those students dismissive of Germany's history (and by implication politics) and those engaged with, and committed to, the nation's (occasionally) progressive traditions.

In this emphasis on students and history, *Und wieder 48!* relies, like *Der Ruf*, on a dual representation of the student: the film contrasts the historically and politically committed Else to the problematically apathetic Heinz. At a time when it was difficult or discouraged to represent the postwar's most obvious conflicts—between Nazis and better Germans or between the Nazis and the Allies or even between returning soldiers and their wives—the conflicts between generations and among students served usefully and often paradigmatically. More precisely, in a cultural context in which it was essential to represent politically compromised characters but also to redeem them, the negatively coded student as young person served perfectly: as I underscored with the Niemöller episode and in *Der Ruf*, the public sphere was full of self-serving critiques of the young, but coding students as emphatically young rendered them likewise malleable, teachable, above all rehabilitable, just as they prove to be in these two films. Interestingly, *Und wieder 48!* similarly problematizes the male student and proscribes, in contrast to *Der Ruf*, a female student to remedy what ails the German young man. Tellingly for this context, the tension between them, albeit gendered, is not romantic, but rather educational.

Politicizing Postwar Universities

While Mauthner undertakes a deliberate attempt to restore the trust of the students in Germany's classical tradition, Else tries to restore the students' faith in Germany's "better" history, a history brushing against the grain of, as Else puts it succinctly, the "the Prusso-German legend." In discussing their films, both Kortner and von Wangenheim were careful to mention the ruptured relationship of the students to Germany's historical tradition as motivating factors in their respective films (respectively, "Fritz Kortner diskutiert über *Der Ruf*," *Die neue Filmwoche*, 14 May 1949; "Hundert Jahre wie ein Tag: Wie Wangenheims Film *Und wieder 48* entsteht," *Berliner Zeitung*, 28 March 1948). In both cases, this ruined relationship becomes a synecdoche for German culture's more general coming to terms with the past in the postwar period. But the differences therein—reestablishing the tradition of German *Bildung* (education) versus faith in the revolutionary potential of Germany—were growing increasingly resonant in the political and cultural events of late 1947 and 1948, when *Und wieder 48!* was shot and released. Events in the Soviet and in the Western zones exacerbated political and cultural tensions such that *Und wieder 48!* manifests markers of these rapidly emerging discursive changes, changes hardening into the ossified positions of the Cold War.

For the first few years of the occupation, the Soviets had been careful, like the Western allies, to acknowledge the traditional autonomy of the German university. Just as in the Western zones, the Soviets believed that the university was instrumental in their efforts to remake Germany, particularly in their articulated goals to produce a new German intelligentsia, and so were careful to honor its traditions (Naimark 1995: 441). In the early years of the occupation (1946–47), this honoring of the traditions of the German university was intertwined with a more general tolerance for things German as part of the "German" (i.e., non-Soviet) road to socialism, a peaceful and expansive path Soviet officials hoped would attract Germans from the other zones (Pike 1992: 250). But by late 1947, the Soviets had grown increasingly dissatisfied with these policies in general and with the university in particular. Reports from the end of 1947, in fact, revealed an increasing frustration with the effectiveness of the SED (Sozialistische Einheitspartei) party in the university, with its inroads into either students or faculty. Some accounts told of student members of the SED being beaten up at the university; others complained primarily about these party members' apathy in recruiting other students for the party (Naimark 1995: 445–46). In the context of the debate about the "German student," these worries resonated with general concerns about students' political indifference, but also reflected the growing conviction that more aggressive political persuasion within the university was called for. At the end of 1947 and at the beginning of 1948, there was to be increasing cultivation of the German university as a resource for the SED party, which itself, in the twilight of the policy of "national" roads to socialism, was being recast in a more Soviet mode (Pike 1992: 359).

Not coincidentally, it was in the spring of 1948 that these issues came to a head with the Western allies, who had already been piqued by the Soviet's taking unilateral control of the famous Berlin University (later the Humboldt University) (Tent 1982: 288). Suspicions about the cooption of universities were spreading rapidly among both Soviet and U.S. officials: the Soviets were convinced that U.S. "agents" among their students were impeding SED recruitment, while U.S. officials were convinced that the Soviets had turned the university into a "breeding ground of hatred of the United States" (Tent 1982: 289). In light of their concern about an SED-dominated university, U.S. officials had already initiated and fostered numerous discussions on founding a new research university that would circumvent both the academy's traditional autonomy as well as more recent SED control (Tent 1982: 286–87).

The mutual suspicions and reciprocating tensions exploded, unsurprisingly, in Berlin, where—besides the obvious symbolic centrality of the four-power capital—the ability of students from the Western zones to study at the Berlin University exacerbated matters. On 16 April 1948, the SED-controlled Berlin University expelled three students for "publication activity that acts counter to the good manners and dignity of a student," an action that cut at the traditional political autonomy of the university and its community (Tent 1982: 288). Large student protests followed a week later, and U.S. officials quickly capitalized on this groundswell of student discontent to call for a new, "free" university in their own sector of Berlin. Even as the Berlin University (and therefore the SED) made "extraordinary efforts" to conciliate the students, U.S. officials continued to exploit the initial student criticisms of the Soviet-sector university (Tent 1982: 293). As James Tent notes, the founding of the "Free" university, was unusual in that its founders were "students, politicians, journalists, and businessmen" (297) rather than faculty or academic administrators. Against the wishes of the Soviets and original inclinations of the British, the United States was happy to encourage and ultimately to enable the Germans inclined to founding a new university. The military governor Lucius Clay himself put aside RM 20 million—worth DM 2 million after the June currency reform—for the new Free University of Berlin, a U.S.-subsidized and fostered, if not entirely initiated, shot across the Soviet reeducational bow.

Restaging 48 at the Cold War University

It was against this tense political and cultural backdrop that *Und wieder 48!* was shot and released: in fact, the week it premiered in Berlin was the same week in which the Free University celebrated its official opening, astoundingly a mere seven months after the student protests. These events, particularly the SED's new commitment to recruiting more students, helps explain the general conceit of the film, namely, a history student who insists on persuading disillusioned and apathetic students around her. The early Cold War context also illuminates more subtle aspects of the film, for instance, the film's historical interpretation of events in 1848, its deliberate critique of the film director within the film, as well as the casting of Ernst Wilhelm Borchert in the role of a politically indifferent medical student.

In his account of Soviet cultural policy between 1945 and 1949, David Pike describes how the "doctrinal" changes of late 1947 and 1948 galvanized (and instrumentalized) a new interpretation of the historical past (1992: 394–96). Foremost among these was a new interest in the revolution of 1848, particularly the complex relations between bourgeois and working-class elements in the ill-fated events. The topic became so important that the SED offered evening courses on the "Bourgeois Revolution of 1848"; also revealing were sudden discussions of Karl Marx's *Communist Manifesto*, whose class-emphatic approach had been avoided in the "national unity" years of 1945–47. As I just noted, these wider discursive changes dovetailed with evolving policy on the university, in this case as Soviet and German officials were taking much more seriously the threat of "bourgeois" elements to effective recruitment within the university (Naimark 1995: 444). In this light, it is telling and revealing not only that *Und wieder 48!* utilizes 1848 as a means for student conversion and recruitment, but that Else comes from a working-class background and that her historical interpretation highlights, against the conventional historical wisdom, the active role of students rather than the bourgeoisie in the revolution of 1848. The general plot lines, the specific character backgrounds, and the peculiarities of German history all resonate with new SED efforts to recruit students and faculty they had found surprisingly obstinate in their independence.

This new stance toward "bourgeois" elements informed not only the film's position toward the academy, but also toward filmmaking. Earlier in the occupation (1945–47), in fostering a "national unity" front that would rehabilitate artists from a diversity of backgrounds, Soviet and later DEFA officials had been willing to recruit "bourgeois" directors long before the Western allies (Mückenberger and Jordan 1994: 34). This openness helped DEFA produce the first postwar feature, *Die Mörder sind unter uns* (The Murderers Are Among Us, 1946), well before any U.S. licensed feature. In fact, U.S. officials had told Wolfgang Staudte, the director of *Die Mörder sind unter uns*, that it would be twenty years before a German was again allowed to make a feature film (Mückenberger and Jordan 1994: 22). *Die Mörder sind unter uns* reflects this broad definition of "national unity" both in the political and economic background of Staudte (who had acted in UFA productions before 1945) and in its content (a protagonist who is a medical doctor). The film's bourgeois protagonist was in fact circuitously criticized when later DEFA films more committed to working class-milieus, like *Irgendwo in Berlin* (Somewhere in Berlin, 1946) and *Rotation* (1949), were released. By the time of *Und wieder 48!* class perspectives were hardening, such that Else's disagreement with a bourgeois film director seems a deliberately staged departure from, even a critique of, the early years of DEFA. Revealing in this context, too, is the curious casting of Borchert as a medical student insulated from progressive interpretations of German history. Borchert was one of DEFA's best-known actors for his work in *Die Mörder sind unter uns*, but his role in *Und wieder 48!* offers what seems a deliberate reprisal and revision of his most famous character: here he is an apolitical and apathetic medical student who learns lessons of Germany's progressive history from a fellow working-class student at the university. Here, revealingly, the tensions with the female lead are more educational than in *Mörder sind unter uns*, though Else, like Susanne, ultimately has a felicitously civilizing impact on the wayward male. His comparisons between German history and human anatomy on his medical exams actually raise his exam grades and, presumably, improve (as well as rejuvenate by juvenilizing) the memorable Mertens from *Die Mörder sind unter uns*.

Conclusion: Conditioning the German Student for the Cold War

Among the thoroughgoing political changes in 1948, Soviet and SED officials made a new commitment to reforming the "student type." Paramount among these changes was the kind of student to be admitted to the university. Soviet officials had declared early in the occupation that they would admit more students from worker and farmer backgrounds, but the numbers of such students had remained relatively small (albeit much higher than in the Western zones) (Naimark 1995: 445). In 1947–48, Soviet and SED officials became more determined than ever to admit more students from such backgrounds because it seemed, increasingly, a mistake to have admitted so many, as Naimark puts it, "representatives of the bourgeoisie and petit bourgeoisie," of which *Und wieder 48!*'s Heinz is certainly one (1995: 444).

Both the film and the publicity materials used to market it subsequently heralded the new type of student that Else represented. Here, too, her gender is relevant as a revision of the ubiquitous stereotype— familiar from the Niemöller episode—of the politically apathetic male veteran as university student. At the moment Berlin was being polarized by the blockade of provisions and hardening of positions—a city polarized, as one article put it, "in politics, in press, even in film-going audiences"—Else was rolled out as the perfect representative of "this side" of the growing political and cultural gap (Steinhauer 1948: 25). Doggedly toiling away at her studies while supporting her sister and her nephew, maintaining a *Gefühlskälte* (coldness of feeling) over the loss of her own husband and child, Else remained an engaged student committed to becoming a teacher. Her pedantic posture and professional ambitions throughout the film reinforce, like Kortner's Mauthner in *Der Ruf*, a teacherly posture as the preferred subject position in an environment of severely limited options. But zonal differences in the pedagogue were also growing clearer: two articles featuring *Und wieder 48!* opened by contrasting Inge von Wangenheim's Else with conventional film stars, stars already making their appearances in Western sectors films like *Und über uns der Himmel* (And the Sky above Us, 1947), *Wege im Zwielicht* (Paths in Twilight, 1948), and *Der Ruf*, in which Hans Albers, Gustav Fröhlich, and Fritz Kortner starred, respectively (see Fisher 2004).

At the end of December 1948, at the conclusion of this tumultuous political and cultural year, a guest column in the *Tagesspiegel* (West-Berlin) celebrated "the Berlin student" as the paradigm for the new Berliner. Not only had Berlin students been compelled to endure the hardship of all Berliners during the blockade but they had even rejected the tempting traditions of Berlin University, where studying would mean inevitable service as a "Soviet mouthpiece" (Hans-Joachim Boehm, "Der freiheitliche Typus," *Tagesspiegel*, 30 December 1948). Almost three years after the Niemöller episode, German students were still at the center of political and cultural debates, confirming the continuing symbolic centrality of universities and students for this context in general. In this evolving environment, however, new battle lines were rapidly being drawn. No longer did students serve simply as a convenient, constitutive contrast to the wise elders embodying a better, lost, *Bildungsbürger* (educated citizen) or Christian Germany. The discourse about students and higher education was landing in an altogether different place: in late 1948 and in the middle of the Berlin university crisis, critics in the Western zones attacked the propagandistic use of the students and universities in *Und wieder 48!* to whose defense Soviet zone critics quickly rose (Menter 1948: 1458). One "Eastern" critic claimed that *Und wieder 48!* was the only postwar feature to represent the "new academic youth," but this essay ought to make clear just what a discursively contested site the postwar student as youth was (Hans Ulrich Eylau, "*Und wieder 48:* Der Revolutions-Gedenkfilm der DEFA im Babylon," *Tägliche Rundschau*, 9 November 1948). Young people had figured prominently in coming to terms with the recent past and German guilt, and now students were deployed on the front lines of the coalescing Cold War. Early postwar discourse about youth displaced and diverted various postwar crises and thereby served as a cornerstone for coming to terms with both the past and the future of German national identity. It was, moreover, mechanisms such as these that lent youth, students, and education an explosive potential that provoked the well-documented, histrionic response to the *Mischlinge* and *Halbstarken* in the 1950s.

Notes

1. "Die Folgerungen, die in den Zeitungsartikeln meistens aus den Vorgängen gezogen werden, kann ich nicht ziehen, wonach die Dissentierenden gewissermassen als verkappte Nazis oder unverbesserliche Militaristen hingestellt werden." See Martin Niemöller, Letter to the Rector of the University of Erlangen, quoted in Hay et al. 1973: 174. All translations are mine unless noted otherwise.
2. Although Fehrenbach does address, in part, an earlier moment in the occupational period, she does not attend to discourse about youth as it was inflected through the discussion on reeducation and the past; her analysis carries her through the early 1950s without fully examining the discourse of youth as it first appeared after the war. Her investigation is rich and revealing, but ultimately she does not address the ways in which German children and youth were already highly contentious categories after the war. The present study will attempt, as it does with Poiger's work, to provide background for the surprisingly emphatic treatments of the young in the controversy about the *Mischlinge,* the "mixed-race" children discussed in Fehrenbach's work, and the *Halbstarken,* the hooligans studied in Maase's and Poiger's work. It is my hope that this essay will help explain why the young came to play such central roles in the materials analyzed by those scholars. See Fehrenbach (1998, 2001).
3. On the other hand, Thomas Koebner, Rolf-Peter Janz, and Frank Trommler did offer an extensive analysis in an earlier work of the "myth of youth" in the fin-de-siècle, 1920s and Nazi periods, though without taking up the fate of this uniquely German discourse after the war. The present essay aims to help fill a gap among these works by investigating the pronounced afterlife of emphatic discourse about youth in the early reconstructive years. See Koebner, Janz, and Trommler (1985).
4. Though I do not have space herein to elaborate, all of these theorists have underscored how children and youth figure centrally in the emergence and constant reconstitution of modern European society. Though his historiography is famously suspect, Michel Foucault's generalizations have been filled in to a large degree by Jacques Donzelot and George Mosse. See Foucault (1978); Donzelot (1979); and Mosse (1985).
5. The packet sent to theater owners quotes from interviews with Kortner in which he spoke of the very personal meaning *Der Ruf* held for him as an exile returning to a land he could never really abandon: "The driving force in this film is Fritz Kortner. *Der Ruf* is a passionate testimony for the country of his mother tongue, for the country of his artistic roots, for the country of undestroyable ties—Germany! The homesickness of the university professor returning to Germany was his homesickness, and the character's attempt to reconnect to the homeland was his own attempt. We know that Kortner created the role of his life in this confessional(!) film."
6. The editing of the restaurant scene casts Fechner as Walter's false Aryan father via intercutting: the film cuts away from Mauthner's demanding to know the identity of the false father to Fechner in the next room. I have noted elsewhere, since *Hitlerjunge Quex* (Hitler Youth Quex, 1933), the anxiety surrounding false fathers in these postwar films (Fisher 2001). There are false father figures in a number of postwar films: Birke and Waldemar in *Irgendwo in Berlin* (Somewhere in Berlin, 1946), Hans's friend Fritz in *Und über uns der Himmel* (And the Sky Above Us, 1947), and brigade leader Udo in *Rotation* (1949). Pedagogues as false father figures can be found in *Germania anno zero* (Germany Year Zero, 1947), with Edmund's teacher, and *Und finden dereinst wir uns wieder* (And Someday We Shall Find Each Other Again, 1947), in the figure of Assessor Paulke.
7. Compare the remark by Fritz Mangikamp in"'Da reist ich nach Deutschland hinüber,'" *Der neue Film,* 20 October 1948: 2.

Chapter Two

RETURNING HOME:
THE ORIENTALIST SPECTACLE OF
FRITZ LANG'S *DER TIGER VON ESCHNAPUR*
AND *DAS INDISCHE GRABMAL*

Barbara Mennel

Introduction

Fritz Lang is not a name associated with West German cinema of the 1950s. Instead, his name is synonymous with visions of modernity expressed in such Weimar film classics as *Metropolis* (1927) and *M* (1931).[1] In addition, his twenty-three Hollywood films directed during his time as an émigré between 1933 and 1958 established him as a master of American film genres, such as film noir and the Western. His socially critical films made in the United States, such as *Fury* (1936), which portrays the persecution of an innocent man accused of a crime he did not commit, and his cooperation with Bertolt Brecht on the anti-Nazi film *Hangmen Also Die* (1943) are generally seen as indicators of Lang's increasing social awareness and politicization in exile.[2] Thus, traditionally Lang's oeuvre is understood on a continuum from his innovative modernism of the Weimar Republic to his mastery of Hollywood genre film that also traces a path from an apolitical aesthetic to a more progressive political position expressed through popular forms. In this conception of Lang's oeuvre, his re-émigré films acquire the status of an afterthought and, as I will show in this essay, pose a methodological problem, since they cannot be assimilated into the master narrative of Lang's oeuvre as modernist auteur.[3]

Lang's films *Der Tiger von Eschnapur* (The Tiger of Eschnapur, 1959) and *Das indische Grabmal* (The Indian Tomb, 1959) are orientalist spectacles that

are mostly remembered for their continued reruns on television throughout the 1960s and 1970s. Lang had written the original script with Thea von
Harbou in the early 1920s based on the latter's novel, *Das indische Grabmal*
of 1917 (von Harbou 1922). His other film directed in West Germany, *Die
tausend Augen des Dr. Mabuse* (The Thousand Eyes of Dr. Mabuse, 1960),
harks back to the character established in the last film he made in Germany before he left, *Das Testament des Dr. Mabuse* (The Testament of Dr.
Mabuse, 1933). Lang's re-émigré films thus invite obvious biographical
readings. For instance, Patrick McGilligan sees Lang's re-émigré films as a
"circle [that] was closing" because "remaking *The Indian Tomb* was a way
of remaking his fate" (1997: 428).[4] Tom Gunning locates "the uncanny" in
"Lang's return to Germany" (2000: 457).[5] Thus, those authors who praise
the films anchor their readings in psychobiographical approaches and
consequently downplay concerns regarding orientalism and postcolonial-
ism, which would question the status of Lang as modernist and political
auteur. In contrast to film scholars' almost mythical biographical accounts
of Lang's late works, the West German press at the time reacted—almost
in unison—with harsh criticism. This criticism was countered just a few
years later in Paris in the early 1960s with the "canonization" of Lang, as
McGilligan terms it (1997: 442), through Jean-Luc Godard's film *Le Mépris*
(Contempt, 1963), in which Godard cast Lang as an aging film director of
international stature. The Nouvelle Vague's (New Wave) celebration of
Lang's *Der Tiger von Eschnapur* and *Das indische Grabmal* I argue, however,
hinges on the precarious relationship of French intellectuals to orientalism
following France's loss of its Southeast Asian colonies and the negotiation
of postcoloniality and national identity in French 1950s culture.

Beyond these two waves of German and French reviews, *Der Tiger
von Eschnapur* and *Das indische Grabmal* have escaped academic attention
because, I surmise, the films' orientalism challenges the canonical understanding of Lang as modernist auteur. The current state of research on
any of Lang's India films is best summarized in the succinct statement:
"This film was underrated by contemporary critics" (Aurich, Jacobson,
and Schnauber 2001: 35–36). The notion of "underrated" implies that a
serious engagement with the films could lead to a rehabilitation of sorts.
Instead of reevaluating Lang's orientalist spectacles in order to make them
conform to the paradigmatic accounts of his modernist auteurism, I analyze the similarities between Langian modernist style and his orientalist
spectacles, not to elevate the popular film but instead to question the formalist account of the modernist auteur's oeuvre.

Der Tiger von Eschnapur and *Das indische Grabmal* continue German
twentieth-century orientalism in the context of the late 1950s by offering India as a projection of desires that provide spectatorial pleasures

incongruent with high culture of the 1950s. I begin with the genealogy of the films, which were produced three times in representative periods of German film history. First, during the Weimar Republic, Joe May directed the film *Das indische Grabmal* (The Indian Tomb), which was shown in two parts, *Die Sendung des Yoghi* (The Mission of the Yogi, 1921) and *Der Tiger von Eschnapur* (The Tiger of Bengal, 1921). Second, during the Third Reich, Richard Eichberg directed two-part, two-language versions with German actors entitled *Das indische Grabmal* (The Indian Tomb, 1937) and *Der Tiger von Eschnapur* (The Tiger of Eschnapur, 1937) and with French actors entitled *Le Tombeau hindou* (1938) and *Le Tigre du Bengale* (1938) (see Spazier and Wedel 1984: B8-B9, F26-F28).[6] This was the last film Eichberg completed before he left Germany and—not unlike Lang—the film he revisited when he returned to West Germany in 1949. In the early 1950s he created a single version out of the two parts with the title *Indische Rache* (Indian Revenge, 1952), which was, however, not successful at the box office (see Spazier and Wedel 1984: B9).

Finally, in the late 1950s, Lang remade the double feature entitled *Der Tiger von Eschnapur* (1958) and *Das indische Grabmal* (1959). The production and reception of Lang's films are characterized by tensions between art and popular cinema embodied by the conflict between producer and director, on the one hand, and by the transition from film to television as the popular visual medium in West Germany, on the other hand. The films are rooted in the orientalism of the Weimar Republic but foreshadow a new generation of filmmakers represented by Alexander Kluge's apprenticeship on *Der Tiger von Eschnapur* (see Aurich, Jacobson, and Schnauber 2001: 408). I conclude this essay with an interrogation of the continued popular appeal that the films enjoyed as television reruns throughout the 1960s and 1970s in West Germany.

Genealogy

Lang's two India films continued the orientalist styles of Weimar cinema into the aesthetic registers of postwar popular cinema. In contrast to French and English cultural production concerning Southeast Asia, German cultural producers did not have to negotiate the production of meaning about "the Orient" with postcolonial subjects and were thus able to continue "colonial fantasies" without contestation. Susanne Zantop, who has discussed the term colonial fantasy extensively in the German context, argues that "by virtue of existing in the 'pure' realm of the imagination, 'untainted' by praxis, German fantasies were not only differently motivated, but had a different function: to serve not so much as ideological smokescreen or cover-up for colonial atrocities or transgressive desires, but as *Handlungser-satz*, as substitute for the real thing, as imaginary testing ground for colonial action" (1997: 6). Brigitte Schulze explains that the particular motif of India in the vast output of films of the 1910s and early 1920s relies on 150 years of history during which "the desire for 'India' that consumed the romantic, 'rational' self of the European urban subject played an important role in the contradictory reflection of the modern individual" (1997: 72).[7] This construction of India was reflected in public opinion that saw India as a "land of miracles" and "a mystery" (Schulze 1997: 73).

This imaginary India is the material of Harbou's novel *Das indische Grabmal*, which provides the key narrative strands and motifs for all of the various film versions. The novel opens with the main character, the architect Michael Fürbringer, who lies sick in bed in Germany when he is visited by an Indian yogi named Ramigami, who mysteriously trans-ports Fürbringer to India, where he meets the Maharaja Arada, Prince of Eschnapur. Arada requests that Fürbringer build a tomb for a woman he loved but who betrayed him with his friend. Because Fürbringer resists the maharaja's orders to build a tomb for a woman who is still alive, he is kept a prisoner. Fürbringer's wife, Irene, arrives at the palace and is united with her husband. When Fürbringer and his wife flee on horseback through the night, Fürbringer awakes, exposing the adventure as a fever-induced dream.

The contrast between East and West in Harbou's novel maps several binaries of orientalist tropes onto each other: vision versus blindness, unveiling versus veiling, rational democracy versus irrational domina-tion and subordination, and masculinity versus femininity. Edward Said defines orientalism as a system of thinking that relies on "an ontologi-cal and epistemological distinction made between 'the Orient' and (most of the time) 'the Occident'" that enables Westerners to dominate and to have authority over the Orient (1978: 2–3). Orientalism, which facilitates imperialist accounts of the Middle and Far East, provides the ideological underpinning of an imaginary that maps stereotypes onto an East/West dichotomy. According to Said, the primary model of the "Oriental" since the nineteenth century is that of the Oriental woman without history, who does not represent herself, but who is represented. The novel juxtaposes the maharaja's excess of feeling with a rational modernity represented by Fürbringer's room in India, in which every piece of furniture is of "that binding practicality, which in its perfection borders on beauty" (von Har-bou 1922: 38). While the Orient is characterized by violent subordination and domination, the West is portrayed as democratic. Thus, while the West is aligned with modern democracies embodied by the rational male, India is cast as "the woman among the Asian countries" (von Harbou

1922: 54). The maharaja explains to Fürbringer: "Once the soul of India has unveiled itself to you, you will discover that it has no other beauty than your dream of its beauty, no other mystery than its betrayal and no other religion than craziness" (von Harbou 1922: 54). The gender stereotype at the heart of orientalism casts India as feminine, which is characterized by pretense and seduction. However, underneath the veil are only projection, betrayal, and craziness.

"The apparently good and fruitful cooperation" on the script of *Das indische Grabmal* marked "the official beginning of Lang's and Harbou's collaboration" until Lang's emigration in 1933 and thus played a pivotal role for their working relationship, on the one hand, and Lang's career, on the other hand (Keiner 1984: 46). Joe May, who subsequently produced and directed the films, was one of the first contacts with the film industry that Lang made in 1916 in Vienna where May bought two scripts from Lang (Aurich, Jacobson, and Schnauber 2001: 31). Relying on two interviews given by Lang late in his life, Michael Töteberg maintains that May had intended to shoot the films himself, while he pretended toward Lang that the production was too expensive (1985: 30–31). Lang himself alleges: "Basically my script was stolen from me" (Töteberg 1985: 31). According to Töteberg, May's decision occasioned Lang's and Harbou's departure from May-Film GmbH to the Decla-Bioscop (1985: 30).

May's film version relied on the novel's basic plotlines but changed some narrative developments, added characters, and shifted nationalities. The main character becomes an English architect named Herbert Rowland, and the maharaja, now named Ayan, wants a tomb built for his wife Savitri, who has betrayed her husband with an English officer called MacAllan. The escape of Rowland, his wife Irene, and Savitri ends with Savitri's sacrificial suicide, and Ayan becomes a penitent. The double feature is one of several orientalist spectacles in the post-World War I period, which were made in response to expectations created by the importation of big productions from the United States. In the opening Rowland looks at a picture of the Taj Mahal and desires to build such a monumental building, foreshadowing the main theme of the film: architecture as a medium for Western desire for the beauty of the Orient, which appears in the excessive mise-en-scène.

Orientalism held special significance for the shift from print to visual culture because the stereotypes that underlie orientalism connect visual indecipherability with simultaneous visual excess. Since indecipherability lends itself to creating suspense and visual excess lends itself to showcasing the fantastic abilities of the new medium of film, orientalism was an ideal object for emerging cinema, especially as a silent medium.[8] May shot *Das indische Grabmal* in Woltersdorf, a location outside Berlin where he constructed eighteen monumental buildings between May 1920 and April 1921. The total cost of RM 20 to 24 million exceeded the cost of most American films at the time. Since the question of whether to "travel for film or construct artificial buildings" was widely discussed despite the recession (e.g., Wolff 1922), May himself addressed the relationship between mise-en-scène (*Ausstattung*) and performance (*Spiel*): "The task of the director is to integrate the mise-en-scène and the performance of the acting characters so tightly that the viewer is not distracted by the mise-en-scène" (1922: n.p.).

It is one of the paradoxes of orientalist films that their excessive mise-en-scène can distract from the narrative, as Urban Gad articulates in a critical perspective on orientalism: "Orientalist stuff . . . is the pure ruin of cinematography" (1920: 126). The mixed reviews of *Der Tiger von Eschnapur* and *Das indische Grabmal* reflect this conflict. Besides much excitement about the orientalist spectacle, contemporary critics also reacted negatively to the excessive mise-en-scène, either by foregrounding the money spent or by contrasting the emphasis on exterior effects with the characters' lack of interiority. This criticism was leveled with even more intensity at Eichberg's 1937 remake of *Der Tiger von Eschnapur*, which one reviewer labeled "exterior pomp without interior content" (*Film-Dienst* 365 [1949]: n.p.). In contrast to May, Eichberg relied on extensive on-location shooting in Udaipur and Mysore and only finished his script with Hans Klaehr and Arthur Pohl after his return to Berlin (Spazier and Wedel 1984: B8-B9). Eichberg edited the footage shot on location that was not of use for his feature film into a cultural film (*Kulturfilm*) shown before the feature film (Spazier and Wedel 1984: B9).

Lang's Double Feature

The choice of Lang as the director of these India films continued the Weimar tradition of modernist auteurism, while the choice of the film subject continued Weimar's cultural imaginary of orientalist fantasies. Artur Brauner from the production company CCC (Central Cinema Company) had seen *Der Tiger von Eschnapur* and *Das indische Grabmal* in his youth and asked Lang to shoot the films.[9] From the outset the work on the double feature was characterized by conflicts between Lang and the production team. Brauner had imagined parallel shooting and editing in order to release the films by Christmas 1958. Lang's own shooting diary (*Drehvermerke*) in the studio and on location in India shows a tight schedule. The first shooting diary (6 August to 10 September 1958) remarks on few exceptional events, such as a visit by Lotte Eisner or Debra Paget's birthday. In addition, Lang writes memos to remind himself to take his passport and to get a shot against smallpox for the trip to India. The second diary, which covers the period of 11 September to 13 October 1958, mostly refers to the uneventful shooting of interior scenes. The last shooting diary covers Lang's time in Udaipur from 23 October to 29 November 1958, when he struggled with organizational and health problems. On the second day in Udaipur, Lang remarks, "still about thirty meters of film!!" and "waiting for the sun for over an hour" (1959: n.p.). Lang refers repeatedly to having the flu and diarrhea. In addition to his problems with his team of producers, he had to negotiate with the chief of police and political representatives in India about receiving elephants and horses for shooting scenes with animals.

The plot of Lang's *Der Tiger von Eschnapur* and *Das indische Grabmal* is set entirely in India. The first film, *Der Tiger von Eschnapur*, introduces the German architect Harald Berger and the palace dancer Seetha (notice that Lang changed the names of the characters), who fall in love when they meet in a small village on the way to Eschnapur to visit the Maharaja Chandra. Before they arrive at the palace, Berger rescues Seetha from an attack by a tiger and discovers Seetha's hidden Irish heritage. During their stay at the palace, the maharaja realizes that Seetha and Berger are in love and forces them to flee, pursued by his soldiers. The cliff hanger of *Der Tiger von Eschnapur* shows Seetha and Berger lying in a desert during a sandstorm. They are saved at the beginning of the second film, *Das indische Grabmal*, while Berger's sister, Irene Rhode, and her husband, Dr. Walter Rhode, arrive at the palace. Seetha and Berger return to the palace, where Berger is jailed and Seetha is forced to perform a dance ritual with a snake in front of the goddess in a subterranean temple. Chandra intervenes to save her, Berger escapes, and conspirators against Chandra attack the palace. Their coup fails, but the palace collapses while the labyrinthine tunnels are flooding. The film closes with the maharaja becoming an ascetic and Berger returning to Germany with Seetha.

The reviews at the time rejected the film because it did not live up to the West German expectations of Lang as auteur and because the orientalist image of India was outdated: "India is now closer to us as a social problem and as a world power. We have plenty of accurate information about this country, not least through the Indian national film culture" (*Der Tag*, 3 June 1959). Some reviewers reacted with sarcasm and irony to the film's orientalism: "an orientalist dream world, in which every Indian is Teutonic" (*Neue Zürcher Zeitung*, 1 May 1959). Rino Sanders stated that "the priests seem like Sub-Saharan medicine men who perform for tourists, and Debra Paget seems to have been hired at the Reeperbahn [famous red-light district of Hamburg]" (*Die Welt*, 24 January). The disappointment in Lang's craft once he returned home leads Enno

Patalas to blame Harbou: "Thus, *Das indische Grabmal* (to be continued!) signifies the posthumous victory of Thea von Harbou, that eternal leader of womanhood (*Frauenschaft*) of the German cinema over the emigrant Lang" (1959: n.p.). Sabine Hake has pointed out that "Harbou is often held responsible for the shortcomings of Lang's German films" (1990: 48), in this case even after her death. If contemporary German criticism addresses the film at all, it remains negative. Ursula Czernitzki, for example, values May's version over Lang's: "If one looks at the weaknesses of skill, such as the artificial snake on a string and the unbelievable dialogues, one cannot believe that this is a Fritz Lang film" (1995: 104).

In contrast to negative West German reviews and to a lack of academic engagement, French critics embraced Lang's India films.[10] In 1959, a retrospective of Lang's films, initiated by Lotte Eisner, took place in the Cinémathèque in Paris. *L'Avant-Scène du Cinéma* published the entire script of Lang's double feature in 1985 in two respective volumes. The status accorded to Lang's version extends to Eichberg's French-language version. Each volume of *L'Avant-Scène du Cinéma* includes a reprint of *Le Film Complet du Mardi* from 1938 with an extensive retelling of Eichberg's French-language version by Robert B. Lesieur (*L'Avant-Scène du Cinéma* 339 [1985]: 83–96, 340 [1985]: 81–96). Thus, Eichberg's French-language version is currently available in France on a DVD set with Lang's version, whereas in Germany and the United States, Eichberg's 1937 version is the only one not in distribution. In *Cahiers du Cinéma*'s lists of "Annual Best Films from 1955–59," Lang's *Tiger von Eschnapur* is the only German film included (Hillier 1985: 287). France's complicated relationship to orientalism in the late 1950s, I suggest, led critics to disavow the film's orientalism in favor of a formalist reading while also proposing a universal human desire for exoticism (e.g., Weinberger-Thomas 1987; Garsault 1994). In May 1954, France had lost the critical battle at Dien Bien Phu and consequently had to give up its Indochina colonies at the 1955 Geneva summit. According to Sylvie Blum-Reid, the retreat from Indochina led to increased "orientalizing [of] the East" throughout the 1960s and 1970s, and in the case of Marguerite Duras, for example, to "discussing Indochina by transposing it to India" (2003: 7).[11]

The French critics thus show an inverted reaction to that of their West German colleagues. While West German critics saw the films' excessive exteriority as reproducing the orientalist stereotype of a lack of interiority and subjectivity accorded to the Other, French critics viewed the excessive exteriority as a conscious simulacra pointing to the lack of interiority accorded to the Other in orientalist stereotypes. This perspective results from a hypersensitivity vis-à-vis orientalism in late 1950s France but at the same time reproduces the deep-seated orientalism of French society. In addition, the positive readings in France are based on a primary focus on the mise-en-scène and on a disregard for the narrative. Fereydoun Hoveyda in *Cahiers du Cinéma* emphasizes the mise-en-scène and stylization, which expresses an "anti-realism that rubs off even on the décor." He concludes: "The idea of having Debra Paget dance in a Folies-Bergères style negligee (by the end of the second period) is absolutely brilliant" (1959: 57).[12] Philippe Demonsablon also asserts that "[t]he real . . . does not interest Fritz Lang" (1959: 59). Catherine Weinberger-Thomas argues that Lang "constantly plays on the distancing between reality and cinematic fabrication," and she accords "antirealism" the ability to "cleanse the rhetoric of exoticism" (1987: 78). The Goddess, described by Weinberger-Thomas as a "kitschy expressionist metamorphosis of the Hindu Goddess, more pictorial than sculptural," illustrates Lang's "willingness to make everything look excessively fake in order for us to see the other side of the simulacra instead of pleasing our phantasmagoria" (79). Yet, while Weinberger-Thomas argues that Lang deconstructs orientalism, she also applauds his mastery of its conventions: "Lang masterfully uses the oriental motif of the *moucharabieh*—subterranean labyrinths that hide a world of monsters (the crocodile) and of death" (80). In the end Weinberger-Thomas, unable to advance a political, historical, or sociological argument for this emptying out of orientalism, concludes with a biographical moment, Lang's loss of his eyesight, which she asserts haunts the film "off-camera," and which she calls "the intimate drama of the vision" (88). In a telling slip, she ends her essay with quotations from François Jullien about "a Buddhist formula, which results from Chinese aesthetic reflection" on the "elusive distance of the Japanese tradition" (88). Thus, after disavowing a political dimension of the appropriation and projection of cultural alterity, Weinberger-Thomas collapses Lang's loss of eyesight in a mélange of Japanese, Chinese, and Buddhist Asianness.

Langian Orientalism

Having outlined the particular French reception of the auteur's India films, in this section I show how the films' orientalism is specifically located in their formal spatial compositions, which also characterize Lang's trademark modernist films. The narrative of *Der Tiger von Eschnapur* and *Das indische Grabmal* combines two forms of orientalism: the mise-en-scène and location reflect the populist and melodramatic aspect of orientalism, while the architectural interest of the German characters echoes the anthropological and ethnographic aspect. *Der Tiger von Eschnapur* and *Das indische Grabmal* are structured by a gendered binarism of East and West, embodied by India and Germany, in which India is feminized and Germany is masculinized, even though male and female characters occupy either side of the binary of nationality. Schulze maps out two sets of motifs concerning India: "the dark male, threatening India" and "the light female, desired India" (1997: 75).

In this film the German woman Irene is masculinized, for example, while Chandra is feminized. The German characters embody German values of the 1950s, such as frugality, cleanliness, hard work, and efficiency—qualities that were a source of West German pride, as Erica Carter points out, especially given the taboo on nationalism in the late 1950s (1997: 21). Since the films end with the return to Germany, the narrative structure implies that Germany contains the excess of the orientalist visual spectacle and simultaneously allows for its fantasy. Shots of Seetha's first dance in front of a huge statue of the goddess, the maharaja, and the priests are intercut with shots of Berger investigating the old tunnels in the catacombs. This crosscutting reinforces the two main characters' romantic attraction and their gender traits: Seetha is the embodiment of the orientalist spectacle, while Berger is the investigating and active German male. The fact that entering the temple and watching the dance is forbidden to Europeans with the punishment of death raises the stakes for Berger, who ultimately finds his way through the underground catacombs to the temple and sees Seetha dancing. Spectators are already engaging in the forbidden pleasure when Berger arrives, since his search is crosscut with the dance.

The film allows spectators to indulge in the kind of visual splendor that is renounced at the end in favor of a return to Germany, a place implied to be scientific and practical throughout the films' narrative. The visual excess that characterizes the films is coded as feminine, typical of melodrama, and Indian. While Chandra sacrifices his desire for Seetha when he becomes an ascetic, Seetha sacrifices her luxurious life in the palace for her future life in Germany. The excess that is projected onto the feminine and ethnic Other is coded as a pleasurable, yet dangerous fantasy and leads to the violent destruction of all that represents India in the films except for Chandra. At the end, Seetha is incorporated into the German family. The last shot shows Seetha and Berger in a small carriage on their way back to Germany, which also invites spectators to return to Germany. The shot encapsulates their containment and foreshadows the vision that Berger has articulated earlier in the film: a small house he will build in Germany, filled only with love.

The geographical lateral binarism that juxtaposes East and West is reproduced through the architectural and vertical divisions between the upper and lower worlds that structure the film.[13] Material excess, namely, the palace, resides in the upper world, while sexual and physical excess reign in the lower world. The lower world contains the catacombs with crocodiles, the temple where Seetha dances, and the lepers locked into an underground cave. This architectural division mirrors the stereotype of the Eastern psyche as inaccessible to Westerners. The technology of mapping allows them to master the subterranean territory—but only to a degree. Berger creates maps to master the topography of the underground world. When Berger's sister and brother-in-law search for him, they read Harald's map, yet during her search, Irene misses her brother Harald and subsequently falls through a hole into the lepers' colony. Not only are the catacombs a space of disorientation but also of anxiety-producing danger and contamination. Besides crocodiles and tigers, the heart of the underground world contains the leper colony. Toward the climax of the film, the sick free themselves and kill Asagara, Rhode's assistant. An excess of water and dynamite destroys the upper and lower worlds at the films' close.

The films combine the epic genre and the family melodrama. The epic is associated with India, historically unspecified and coded as mythical, whereas the melodrama concerns the German characters. *Der Tiger von Eschnapur* begins with shots of the Indian countryside, which serve to authenticate India. The monumental architecture and the choreography of masses of Indians against the Indian landscape characterize the epic aspect of the films.[14] India serves as the epic backdrop for the melodrama, in which primarily European characters are accorded psychological complexity. The melodrama is performed by European actors (no matter whether the characters they portray are Indian or German), whereas the extras—the masses—are Indian.

The two nations, Germany and India, are represented by the familial relationships of siblings and married couples, typical for melodramas, which transform political themes into personal relationships. Since a musical accompaniment to emotions is integral to melodramas, music serves to mark the mise-en-scène as "oriental" by accentuating the expression of emotions by the characters. The musical motif that underlies the plot is the juxtaposition of the Irish folk song that reveals Seetha's European roots with the melodies coded as Indian accompanying the epic and dance scenes. The melodrama, according to Thomas Elsaesser, foregrounds mise-en-scène, music, gesture, and color and privileges the rhythmic and musical qualities of speech as opposed to its status as dialogue (1987: 53). The melodrama's emphasis on the mise-en-scène appears in repeated shots that do not advance the narrative: the palace, its interior, and the garden. In the melodrama, the mise-en-scène portrays "women as caught in a world of objects in which they are expected to invest their feelings" (Carter 1997: 62). An example of this is a golden birdcage, which symbolizes Seetha's existence.

The plethora of objects in the highly ornamental mise-en-scène surrounding Seetha frame her as the embodiment of orientalism. Her costume, jewelry, and dance encode her as the "oriental" woman, sexualized, erotic, and sensual, with a "primitive" belief system. The trope of the exotic woman with hidden European roots allows for an orientalizing gaze at the exotic character while legitimizing Berger's desire for her. Thomas Brandlmeier characterizes the trope of the "exotic" woman as representing "high culture within the foreign space" and "colonial spoils at home" (1997: 35). The first shot of Seetha shows her adorned with a see-through scarf, looking at Berger through a hole in a dilapidated wall. When Berger turns for a moment, she has disappeared. Her sudden appearance and disappearance, her veiling and unveiling, mark her as the mystery of the Orient. Even though it is revealed early on that Seetha is not Indian, she still performs Indianness. Berger triggers Seetha's memory when he recognizes an Irish folk song she is singing and reads the inscription on her guitar.[15]

Lang traditionally casts his female lead characters as "double women" (see Huyssen 1981; Lungstrum 1997): here the double is specifically that of India and Germany. "The Other, the double, the dual personality, the return of the repressed" are listed by Brandlmeier as favorite tropes for exoticism (1997: 39). The architectural construction mirrors the split of femininity. Irene lives in the upper world of material rationality and can only attempt to negotiate the lower world of danger and excess with maps, whereas Seetha is positioned in the lower world of the temple and seems unhappy in the upper world of worldly goods. According to Carter's analysis of German melodrama in the 1950s, female heroines are caught between "the domesticity of heterosexual coupledom" and "the nether region of perverse and inchoate desire" (1997: 177). In *Der Tiger von Eschnapur* and *Das indische Grabmal*, this binary of female identity is projected onto Seetha and Irene. While the former is sexualized, the latter is desexualized. Whereas Seetha's costumes are adorned with jewelry and change throughout the film, Irene's outfits are plain and emphasize her practical nature.

The film reinstates a male heterosexual gaze especially in those scenes where the films' orientalist staging produces homoerotic moments between female characters. Not only is Seetha sexualized through the staging of her dance and her costume, but the female goddess is also sexualized: the goddess is a naked statue with exaggeratedly large, round breasts that takes up one wall of the underground temple in a grotto.[16] The extensive dance scenes are explained by Laura Mulvey's feminist account that in dominant cinema, women's "to-be-looked-at-ness" creates a spectacle that arrests the narrative (1988: 62). Seetha's dance combines traditional Indian and modern dance elements with sexually explicit movements. The homoeroticism of the dance's climax, when Seetha seems to be offering her body to the goddess with a thrusting movement of her pelvis, is contained as a spectacle for the all-male crowd of priests, heterosexualizing the homoerotic spectacle. Similarly, Seetha and her servant Bahrani are accorded intimacy, while Berger and Seetha's love is illegitimate, and Chandra and Seetha's love remains unfulfilled. Thus, the relationship of the two women is an entryway for female spectatorial desire and identification with the female characters. Even though their relationship is coded as master-slave—a power asymmetry projected onto India—this fact is simultaneously disavowed by the portrayal of intimacy between the women. Seetha's and Bahrani's homoerotism results from the sexualization and feminization of the Orient. Bahrani is sacrificed for Seetha in a highly staged spectacle when Bahrani is killed at a seated dinner by a fakir during the performance of a magic trick. Her absence creates a strategic lack in the narrative to be filled by Irene, who will become close to Seetha. Bahrani's character represents a femininity that is not contained in the image of European heterosexual patriarchy encapsulated in the last shot. Bahrani's death carries with it the ambivalence of sacrifice and murder. Identification with her exceeds the heterosexual coupling of the film but does not offer any resistance to the film's orientalism, since the sacrifice is projected onto the only female Indian character and is thus open to masochistic identification.

Bahrani's murder/sacrifice and Chandra's self-renunciation enable the doubling of heterosexual European couples on their way home to Germany. The feminization of India as a nation allows for an implicit need of the Europeans to dominate, a need masked by an ideology of protection. This structure has been analyzed by Susanne Zantop in her study of colonial fantasies as "stories of sexual conquest and surrender, love and blissful domestic relations between colonizer and colonized, set in colonial territory, stories that made the strange familiar and the familiar 'familial'" (1997: 2). The representation of the return home and the integration of the "Indian" woman into the German nuclear family were not part of the film and book versions from the Weimar Republic. The return home can be further illuminated by Heide Fehrenbach's explication of West German cinema in the 1950s as a "response to the new Cold War paradigm," which creates "the notion of a 'moral nation' based upon the patriarchal family" (1995: 7). The return home from the colony rejects the role of the colonizer, representing Germany as able "to reenter the international order as a proud but peaceable *Kulturnation*," an agenda that emerged, according to Fehrenbach, in the West Germany of the postwar period (9).

Afterlife: Reruns on West German Television

Despite the negative reviews in West Germany at the time and despite *Der Spiegel*'s description of the double feature as a "misguided attempt by film producers to wean people away from television," the films continually reran on West German and, later, on German television, beginning in the early 1960s and continuing up to this date (Kaplan 1981: 210). The films' melodrama posed a stark contrast to the intellectual discourse of high culture associated with West Germany of the 1960s and 1970s. Just as the films offer India as a projection of forbidden desires for a postwar audience, so does the melodrama present a secret underbelly of (West) German culture. The success of the films on television, a populist medium distinguished by its private mode of reception, in contrast to their failure in movie houses and particularly with West German film critics, mirrors the binarism of public rationality and hidden seductive desires that holds together the films themselves.[17] Their narrative and mise-en-scène are structured by a hierarchy of the visible, rational, masculine upper world, identified as German, and the secret, seductive, dangerous, sexual, and female lower world, identified as Indian. The continued life of *Der Tiger von Eschnapur* and *Das indische Grabmal* on German television links the different postwar periods, while the films themselves carry forward the cultural imaginary of the Weimar Republic. While much of German film historiography focuses on the discontinuities between different periods, the films' orientalism in their different incarnations offer continuity for a familial and familiar colonial fantasy throughout the twentieth century. The characters' triumphant return home provides a narrative and ideological closure that was not accorded to the narrative of Lang's biography, since his "return home" failed miserably with the West German cultural establishment. Yet, that neatness of narrative and ideological closure was accorded both to Lang as auteur and to his oeuvre, a neatness that my essay has attempted to disrupt.

Notes

I am grateful to Elke Heckner, Amy Ongiri, and Sandra Shattuck for their readings of earlier drafts. I also appreciated the help of the archivists Ned Comstock at the Cinema and Television Library Archive of the University of Southern California and Gerrit Thies at the Nachlaßarchiv of the Filmmuseum Berlin. In addition, I thank the anonymous reader for incisive and productive observations and suggestions.

1. This understanding of Fritz Lang is indicated by the title of Tom Gunning's canonical book on Lang, *The Films of Fritz Lang: Allegories of Vision and Modernity* (2000).
2. For example, Gunning's book includes a section entitled "Fritz Lang's America—The Social Trilogy," which includes a discussion of *Fury* (1936), *You Only Live Once* (1937),

and *You and Me* (1938) (2000: 203–82). My own essay on *Fury* questions Lang's political progressiveness in relationship to the representation of racist politics of lynching in the United States (Mennel 2003).

3. Even though Lang made two films in postwar Germany, he continued to hold American citizenship. He died in Hollywood in 1976.

4 Canonical works on Lang use a variation of the phrase "the circle had closed," referring to Lang's own statement about his return: "like a circle that was beginning to close—a kind of fate" (Bogdanovich 1967: 111; see also Eisner 1976: 384; Gunning 2000: 458; McGilligan 1997: 428).

5. Lang left Germany for Paris in 1933 and sailed from Le Havre, France, to New York on 6 June 1934.

6. Maurice Bessy in his comprehensive encyclopedia on French films lists Eichberg's *Le Tigre du Bengale* as a film produced by the Société des Films Sonores Tobis in two episodes for the year 1937 (rather than 1938) (Bessy and Chirat 1987: 276).

7. All translations from German, except otherwise marked, are by the author.

8. Nick Browne considers "the Figure of the *East*, of Orientalism, at the origin of the tradition of Western film theory" (1989: 24), integrating the significance of hieroglyphics for early film theory, the racism of immigration and exclusion of Asian immigrants at the beginning of twentieth-century United States, and the discovery of King Tut's Egyptian tomb in 1922 with the "design and ornamentation of the American movie palaces" (26). He concludes: "The 'Orient' was dispersed into multiple sectors of the film institution as an investment in theater design, in films themselves and in theory" (25).

9. Artur Brauner had attempted to recruit Lang for an earlier directing job in 1955 about the assassination attempt on Adolf Hitler. After completing *Beyond a Reasonable Doubt* (1956) in Hollywood, Lang flew to India to "lay the groundwork to *The Pearl of Love*, a story about the Taj Mahal in Agra, which he was to direct for Taj Mahal Productions" (Aurich, Jacobson, and Schnauber 2001: 457).

10. While most academic discussions of the films and Lang's work acknowledge that the French reception is positive, there is little engagement with the actual argument. To my knowledge none of the French reviews have been translated and published in English and only two of the French texts (Demonsablon 1959; Hoveyda 1959) have been translated into and reprinted in German (Fischer and Eckl 1964).

11. Blum-Reid (2003) is making a larger and more complex argument about French theory than I can account for in the scope of this essay. Her specific reference here is to Marguerite Duras's books *Le Vice-consul* (1965) and *India Song* (1973). For a discussion of the function of emblematic writer Duras for postwar French relationship to orientalism, see Ha (2000) and McNeece (1996). For an account of the relationship of France and Indochina in the period in question, see Sagar (1991). For a discussion about the significance of the Geneva summit, which, in addition to the decision of France's loss of colonies, was also important in regard to the two separate German states and the beginning of the cold war, see Varsori (1994). For an insightful account of the significance of Duras's writing for a working through of French orientalism and the appropriation of her persona by French right-wing politics in the 1950s and 1960s as a stand-in for the French nation, see Winston (2001).

12. All translations from the French are by Chantal Rodais (unpublished).

13. For a general discussion of "the role of sexual differences in the construction of a number of superimposed oppositions—West/East, North/South not only on a narratological level but also on the level of the implicit structuring metaphors undergirding colonial discourse," see Shohat (1997).

14. The epic nature of these films connects them to Lang's other two-part epic, *Die Nibelungen* (The Nibelungs) which consists of *Siegfried* (1922) and *Krimhield's Rache* (Kriemhild's Revenge, 1924) (see Hake 1990).

15. "Half-Irishness" as a trope in colonial literature about India does not appear only in Lang's films. In *Imperial Leather* Anne McClintock analyzes the function of the half-Irishness of Kim in Rudyard Kipling's eponymous novel as placing "him racially closer to the Indians than if he had been wholly English" (1995: 69).

16. For a discussion of popular ethnography, specifically the use of pictures of "bare-breasted native women" in journals and their function as "soft-core pornography" in the 1950s, see Gates (1998).

17. "Success" in this context refers not only to the frequency of reruns of the Lang version on German television, but also to the hold the film has on viewers' imaginary and memory. Even though my claim relies on anecdotal evidence of those who vividly remember tiger hunts and dance scenes from childhood viewings, it is precisely this phenomenon that motivates contemporary discussions about the films and that troubles its reception. For example, at a multinational event entitled "Import-Export: Cultural Transfer between India, Austria and Germany," which took place in Bombay, Vienna, and Berlin in May 2005, the media scholars Vinzenz Hedinger and Meenakshi Shedde addressed the question, "how this film in particular could develop such a power in regard to the reception of India in German-speaking Europe" (2005).

Chapter 3

THE PASSENGER: AMBIVALENCES OF NATIONAL IDENTITY AND MASCULINITY IN THE STAR PERSONA OF PETER VAN EYCK

Tim Bergfelder

West German cinema from the late 1940s to the mid 1960s has often been conceived of as a cinema of reconstruction. This is understood to encompass both the rebuilding of an indigenous film industry and cinematic infrastructure after the war, and the period's ideological aims. The latter combined the suppression of the memory of the "Third Reich" with an active promotion of a new capitalist society, albeit with a very German emphasis on ordered, rational, and sensible consumption behavior (see Carter 1997). The cinema of the era has been seen as responding to this purpose by creating a gallery of popular actors and actresses conforming to ideal social types, which were placed in scenarios designed to promote the restoration of national identity and normative gender roles.

One problem with such a conceptualization is that it conflates complex historical, cultural, and social processes with unambiguous motivations and correspondences, a critical strategy that has frequently underpinned the dismissal of 1950s cinema as conformist and reactionary (e.g., Bongartz 1992). Over the last decade, this strategy has been challenged by a number of revisionist studies of the period (e.g., Carter 1997; Fehrenbach 1995; Westermann 1990), even where their conclusions ultimately reaffirmed previous perceptions of the era. It is worth noting that many studies have focused primarily on issues of female experience, female-centered genres, and female representation. Through an investigation of the relationship between masculinity and national identity in star images of the 1950s, this article aims to expand on those previous studies, but also to query some of their conclusions. The article's subject, the actor Peter van Eyck, may seem at first an unusual choice in that he never attained the popularity of contemporaries such as Curd Jürgens, O. W. Fischer, or Dieter Borsche or the cult following of a Horst Buchholz. Nevertheless, van Eyck was a leading star of the 1950s and 1960s and in constant demand almost up to his death from cancer in 1969. At the same time, he represents a liminal star persona in terms of his career's highly complex take on masculinity and national identity. As such, his case may be used to modify some preconceptions of the West German cinema of the 1950s, in particular the assumption that the only function of male (or female) stars in this period was to promote traditional values and hierarchies in gender relations, or to reconstruct (or rehabilitate) outmoded notions of German identity. In other words, van Eyck's liminality vis-à-vis nationhood and gender allows contradictions to emerge in the supposedly monolithic ideological discourses of the decade, and it brings to the surface the tensions between films' textual and narrative properties and historically and culturally determined instances of reception and interpretation.

Van Eyck's on-screen image was often that of an outsider (either in sexual or in national terms), a cool, arrogant, elegantly dressed, cosmopolitan dandy with an aristocratic demeanor, whose behavior could shift between laid-back charm, narcissist vanity, brooding cynicism, and outbursts of ruthless brutality and physical violence. As such, van Eyck's roles alternated between villains and heroes (an example for the latter is his proto-James Bond in the Dr. Mabuse series of the early 1960s, beginning with Fritz Lang's *Die tausend Augen des Dr. Mabuse* (The Thousand Eyes of Dr. Mabuse, 1959), but more often than not, their very essence was their ambivalence. Good examples for the latter are his roles in the *Wirtschaftswunder* satire *Das Mädchen Rosemarie* (The Girl Rosemarie, 1958; see also Larson Powell's contribution in this volume) and in what is possibly his internationally best known film, *The Spy Who Came in from the Cold* (1965), in which he plays an inscrutable East German spymaster.

The strangeness of van Eyck's on-screen persona was accentuated by his striking physical appearance. Tall, broad-shouldered, with luminous, near fluorescent white hair (which he had first bleached for his role in *Le salaire de la peur* [The Wages of Fear, 1953]), and piercing eyes, van Eyck did not conform to conventional notions of handsomeness. Occasionally he approximated an almost caricatured version of "Aryanness," or the stereotype of a Prussian officer. At the same time he exuded (especially in his villainous parts) a feline, sexually ambivalent attractiveness, comparable to that of Weimar stars such as Conrad Veidt. Many press portraits of him asserted that female audiences were his main constituency, whereas men responded more cautiously, and even suspiciously, to his masculinity. The following quotation from a newspaper portrait sums up this dichotomy: "Is he the male role model for our time? Hardly. Does he look like the man today's women dream of? More likely" ("Einer vom Filmhimmel unserer Tage: Peter van Eyck—Leinwandheld zwischen den Kontinenten," *Tagesspiegel*, 19 July 1959). Van Eyck's sexual ambivalence articulated itself in a seemingly excessive attention toward personal appearance and grooming. The following comment on van Eyck's trademark bleached hair is typical in this respect: "One has learned to live with the fact that dark-haired women dye their hair blond, because they think it might look more effective, that blondes go for red, and redheads go for black. But now cinema's leading men follow suit . . . Peter van Eyck whose hair originally turned snow-white only for one film role cannot bring himself to go back to his natural color. Because the white hair makes him more 'interesting.' That's at least what his female fans claim" (Neue Filmverleih Gmbh-Zentralpresseabteilung, 1958).

Van Eyck himself spoke publicly, often, and at great length about dyeing his hair (e.g., "Karrieremachen heißt blond sein," *Frankfurter Neue Presse*, 8 May 1959), while press reports revealed that he frequented a women's hairdresser for that purpose (the implication being that normal men don't dye their hair). Such publicity ephemera added to the perception of him as possessing an excessively vain as well as slightly effeminate character. One film that made deliberate use of van Eyck's hair to signal a deviant side to his onscreen personality was *Das Mädchen Rosemarie*, where his hair color perfectly matched that of his protégée, the film's prostitute heroine Rosemarie (Nadja Tiller), thus underlining their status as partners-in-crime, but also subtly blurring the gender distinctions between them.

Van Eyck's status as an outsider was heightened further by his placeless accent (typical of someone who has lived abroad for a long time), his slurred diction (likened by some critics to the pronunciation of a drunk), and by his deadpan manner of acting, which relied more on the projection of overall body posture and physical presence than on either facial mobility or declamatory qualities. The latter was of course typical of the understated style of contemporary Hollywood stars such as Gary Cooper or Robert Mitchum, but in the context of German cinema, and German acting conventions more generally, van Eyck's minimalism was unusual; as was his exclusive commitment to the screen. Unlike the majority of West German film actors, van Eyck never appeared on stage (see Dombrowski 1965). Given the high prestige accorded to stage training in the German context, this would lead to repeated challenges from critics as to his abilities as an actor. Typical in its disapproval of van Eyck's acting style and of his perceived vanity is a comment from a review of *The Spy Who Came in from the Cold*, which opines that "Peter van Eyck does nothing but prance about" (U.N. 1966: 212–13). The film historian Lotte Eisner was not well disposed toward van Eyck either. In her memoirs she recalls a visit to the set of Fritz Lang's *Die tausend Augen des Dr. Mabuse*, prompting her to dismiss van Eyck along with fellow actor Gert Fröbe as part of the "scum" of the West German film industry at the time (283).

Such criticisms notwithstanding, unlike few other postwar West German male stars (exceptions include Jürgens, Hardy Krüger, and, for a brief period in the early 1960s, Buchholz), van Eyck managed to maintain an international career throughout the 1950s and 1960s, with a prolific record as a character actor in American, British, French, and Italian productions, while performing leading roles in West German films, and moving between residences in Switzerland, the United States, and Paris. At least to some degree, van Eyck's seemingly effortless segueing between national cinemas and identities had to do with the fact that he belonged to a very select group of émigré actors whose return to postwar European cinema had been successful—indeed as far as remigrant stars (rather than supporting actors) in the West German film industry of the time are concerned, the only other example of note is Lilli Palmer. It is significant that neither had had a career in prewar German cinema (although van Eyck had at least orbited the Weimar film scene in Berlin in the early 1930s), which probably rendered them easier to reintegrate.

While Palmer was Jewish, van Eyck was not. Born in 1913 into a landowning aristocratic family in the Prussian region of Pomerania and originally expected to pursue a military career, van Eyck left Germany and his musical studies before the Nazis came to power. He traveled across Europe, North Africa, and the Caribbean, before settling in the United States in 1937. In New York he worked as a musical arranger for, among others, Irving Berlin, and collaborated with the composer Aaron Copland, and with Orson Welles's Mercury Theatre (van Eyck would later have a cameo part in Welles's *Mr Arkadin/Confidential Report*, 1955). It was during World War II that he became an actor in Hollywood, where he was usually cast in supporting roles as a youthful Nazi (e.g., in Billy Wilder's *Five Graves to Cairo*, 1943). Through his connection with Wilder, van Eyck found himself working as an U.S. Army officer for the Film Section of the Information Service Control Branch in Berlin between 1945 and 1948, and subsequently decided to remain in Europe.

Van Eyck's background of a Pomeranian aristocrat (i.e., originating from a German province that had been lost to Poland after the end of the World War II), combined with his initial status as an American officer and his years in exile complicated his reintegration in West German film culture. (Indeed, as I will argue below, it took until the late 1950s before van Eyck was claimed in the West German press as a "prodigal son.") This contributed to him being cast as a foreigner in the majority of his West German films in the 1950s, while making him at the same time the "very epitome of the Teutonic Terror type" (Maltin 1994) in most of the international productions in which he appeared. The contrast in roles and genres between his West German and his international productions in the 1950s is indeed striking. The majority of his international films were either thrillers or war films, where van Eyck played an assortment of German soldiers (e.g., *Single-Handed*, 1953), foreign legionnaires (*Le grand jeu* [Flesh and the Woman], 1954), SS officers (*Attack*, 1956), Nazi psychopaths (*Run for the Sun*, 1956), and criminals (an arms dealer in *Le feu aux poudres* [*Burning Fuse*], 1957, or a wife-killer in the British film *The Snorkel*, 1958).

In West German productions of the same period, on the other hand, van Eyck was typecast to a lesser degree, both in terms of genre and role. His work encompassed, apart from war films and thrillers, also melodramas, musicals, and historical costume pieces such as Walter Reisch's unusual Rilke adaptation *Der Cornet* (The Cornet, 1955). However, unlike in the case of his international productions, he rarely played Germans. Among the nationalities van Eyck portrayed in West German films of the 1950s are Americans/Brits (e.g., *Der gläserne Turm* [The Glass Tower], 1957; *Labyrinth*, 1959; *Die tausend Augen des Dr. Mabuse*, as well as two further Mabuse sequels in the 1960s); French characters (*Dr. Crippen lebt* [Dr. Crippen Lives], 1958; *Das Mädchen Rosemarie*); Hungarians (*Rommel ruft Kairo* [Rommel Calls Cairo], 1959); or unidentified foreign nationals (e.g., *Abschied von den Wolken* [Rebel Flight to Cuba], 1959 and *Geheimaktion Schwarze Kapelle* [The Black Chapel], 1959). In some cases, the film scripts appear to have almost willfully obfuscated the identity of van Eyck's roles in the desire to make them more liminal, as in *Das Mädchen Rosemarie*, where his character, the industrial spy Alfons Fribert, is initially introduced as French, but later pointedly insists on originating from Lorraine, a region both rich in resonances in French national mythology (as the home of Joan of Arc), but at the same time constituting a border province between Germany and France with historically and culturally shifting boundaries and allegiances. As I will demonstrate in the following pages through a discussion of three key films in van Eyck's career (two West German films and one European coproduction), the textual ambivalence of his characters was matched by an equally ambivalent and shifting reception of his image in the West German press of the time.

The difficulty for West German producers to place van Eyck in terms of national identity is already evident in his first postwar film, Rudolf

Jugert's *Hallo Fräulein!* (Hello Fraulein, 1949). In this rather didactic back-stage musical, van Eyck plays American town-major Tom Keller, responsible for reeducating a provincial southern German town in the months after the end of the war. Democratization is primarily achieved through the staging of a "jazz revue" promoting fraternization, which is organized by a German musical student, Maria (Margot Hielscher), who previously was entertaining German troops at the front. Incongruously, considering the film's setting in 1945, yet constituting a telling redemptive fantasy in the context of the postwar German psyche, Maria organizes a tour of a multinational orchestra, comprising Hungarians, French, and Czechs alongside German musicians. Although Tom's educational mission succeeds, he ends up empty-handed as far as the film's central romantic triangle is concerned. Maria chooses not him, but the earnest and mature German architect Walter (Hans Söhnker); Tom gives his blessing to this decision. Thus, American popular culture may be palatable once it has been rearranged to suit German tastes (as Sabine Hake has argued, the film promotes a "happy compromise between American big band music and German folk song" [2002: 111]), but international romance is not on the film's agenda.

Contemporary West German critics echoed the film's view on fraternization, praising the film for avoiding "the uncomfortable reality of the *Ami-Fräulein*," German women fraternizing with American soldiers, and instead presenting as its main protagonist "an honest, decent woman" (W. W. Koch, *Rheinische Zeitung*, 16 May 1949). It is also interesting how the two main male characters, Tom and Walter, and their respective performers, are judged. Although both characters are meant to be sympathetic in the film and were understood as such by the press, there are some telling differences in what amounts to stereotypical perceptions of German versus American masculinity. Thus, one reviewer compares van Eyck's "authentic American swagger" with Söhnker's "pleasant virility" ("Der versöhnende Jazz," *Telegraf*, 3 June 1949), while another contrasts Söhnker's "agreeable simplicity" with van Eyck's character being "free and easy (*salopp*)" ("Hallo Fräulein," *Film Illustrierte*, 26 May 1949). Throughout such oppositions, the emphasis is on arguing for, and championing, a superior German masculinity, characterized by principles of emotional control, renunciation, and duty. This national male ideal is set against the more spontaneous, carefree, but also more immature American version of masculinity that van Eyck embodies.

In the promotional brochures circulated by the film's distributor and in most of the available press reviews, van Eyck's real biographical background was camouflaged in an attempt to conflate on-screen and off-screen identity. Thus, the distributor's promotion insisted with regard to van Eyck, that "an American plays an American," and continued, "Peter van Eyck is the laid-back, open-minded, and boyish type of the American screen. In German cinema his type constitutes a novelty of specific appeal, and he will undoubtedly become an audience favorite with this film" (Zentral-Presse- und Werbeabteilung der Herzog-Film GmbH, 1949). While van Eyck's postwar activity as an officer with the U.S. occupation forces was acknowledged in several newspapers (indeed this contributed to his performance in *Hallo Fräulein!* being praised as particularly authentic), his German origins were not mentioned once, which may hint at the sensitivities involved in addressing issues of exile, remigration and the loss of national territory (van Eyck's home province of Pomerania) in the immediate postwar period.

Following his debut in Jugert's film in 1949, van Eyck's career as a youthful hero in German films did not take off. He appeared in a few films, among them two directed by Helmut Käutner: he played the romantic lead, this time as a German, in the comedy *Königskinder* (Royal Children, 1950), and as an American FBI agent in the convoluted thriller *Epilog: Das Geheimnis der Orplid* (Epilogue: The Orplid Mystery, 1950; see also Yogini Joglekar's contribution in this volume). However, both of these films were box office flops. Although van Eyck retained an image of indeterminate national identity in his subsequent West German productions, he abandoned the cheerfully bland and harmless persona on display in *Hallo Fräulein!*—none of his screen characters in the 1950s and 1960s could any longer be described as "boyish," while his onscreen image attained an ethically more ambiguous dimension.

Principally responsible for the change in image was van Eyck's role in Henri-Georges Clouzot's international box office hit *Le salaire de la peur* (The Wages of Fear, 1953). As one of the major "event" films of the 1950s, *Le salaire de la peur*, released in West Germany in a dubbed version with the title *Der Lohn der Angst*, had a significant impact with audiences and critics alike. As I will argue below, the film's West German reception provides an interesting insight into the ideological discourses and taboos at the time that impacted on the reading strategies manifest in the film's reviews. Moreover, the film revitalized van Eyck's career not just internationally, but also in West German cinema.

Clouzot's film is the extraterritorial film par excellence—financed as a European (French-Italian) coproduction and set in an unnamed South American country, the film is peopled by polyglot characters (and actors) of different national backgrounds caught in limbo at a jungle outpost. The film's central narrative concerns four men (played by Yves Montand, Charles Vanel, Folco Lulli, and van Eyck) who take on the suicide mission of driving two trucks of highly explosive nitroglycerin across difficult terrain. None of the men survive the journey. The grimy, testosterone-charged atmosphere, and the merging of the homosocial with the homoerotic (especially in the chemistry between Vanel and Montand), add a quasi-existentialist dimension to the film's action plot, as the suicide transport mission becomes a journey where "true male identities can be fully achieved or lost entirely" (Mazdon 2000: 45).

Within the film's interpersonal dynamic, van Eyck's character with the odd, and somewhat feminizing name "Bimba" is the most enigmatic. Unlike the other three main protagonists who reveal and develop their individual traits and flaws through their—often aggressive—interaction with each other, Bimba's part is more or less self-contained, for the most part a narcissistic and solipsistic presence. Throughout the first half of the film, before the men take off on their mission, Bimba's main activity is to observe the macho posturing of the others from the sidelines, a cigarette in a holder casually dangling from the corner of his mouth (this would become one of van Eyck's trademark gestures). Although the audience assumes, primarily owing to van Eyck's looks, that Bimba is German, this is never made explicit. Although he does speak German on two occasions, he talks more frequently in French and English, and only has cursory contact with the other, more obviously German, characters in town, such as the boorish Smerloff. As ambiguous as his national identity is Bimba's sexuality. Unlike the other men, Bimba never engages in heterosexual banter, and initially seems closest to the young Italian Bernardo (the film drops this subplot soon after and never shows Bimba's reaction to the latter's suicide later on in the film). His dandyesque demeanor, and his implied aristocratic background, too, distinguish his brand of masculinity from the working-class machismo of the other men, which is further accentuated by the contrast between van Eyck's controlled body movements and especially Montand's more erratic and volatile physical expressions.

Crucially, and very much in line with the film's misanthropic philosophy, it is Bimba's gradual emotional softening during the suicide mission, and his incipient interaction particularly with codriver Luigi, which precipitate his death. After Bimba has proven to be as heroic as everyone else, and shortly before their truck blows up, Bimba finally reveals his past to Luigi, telling him that he was once sentenced by the Nazis to three years of hard labor in the salt mines. It is left unsaid what he was sentenced for—was Bimba a criminal, a political prisoner, racially undesirable, a disillusioned soldier, perhaps even committed for charges of sexual deviancy? The film never provides an answer. Fastidiously shaving himself, inspecting himself in the truck's rear mirror, and casually anticipating his death, Bimba's last words, delivered by van Eyck with haughty pride and clipped tones, are: "Before being hanged, my father asked to take a shower. It runs in the family. I like to be clean. If I've got to be a corpse, I want to be . . . presentable."

Given the rather hazy clues the film provides as to Bimba's origins, it is perhaps not surprising to find diverging interpretations of the character in the film's contemporary West German promotion and press reception. On the whole, van Eyck's performance, and the character of Bimba, were valued positively. A number of reviewers contrasted van Eyck's perfor- mance with his previous parts in German films, implying that the latter had been somewhat lacking in appropriate masculinity. Thus, one critic praised his performance, but regretted that in West Germany he had been mainly used as a "male beauty" (Kolle 1953), while one reader's letter to a newspaper found van Eyck in *Le salaire de la peur* "surprisingly mascu- line" (Bletschacher 1953). In contrast, none of the West German reviewers detected any sexual ambiguities in the part of Bimba.

Another interesting aspect of the West German reception of *Le salaire de la peur,* and particularly of van Eyck's role in it, is the emergence of interpretations that do not appear to have any foundation in the film itself. Thus, the film's German distributor refers to Bimba as a "German adven- turer and mercenary" in its promotional brochure, despite the fact that the film never indicates explicitly that Bimba has a military background. The brochure also offers a brief biographical portrait of van Eyck, which mentions his German origins and his stay in the United States, although no specific dates and details are given, and thus any linkage to the Nazi past is avoided. More puzzling is one review in which van Eyck's part is described as a "former German soldier whose hair turned white in the Uranium mines of the East" (Kolle 1953). In fact, none of these observa- tions relates to information provided in the original film.

As Joseph Garncarz has demonstrated (1992), politically motivated alterations of the dubbed soundtracks of foreign films in 1950s West Ger- many were not uncommon, especially where foreign films included rep- resentations of, or references to, the Nazi past, or more generally negative portrayals of Germans and Germany. Notorious examples include the excision of characters, and the revision of dialogue in the West German release versions of Hollywood films such as *Casablanca* (1942) and *The African Queen* (1951). It is thus plausible that in the West German version of *Le salaire de la peur,* Nazis could have been translated into enemies from the East to suit the period's Cold War political agenda; that the salt mines had become, more topical for the nuclear age, uranium mines; and that a gratuitous explanation was inserted to resolve the mystery why formerly brown-haired actor van Eyck, familiar to German audiences, was sud- denly sporting shockingly white hair. However, this explanation loses some credibility since at least one review clearly identified van Eyck's role as that of a German émigré (e.g., *Zürcher Zeitung*, 21 October 1953).

It is difficult to determine retrospectively what caused this divergence in interpretations. However, even if these comments are pure inventions or acts of misremembering, as Janet Staiger has argued, no act of interpretation, including apparently "false" readings or "misreadings" (in the sense of a seeming mismatch between reading and text) "falls from the heavens" but rather emanates "from discourses circulating in the social formation" of that particular interpreting individual at that particular moment in time (1989: 360). In this respect, the frequent associations by West German critics of van Eyck's part in *Le salaire de la peur* with the German military, and the transferal of references to the Nazi period onto references to the Cold War, are particularly telling.

In the early to mid-1950s, attitudes in West Germany toward militarism in general, and Germany's own military legacy in particular, were complex and contradictory. On the one hand, a large proportion of the West German public held strong (if politically diffuse) pacifist views, and opposed the Federal Republic's rearmament (which took place by mid decade with the foundation of the *Bundeswehr*, mostly as means to integrate West Germany into the transatlantic alliance against the Warsaw Pact states; see Westermann 1990: 36–44). Moreover, the memory of the German army was intrinsically linked to memories of national defeat and humiliation as well as to individual hardship and trauma, and thus more often than not suppressed. The traditional army hierarchy and military elite had been morally discredited for having been complicit in the Nazi regime. With regard to the negotiation of van Eyck's star persona, it is worth remembering that the professional soldier class had traditionally been recruited from precisely the same background van Eyck had been born into and that he still epitomized in his looks and appearance—the *Junker* class or landowning Prussian aristocracy. Thus it is notable that throughout most of the 1950s, this aspect of van Eyck's background remained more thoroughly repressed than any other aspect of his biography, including his exile.

At the same time, large parts of the West German population did not accept the culpability of the army per se, or of the "ordinary soldier." In this context, the West German critics' reading of van Eyck's part in *Le salaire de la peur* as a German soldier who possesses qualities of virtue and heroism, who is conveniently detached from any association with the Nazi past but also is not (unlike in the original film) an active opponent or victim of the Nazi regime, offers a way out of the impasse in which the German military legacy was held after the war. One can surmise that the film's textual polysemy, as well as its existentialist emphasis on individual destiny and choice aided such an interpretation. Moreover, this reading anticipated and complemented the narrative strategies of countless West German war films in the second half of the 1950s (see Westermann 1990: 51–95; Hake 2002: 96–97), a genre that actively promoted the rehabilitation of the "ordinary" German soldier and of the traditional professional soldier class; film examples include *Canaris* (Canaris: Master Spy, 1954) and *Des Teufels General* (The Devil's General, 1955).

Ostensibly falling into the category of the rehabilitory war genre is one of van Eyck's West German films in the late 1950s, *Rommel ruft Kairo* (Rommel Calls Cairo, 1959), although the film and its reception perhaps more accurately demonstrate that the discourse on West Germany's position in Europe and in the world, and on its military legacy, had evidently moved ahead since the mid 1950s. This in turn also had an impact on how van Eyck's star persona was negotiated. More of a desert adventure *cum* spy caper than a proper war film, *Rommel ruft Kairo* retells a famous episode of the North Africa campaign during World War II. On Rommel's orders two German agents traversed the Libyan Desert under the nose of the British army, and set up a spying operation in Cairo with the help of Egyptian nationalists (for the most recent historical study concerning this mission, see Kelly 2002). In the film version of the story, van Eyck has again a suitably liminal role, that of the real-life Hungarian explorer Count Almassy (later to be fictionalized in the novel and film *The English Patient*, 1996), who works for the Germans and guides the agents through the desert. Asked by one of them why he is taking part in this conflict as a foreigner, Almassy replies: "Because everyone has to be somewhere today. If I have to play war games, I'd rather do it in Africa. I'm at home in the desert. Also, I believe that they conduct war in a more sporty way here." *Rommel ruft Kairo* certainly works hard to sustain Almassy's impression of a "sporty war." Everyone in the film (whether German, British, Hungarian, or Egyptian nationalist, including Field Marshall Rommel, portrayed with paternal gravitas by former Ufa star Paul Klinger) appears to be noble, chivalrous, and heroic. The operation itself, which ultimately fails, is conducted with good humor and cheerfulness; the enemies consider each other with mutual respect and admiration (there is even a rudimentary romance between one of the German agents and a British secretary); there is hardly any reference to the wider political context; and, thus, the war seems indeed more like an enjoyable and good-natured game or tourist adventure than anything else.

Interestingly, the strongest opposition to the film at the time came not from antimilitarist circles but rather was voiced in the right-wing war veterans' publication *Der Stahlhelm* by one of the original participants in the operation, objecting to what he considered a falsification of the real events. This included the film's assumption that the British army had been aware of the operation from the start (von Steffens 1959). Looking at the film today, however, it is highly unlikely that the filmmakers' primary motivation had been historical authenticity, or even a retrospective rehabilitation of the German *Wehrmacht*. If the film has an ideological project at all, it is to provide a blueprint for amicable and cooperative relations between Britain and West Germany in the context of new Cold War alliances. One review picked up this theme, commenting on the film's curious lack of national hostilities: "it is understandable that in the age of NATO no one steps on each other's toes" ("Spione am Nil," *Frankfurter Rundschau*, 4 May 1959). The story itself certainly did not offend British sensibilities—a British film version was released only two years later under the title *Foxhole in Cairo* (1961), again with van Eyck in the Almassy role. Other reports on the film read like enticements to West German audiences to consider tourist trips to Egypt. The following extract is from a location report published prior to the film's release: "Yesterday a battlefield, today a film location, tomorrow a tourist destination—this is El Alamein . . . European travel agencies are already investigating accommodation possibilities . . . for package tours under the heading 'From the pyramids to Rommel's battlefields.' Attractions are manifold: pharaonic tombs, eternal summer sun, ideal beaches, camel rides, and now too a walk across the battlefield of El Alamein, and a visit to the cemeteries and memorials" (Borgelt 1959).

Indeed, most of these attractions, including the additional one of an authentic belly dancer, were on prominent display in *Rommel ruft Kairo*. What the contemporary reception of the film, and its explicit tie-in with the tourist industry, indicates is that by the late 1950s the thorny issue of national identity in West Germany was addressed by enthusiastically an individualistic, consumer-oriented cosmopolitanism, and deliberately rejecting the notion of a fixed German identity. As I have argued elsewhere, this was to become one of the central characteristics of 1960s popular cinema in West Germany and represented the mind-set with which this type of cinema was received (see Bergfelder 2004). In the case of the report about the making of *Rommel ruft Kairo*, and within the film itself, the emphasis is clearly on transforming the uncomfortable memory of military defeat into a consumable and enjoyably themed tourist experience.

In keeping with this shift in public discourse, the engagement with van Eyck's star persona underwent a significant change in the late 1950s, which constituted the peak of his career in West German cinema, culminating in a number of major roles in high-profile productions. Although van Eyck continued to play a variety of nationalities on screen, from the late 1950s onward, he was equally often cast as a German, for instance as a teacher in the youth drama *Schmutziger Engel* (Dirty Angel, 1958), as a Krupp-like industrialist in Helmut Käutner's *Hamlet* adaptation *Der Rest ist Schweigen* (The Rest Is Silence, 1959), and continuing in the 1960s with the domestic thriller *Ein Alibi zerbricht* (An Alibi for Death, 1963), where he plays an architect. Still, even in these roles he remains an ambiguous and placeless figure, perhaps most poignantly in his part as a Jewish-Prussian civil servant in the Nazi-period melodrama *Liebling der Götter* (Sweetheart of the Gods, 1960).

At the same time, newspaper reports and reviews began to refer to van Eyck more frequently than before as being German, even in those instances where the respective roles were not. For example, in some reviews of *Rommel ruft Kairo*, van Eyck's part is referred to as a "German officer," despite the fact that at several moments in the film his part is clearly identified as Hungarian. Similarly, one can detect in star portraits and promotional brochures of this time a greater willingness to embrace van Eyck precisely because of his nomadic biography, which is now valued positively. Portraits and reports claim the "prodigal son" van Eyck, a successful cultural export of (as well as import in) the Federal Republic, who is confidently compared with international stars, such as equally white-haired Hollywood actor Jeff Chandler ("Ein Pommer in Hollywood: Peter van Eyck wird internationaler Star," *Rhein-Zeitung*, 9 January 1959) or the French Jean Gabin ("Ein Filmstar mit kosmopolitischem Steckbrief," *Saarbrücker Zeitung*, 1 February 1958). In the context of a country that had regained enough self-confidence through the economic miracle, as well as through the entry into NATO and the EEC, to reclaim its importance and equal footing in the world, van Eyck's cosmopolitanism now represented a lifestyle to be aspired to, summarized in romantically embellished descriptions such as this:

> The French, who are of course well known for their poignant expressions, call him the "man from nowhere." One could equally say, a man from everywhere, as Peter van Eyck is a cosmopolitan *par excellence*. . . . He is the modern type of man that Hemingway introduced to literature—the man without illusions, the representative of a lost generation. . . . That he, the quintessential globetrotter with a house in California and a flat in Paris is also German seems initially scarcely believable. ("Star auf der Leinwand und Kosmopolit dazu," *Mittelbayerische Zeitung Regensburg*, 24 December 1959)

If it is true, as many film historians claim, that the main ideological projects of the West German cinema of the 1950s were the readjustment of normative gender relations (i.e., a process of patriarchal relegitimation) and the restoration of national identity, then the very existence of a star image such as van Eyck's, transgressing in varying degrees both norms of national identity and masculinity, could be perceived as an implicit critique of, or at least as a contradiction to, both projects. Alternatively, one could argue that it is precisely the fact that van Eyck was cast so often in foreign roles that allowed the West German films he appeared in to locate any challenges to postwar West German masculinity outside the boundaries of the national. For this strategy to be effective, however, would have required van Eyck to be perceived by audiences as an unreconstructedly negative image, which clearly he was not. His prominence and popularity, particularly with female audiences, suggest otherwise.

Van Eyck's case may in fact be productively compared with the reception in the United States of Erich von Stroheim and his 1922 film *Foolish Wives*, and not just because both actors projected a somewhat heightened stereotype of Prussianism. Analyzing press responses in the 1920s, Janet Staiger has described how Stroheim's star image and on-screen persona contravened and collapsed a number of seemingly fixed binary oppositions in American public discourse at the time (e.g., between American and un-American, between American and foreign, between masculine and feminine, and between hero and villain [1992: 124–38]). Staiger locates the scandal that von Stroheim caused, as well as his appeal particularly to female audiences, precisely in the inability of his star image to be contained by these oppositions, a paradox that becomes encapsulated in the seemingly tautological epithet von Stroheim earned himself during this time as "the man they love to hate."

Similarly, my study has demonstrated that there are a number of binary oppositions operating in the West German public discourse of the 1950s that inform and structure the reception of van Eyck's star persona. Among these, most notably, are German versus foreign, a repressed German past versus an eagerly pursued German future, masculinity versus femininity (as well as competing versions thereof), and the qualities of an actor vs. the personality of a star. Many of these dichotomies were placed on a spectrum between "appropriate" and "excessive," value judgments that corresponded to connotations of national qualities and traditional values versus the specter of crass commercialism and foreign, in particular American, infiltration.

As in the case of von Stroheim, van Eyck's star persona collapsed the distinction between categories believed at the time to be incompatible—he was both an émigré and a Prussian *Junker*; he was alternately German, American, and foreign; he exuded the appeal of the worldly cosmopolitan but he could equally be contained in the domestic, national sphere. He contravened some norms of masculine behavior, while exceeding them in other respects; his sex appeal had a dangerous and adventurous undercurrent, as his ambiguous film roles demonstrated. Van Eyck's more feminized consumption patterns and his associations with fashion and grooming, meanwhile, legitimated and glamorized such behavior for his female fans at a time when dominant social and political discourses attempted to police it differently. It is thus understandable why van Eyck, especially to female audiences, constituted an attractive and liberating alternative to other male star images, masculinities, and national identities in 1950s West Germany. But it is equally clear why it took almost a decade before his persona in its various ambiguities could be fully accepted.

Chapter 4

HELMUT KÄUTNER'S *EPILOG:* *DAS GEHEIMNIS DER ORPLID* AND THE WEST GERMAN DETECTIVE FILM OF THE 1950S

Yogini Joglekar

The sixty-three *Detektivfilme* (detective films) made in West Germany from 1950 to 1955 amount to approximately 15 percent of West German film production during these years (Schuster 1999: 132).[1] On a scale of one to seven, with one being the best, most of these detective films received a popularity rating of between two and three, and a press rating of between three and four (Bauer 1981). In spite of these impressive statistics, a predominant theme in 1950s film criticism was the dearth of detective film in postwar Germany: "No one will deny that postwar German cinema has ignored the genre of detective film in an almost stepmotherly fashion. Imported goods from French and Anglo-American cinema have filled German theater screens in the last decade—such as films by Hitchcock, Huston, Wyler, Reed, Dassin, Cayatte" (*Film-Echo*, 1 March 1958: 86) .[2]

Detective films remained absent from scholarship on postwar German cinema for a long time. While scholars dealt with Weimar detective films to some extent, the prevalence of this genre in 1950s German cinema remains underexplored.[3] This essay takes stock of the detective genre's popularity in postwar film production. I analyze the genre-breaking and politically committed film *Epilog: Das Geheimnis der Orplid* (Epilogue: The Orplid Mystery, 1950) as a trendsetter for the West German antidetective film, which, as I argue in the next section, breaks with both the form and epistemological project of the detective genre. While connecting back to the émigré traditions in Hollywood that will become known as film noir, *Epilog*'s antidetective impulse anticipates the work of New German directors such as Rainer Werner Fassbinder, Rudolf Thome, and Reinhard Hauff in the late 1960s and early 1970s.

Trends in Postwar German Detective Films

In 1949, results from a public opinion survey conducted in the American occupation zone ranked detective films third among the most viewed genres, after romantic films and musicals. The same survey indicated that 51 percent of the viewing public wanted to see entertaining films, while only 21 percent voted for "problem films" (Burghardt 1996: 242). Manfred Barthel lists two common elements of German detective films between 1945 and 1955: (1) they were set in the postwar, rubble-strewn present, and (2) the focus was less on detective work and more on the criminals' self-questioning and self-incrimination (1986: 265). These two characteristics evoke the main features of "rubble" films—namely, their engagement with calamitous destruction and resilient reconstruction, and their imagery of urban ruins. Accordingly, Barthel's characterization fits a generation of rubble detective films that concentrate on surviving the postwar years, such as *Razzia* (Police Raid, 1947) and *Wer fuhr den grauen Ford?* (Who Drove the Gray Ford? 1950). Both films are set against a backdrop of destroyed cities and feature crimes involving profiteering on the black market, smuggling, and shady deals made for bread and liquor. These pessimistic films, where a new life is predicated on petty crimes, treat rubble cinema's message of the new beginning ironically. At the same time, criminals are shown as victims in *Razzia* and *Wer fuhr den grauen Ford?* and treated with sympathy by well-meaning detectives. In fact, the investigators of rubble detective films become blemish-free representatives of a new postwar beginning.

Detective films of the 1950s made in West Germany take economic recovery for granted, replacing the ruined cityscape with posh hotel rooms and elegant apartments. The detective genre resorts to closed-room mysteries and jigsaw-puzzle structures in films such as *Der Mann, der sich selber sucht* (The Man in Search of Himself, 1950) or *Der Fall Rabanser* (The Rabanser Case, 1950). Happy endings further reinforce a sense of security, for instance in the West German/Swiss/Spanish production *Es geschah am hellichten Tag* (It Happened in Broad Daylight, 1958). All of these films unperturbedly gloss over the recent past of National Socialism. In fact, by refusing to admit any doubt about detectivistic acumen or the absolute categories of guilt and innocence, they echo the black-and-white distinctions between crime and detection characteristic of Nazi detective films like *Alarm* (1941) and *Flucht ins Dunkel* (Flight into Darkness, 1939), and the puzzle structure of *Der Ruf an das Gewissen* (The Appeal to Conscience, 1945, released 1949).

Film scholars have often observed that unlike the *Stunde Null* (zero hour) in German literature and art, where an effort was made consciously to evaluate and spurn the legacy of the Nazi past, filmmaking in postwar Germany thrived on a sense of uncritical continuity with the past (Elsaesser 2000: 252). Many of the directors, actors, and technicians had learned their craft in the Ufa studios during the 1930s and 1940s. Within the detective genre, directors such as Erich Engels continued to produce suspenseful thrillers in postwar Germany. Some of the most popular detective films of the immediate postwar period were made in 1945 and released in 1949, such as *Der Ruf an das Gewissen* and *Die Nacht der Zwölf* (Night of the Twelve, 1945).

Films such as *Gesucht wird Majora* (Search for Majora, 1949) are set during World War II but nevertheless dodge memories of the Third Reich. The past appears only in the form of war, which provides the main twists in the detective plot. References to the past serve to indicate that moral decency and individual courage had prevailed during National Socialism. Solving the mystery about a missing chemical formula becomes relevant only with respect to a moral code that prescribes fulfilling a promise made to a fallen war comrade, and enabling his widow's survival in postwar penury. In *Gesucht wird Majora*, the action cuts between the war front and postwar reconstruction in a chemical factory, completely glossing over the political past.

Nonconfrontation with the Nazi past is most evident in the Edgar Wallace films, where the murdered body is displaced from Germany to the home of crime stories in England. The cityscape of London, with its fog-covered streets, shady warehouses along the Thames, and formidable underworld, creates an aura of peril, while the closed world of castles or country houses limits the number of suspects. The mentally and physically agile detective poses questions, follows leads, and reasons adeptly until he uncovers the truth. The criminal is promptly delivered to the law, while the detective and survivors (potential victims and innocent suspects) rejoice in the restoration of order. Although the spine-tingling Edgar Wallace series can be seen as a counterpoint to the mellifluous accord of many postwar films, the series' displacement of crime and detection away from Germany indicates an unwillingness to explore the problematic issue of guilt on home terrain (see Bergfelder 2003; Kreimeier 1985).

It is clear from this brief survey of postwar German detective films that the genre served as a fantasy world and avoided an open political analysis of the National Socialist past. The investigative narrative successfully negotiated the stories of crime and detection to a reified conclusion, including punishment for the criminal and reward for the detective. The few detective films that do talk about the Nazi past use flashbacks to create a safe distance and clear demarcation with relation to the Third Reich. The investigative structure provides suspense, but a resolution of the enigma mitigates the political import in favor of attention to the present, resulting merely in a coherent position of knowledge.

Der Verlorene (The Lost One, 1951), an investigative story *cum* thriller, uses a flashback structure to unmask gradually its main character, Dr. Rothe (played by the actor and director Peter Lorre), as a scientist who metamorphoses into a pathological serial killer during the Third Reich. In the frame narrative, set in the postwar present, Rothe confronts his former laboratory assistant, Hoesch, who is the sole witness to his past crimes. Intercutting between the past and the present leads to the exposure of Rothe's past and culminates with his murder of Hoesch and his suicide. In spite of its confrontation of the past, the film associates the Third Reich with lunacy, and thereby historically qualifies Nazism as an act of madness. Through a narrative structure typical of Hollywood film noir—namely, setting crime in the past and its reconstruction in the present—*Der Verlorene* encourages a reflection on guilt but also precludes historical knowledge of this guilt and, by analogy, of a criminal Nazi regime.

By contrast, *Nachts, wenn der Teufel kam* (The Devil Came at Night, 1957) spurns the flashback, voiceover narration typical to film noir. Robert Siodmak's film signals that the future of detection in the postwar world must be synonymous with an investigation of the Nazi past, thereby questioning every person's complicity in the Third Reich. The film is set in 1944 and revolves around commissar Kersten's investigation, on behalf of the Gestapo, of the murders committed by the serial killer Bruno Lüdke. Siodmak's film, like *Der Verlorene*, makes the connection between the Third Reich and lunacy. However, it critically portrays the Nazi government's fear of Lüdke's and Kersten's criminal and detectivistic lunacies. Lüdke's combination of Germanness and abnormality is considered dangerous and worth eradicating because it contradicts the National Socialist state's fundamental beliefs about race. After Commissar Kersten refuses to compromise his reading of the mystery in favor of the Gestapo's predetermined solution, he is immediately deported to the dreaded eastern front.

Siodmak's pessimistic ending from 1957 builds on tendencies from West German detective cinema begun with the genre subversive tendency of Helmut Käutner's *Epilog* in 1950. Here, running parallel to traditional detective films that affirmed the status quo throughout the 1950s, begins a new subgenre, namely antidetective film, that exhibits the need to incorporate a meticulous stocktaking of political history in the unraveling of mystery. *Epilog* becomes the first example of antidetective film in West

Germany, deviating from the formal conventions that had been the back-bone of the Nazi, as well as the genre-affirming postwar detective films described earlier in this section.

By antidetective cinema I mean films in which the detectives' investigations lead not to a successful solution, but instead to a core of doubt enhanced by two means: (1) a questioning of the traditional detective film form, and (2) a commentary on sociopolitical conditions.[4] Fritz Lang's early detective films, including *M* (1931) and the first two Mabuse films (1922, 1933), foreshadow West German cinema's engagement with anti-detection through their formal transgressions and their perceptive social commentary. Käutner departs from the stilted conventions of West German detective film through his postwar brand of antidetection, which combines references to Hollywood film noir, a subversion of traditional detective film conventions, and a critical connection to the Nazi past.

Antidetective Cinema and Film Noir

Film noir emerged in the 1940s as a visual expression of social and aesthetic concerns, including a collective social angst culminating in World War II, individual alienation, and sexual confusion. The body of film noir, a set of Hollywood films largely influenced by European émigrés, became increasingly familiar to 1950s filmmakers and audiences in West Germany with the import of movies such as *The Maltese Falcon* (1941), *Niagara* (1953), and *Pickup on South Street* (1953) (Seidl 1987: 15).

The detective's exit from the narrative through death is a film noir convention that Käutner appropriates for the German screen in *Epilog* to set critical postwar detective film back on its feet. Käutner chooses to imbue his antidetective film with shades of noir through *Epilog's* expressionist lighting, complicated narrative structure, and its reliance on a (soon-to-be) dead detective as the first-person narrator—a device that had already appeared in films such as Billy Wilder's *Double Indemnity* (1944) and *Sunset Boulevard* (1950). Most of the characteristic American noir techniques are found in Käutner's film: many of the scenes are lit for night; oblique and skewed lines or camera angles are preferred over horizontal ones; and there is an attachment to water, windows, and other reflective surfaces and to a complex chronological order (Cook 1981: 404). Film noir was a highly expressive visual arena for filmmakers who were able to articulate the individual and cultural concerns that troubled postwar America. The foreword to *Shades of Noir* cites the volatile social and economic situation of the decade immediately following World War II as informing the body of classic noir films (Copjec 1993: 4). Such a grounding of noir's cinematic elements within a social context runs parallel to *Epilog*'s juxtaposition of its unconventional film form with contemporary conditions in West Germany.

European filmmakers in exile—the German-speaking directors Fritz Lang, Otto Preminger, Robert Siodmak, and Billy Wilder, among them—played an integral role in the formation of Hollywood's film noir.[5] In a kind of reverse transfer, Käutner sets postwar detective film back on its feet by appropriating noir conventions for the West German screen in *Epilog*. Because the seminal figures developing this film form had been exiled during the Nazi years, *Epilog* can conceive of noir as being unburdened by Germany's immediate historical and cinematic past. Käutner's turn to the legacy of Hollywood noir, then, confirms two things. First, *Epilog*'s noir stylization and blending of hopelessness with irrecoverable time contrasts with Nazi detective cinema's formal techniques and its insistence on closure through the detective's triumph. Second, political concerns permeate *Epilog*'s dark style, departing from Nazi film's disavowal of politics. The dark elevator at the end of the film can be read as a zero hour for antidetection, and the signal for a redefinition of detective cinema's images as the future of West German film.

The path to antidetection in *Epilog* leads back to a Weimar antidetective tradition initiated by Lang and to German expressionist cinema's visual techniques, which in turn connect to film noir in Hollywood. Käutner's emphasis on chiaroscuro in *Epilog* suggests one way out of the demarcations of traditional detective cinema. Yet *Epilog*'s noir connection forms only one part of its broader antidetective tendency. While most of film noir can be classified as being antidetective owing to a sense of past and future disaster and a fascination with unpredictability in form and content, antidetective cinema cannot be reduced to noir. Film noir and antidetective cinema merge in questioning the traditional representation of detection and their common exposure of the links between power, money, and politics. But antidetective cinema's agenda, broadly stated, consists of a revision of film form. The boundaries between theorizing and fictionalizing detection are more or less erased, and the resulting interconnection is linked to historical conditions. In this sense, noir references are only one aspect of *Epilog*'s antidetective character, which combines self-consciousness through film form with self-criticism through tackling the Nazi past.

Epilog and West German Antidetective Cinema

The negotiation of guilt and innocence with regard to the Nazi past was a widely debated theme in the immediate postwar period. By February 1950, 3.6 million Germans were tried in the so-called de-Nazification trials

(Lange 2000: 1): 25,000 were sentenced as *Hauptschuldige* or *Belastete* (highest culpability, category one or two); 150,000 were categorized as *Minderbelastete* (less culpable, category three). One million landed in category four, *Mitläufer* (collaborator), and 1.2 million were declared *unschuldig* (innocent, category five). The sentences corresponded to these five categories of National Socialist involvement, and ranged from fines, confiscation of property, loss of voting rights, loss of the right to practice one's profession, and imprisonment up to ten years. After eight months, in December 1950, the *Bundestag* recommended the following for de-Nazification trials: canceling categories three to five and lifting all sanctions against them by April 1951; continuing trials for categories one and two; and, excusing fines under DM 2000. These sanctions, along with the fact that individuals such as Alfred Hugenberg, who had at one time occupied a prime place in the Third Reich's hierarchy, were declared to be merely category four, destroyed the validity of the Western Allies' de-Nazification and strengthened the emphasis on forgetting. Detective films held up a mirror to the repressive tendency of the times, rendering the political past invisible in their treatment of crime and punishment. However, Käutner's antidetective film insisted on casting a critical glance at the Nazi past and foregrounded the connection between investigation and introspection, between suspicion and self-incrimination.

Epilog was hailed by many as a symbol of a "rebirth" for German detective film after the caesura of World War II (*Der Spiegel*, 24 August 1950: 51). Reviews acknowledged Käutner's unsettling film style, but they did not make any connections to the traditional detective film form. Käutner's unconventional use of lighting and camera angles was compared with French realism, and *Epilog*'s moral ambivalence was read as a reaction to "the typically cheerful American knockout mentality" (51). There were a few initial murmurs of disapproval about the "trashy" quality of Käutner's new product (*Filmpresse*, 29 September 1950: 82). However, *Epilog* soon received an unequivocal stamp of approval after being showered with accolades by the foreign press and being bought by thirteen countries at the Biennale film festival in Venice. The commercial and critical success of the film was evident both in the summary of sales that reported a "business prognosis [of] very good for every theater" (*Film-Echo*, 30 September 1950: 7), and in the inclusion of the film as part of the *Woche des deutschen Films* (German Film Week) organized in Wiesbaden from 29 September to 5 October 1950, which showcased 50 German films out of a total of 203 produced between 1946 and 1950.[6]

Undoubtedly, the most significant aspect of *Epilog*'s reception was the sense of its being "more than a *Krimi* (crime drama)" (*Filmpresse*, 29 September 1950: 82). Reviews focused on the film's intriguing concoction of crime, adventure, scandal, and detection, but they did not give much notice to *Epilog*'s incertitude about genre conventions like happy endings and successful solutions. This neglect probably points to the fact that the film's sensational and fast-paced narrative drew most viewers to the theater rather than to its genre questioning.

Within Käutner's film, "Epilog" is the title of a report composed by the journalist Peter Zabel. Zabel becomes the main detective figure who investigates the mysterious sinking of a cruise ship (the *Orplid*) carrying a wedding party in August 1949. The film quickly reveals that a criminal named Siano, who belongs to a radical political organization, has been given the task of assassinating two corrupt weapons dealers on the ship. Siano plants a bomb on the *Orplid* and escapes. An undercover FBI agent on the ship discovers the bomb and gets rid of it. But the infighting among other passengers, who are unaware that they have been saved, finally leads to the ship's sinking. Zabel reconstructs this solution with the help of sketches drawn by the *Orplid*'s sole survivor, a mute Malay woman, Leata, with whom he becomes romantically involved. In questioning government officials and witnesses about the accident, Zabel stumbles upon secret weapons dealings among influential circles in West Germany. After narrating the story to potential publishers, Zabel fails to sell his report and leaves the magazine's offices, only to be shot in the elevator. His killer, Siano, is subsequently shot by Leata, and the film ends as Siano's accomplices seize Zabel's report and carry it off the screen.

Breaking away from formulaic detective cinema, Käutner suggests that detection means certain failure, and possible death, in the new postwar world, a sentiment that is at the core of antidetective cinema. In terms of film form, Käutner writes an epilogue—or, more appropriately, a requiem—for traditional German detective cinema. *Epilog* achieves this antidetective effect through three means: first, through innovative formal devices that question traditional detective film techniques; second, through its critical view of postwar Germany's attempts to come to terms with the Nazi past; and third, through its deep doubt in the efficacy of concepts like truth and knowledge, which aligns it with the pessimism and cultural critique of film noir.

What characterizes *Epilog* as an antidetective film is its break from traditional detective cinema's straightforward narrative movement from the crime to the solution, mediated through the detective's point of view. *Epilog*'s remarkable editing constantly intercuts between the frame and main narratives. The frame narrative, set in 1950 in the publishing house Mondial, presents Peter Zabel's attempts to sell his politically scandalous exposé. The main narrative presents Zabel's reconstruction of the fatal evening and his solution to the mystery of *Orplid*'s sinking.

The main narrative is clearly distinguished from the frame through distinctions in formal codes. For instance, the scenes in the publisher's office are characterized by zooms, reverse angle shots to simulate dialogue, and natural lighting, all of which imitate conventions of classical detective cinema. By contrast, a tilted camera axis, expressionist lighting, and an effective use of silence dominate the reconstruction of events on the *Orplid*.

Despite these differing techniques, the film persistently makes viewers aware of the fact that the two stories are inextricably interconnected, primarily through the use of parallel editing. The frame narrative from 1950 involving Zabel, Leata, and the publishers continually interrupts the action on the *Orplid* from 1949, most conspicuously through Zabel's voiceover narration. The year 1950 thus becomes the vantage point from which the events in 1949 are reviewed. Käutner uses the detective form to challenge his viewers' acumen, for instance, through metadiegetic devices like making the reel time correspond exactly to the "real time," the 72 crucial minutes (from 10:08 to 11:20) in the film's main narrative, inviting further reflection on the different temporal levels.

The parallel editing between temporal levels heightens suspense by raising audience expectations about a resolution to both sets of action in only one of the narrative levels. In a key sequence, the film gives viewers a clue about its antidetective conclusion. An anonymous telephone call received by the publisher while Zabel is trying to sell his investigative report sets off the sequence. When the caller inquires whether Zabel has several copies of his report, Zabel responds negatively but soon becomes suspicious of the caller's identity. The film cuts to a medium shot of the caller and shows the criminal Siano in deep focus, acting as the mastermind behind the threatening call. The sequence ends with a close-up of Zabel's panic-stricken face.

By revealing the caller's identity to viewers but not to the detective. and by focusing on Zabel's fear, the film exposes the detective's ignorance and vulnerability and usurps his authority. Although they take place in the frame narrative, these shots containing Siano are characterized by expressionist lighting, low angles, and a titled camera axis—all of which make an explicit connection to the main narrative's formal devices and evoke the *Orplid*'s milieu of foreboding and death.

Epilog signals a departure from traditional detective films in its fluctuation between various perspectives, including the points of view of the detective, the criminals, the co–conspirators, and the victims. This becomes evident after the discovery of the hidden bomb onboard, when the camera views the chaotic action from the perspective of different travelers on the ship, held together by Zabel's voiceover as he posits the "moral" of the film: "There was no assassination. The wedding party sank through its own guilt." His observation makes only a subtle reference to collective guilt, yet the allusion to debates about coming to terms with the Nazi past should have rung familiar to postwar audiences. *Epilog* departs from the apologetic, defensive tone of Käutner's immediate postwar films, such as *In jenen Tagen* (In Those Days, 1947), and provides a critical look at postwar German society through its frame and main narratives. Investigation in *Epilog* is revealed to be a two-pronged act of dismembering and remembering the past.

Zabel's deciphering of the *Orplid* mystery exposes the corrupt reality behind the facade of postwar complacency. In the frame narrative, a bureaucrat interrogated by Zabel gives an extensive report on the shady war dealings of the rich businessmen, Hoopman and Hill. The officer asserts: "We carry all records about de-Nazification." By connecting Hoopman's name to the postwar de-Nazification trials, the film implicates him in the crimes of the National Socialist regime. At the same time, Käutner ironically comments on the inadequacy of the de-Nazification process. The film gradually reveals Hoopman and Hill to be greedy profit-mongers who had thrived on dealing weapons during World War II, and who profit from war and death in an ostensibly peaceful postwar world. *Epilog* exposes the fallacy of declaring an entire population as de-Nazified already in 1950 by underlining Hoopman and Hill's continued culpability from the Third Reich to the present.

In fact, the main narrative explores the culpability of each of the ship's members in some detail, tracing their feelings of guilt to their past crimes. This exploration is anchored in the film's form. The camera cuts between different "victims"—the *Orplid*'s travelers, facing potential death—but does not portray them with the genre's usual sympathy for victims. Instead, their contemplation on past guilt and their perpetration of present crimes makes everyone onboard equally guilty. On the other hand, Zabel's voiceover mitigates Siano's guilt: "Siano was not a criminal in the usual sense of the word." The film condemns Hoopman as the true villain onboard, who made a fortune during the National Socialist years through shady weapons dealings and who seems to have survived de-Nazification with an unscathed reputation and conscience.

Another connection that the film establishes to the Third Reich is through the groom, Martin, who, portrayed as a bloodthirsty and bitter *Heimkehrer* (returning soldier) haunted by the past, becomes guilty of two murders in the film. The film also exposes the personal liability of the bride's coworker, whose jealousy of the newlyweds leads him to proclaim, "I am guilty," and to take his life with a revolver. Finally, the film unmasks its women as co–conspirators, sharing guilt and responsibility with different men. The film depicts postwar Germany as a society in which the shadow of war still looms large and the issues of guilt and innocence continue to be negotiated. The deadly residue of past guilt, combined with the heavy weight of present crimes, leads to what Zabel calls the ship's "sinking through its own burden."[7]

While there is a strong critical thrust in *Epilog*, it would be going too far to claim that Käutner's film overtly challenges the dominant mindset of its day. The film loses some of its edge by refusing to name names, although its allusion to a problematic past constitutes an important gesture for 1950s detective cinema. In this regard, it is interesting to note Käutner's choice of Carl Raddatz, the veteran actor from Nazi films, to play the part of the criminal, Siano, and his use of a young actor like Peter van Eyck, whose career is associated with the postwar German film industry, to play the part of FBI agent Banister. *Epilog* rapidly moves from personal intrigue to corrupt political dealings in its investigative narrative. Yet the return to the postwar present in the closing sequence appears to be a stylized noir gesture, packaging the past as a distant and neatly deciphered mystery.

In fact, *Epilog*'s conclusion contains the film's strongest social commentary and resonates with all three aspects that helped create its antidetective effect, namely, its disruptive film techniques, noir citations, and its critique of West German society's attempts to deal with the Nazi past. The "open elevator" sequence shifts the filmic perspective thrice, moving from an objective perspective to Leata's POV and then back to a new objective perspective in the final frame. In the course of these perspective shifts, the film violates the 180-degree rule, used in traditional detective cinema to maintain the audience's surety about where they are in relation to the on-screen action. By abandoning rigidity of (camera) position, the film refuses, in effect, to "take sides," and underscores its ambivalence about guilt and innocence.

The concluding scenes of the film occur in the following order:

a. Low-angle shot up the stairwell of the publishing house, foregrounding the rear close-up of a man; the man turns to face the camera and is identified as Siano; CUT TO

b. Medium shot of Zabel and Leata (filmed from the lobby looking into the elevator); the next few frames show Siano entering the elevator, stabbing Zabel and moving toward the building exit; Leata discovers Zabel's revolver in deep focus; CUT TO

c. Leata's POV, long shot of Siano from elevator; CUT TO

d. Close-up of tiles on the floor, fade out as the *Paternoster* (open elevator) passes between floors; FADE IN TO

e. Long shot from elevator of Siano handing over Zabel's manuscript to an accomplice, sound track playing revolver shot, and
Siano falling down; CUT TO

f. Traveling shot of elevator in the background moving up to the
eighth floor, with Zabel's corpse and Leata in darkness. Credit sequence begins.

While offering a semblance of closure for the *Orplid* mystery by punish-
ing the criminal Siano with death, the film also subverts the impulse of
traditional detective narratives in awarding the same fate to Zabel. The
extreme close-ups used throughout the film are replaced in the end with
a long take, a traveling shot that shows the dead reporter as yet undis-
covered in the dark, narrow space of an elevator, moving between floors,
while the results of his investigation are condemned to silence. The elevator "that moves upward, but not forward" brings to mind Hans Magnus
Enzensberger's formulation regarding German society's economic recovery and its upward mobility in the 1950s, despite its drifting in a state of
moral limbo (cited in Bänsch 1985: 27). The final frames capture the undis-
turbed daily life of the publishing house, even after two murders have
just been committed on its premises. The elevator in deep focus remains
submerged in the darkness of the background, perhaps signaling contemporary reactions to dealing with the past. Finally, the film undermines
Zabel's solution by making his investigative report disappear from the
screen in its final sequence, leaving viewers with a gaping void in place
of closure.

Käutner's depiction of the investigator's death negates not only the mystery and its reconstruction but also the entire filmic project of detection in
Epilog, which has been sustained on the various narrative levels through
his voice over. The convoluted chronology, combined with the detective's
death, creates the disturbing feeling that no one, especially the detective
who eventually reconstructs the past, can affect that destiny. The reliance
on a dead detective as the first-person narrator culminates the antidetective,
anti-epiphanic statement of the film. It also sets *Epilog* apart from traditional
West German detective films from the 1950s, which insist on providing
closure to all of the narrative strands they introduce. By making the detective himself pay dearly for his solution, namely, with his own life, and by
emphasizing the indifference of surviving witnesses, *Epilog* raises poignant
questions about the function of detection in 1950s society. Through the dead
end of the film, which abandons viewers without any solution, Käutner
casts doubt on the epistemological project of classical detective films as well
as on the efficacy of concepts like truth, enlightenment, and justice, even
while, in some sense, still insisting upon their pursuit.

Käutner's film subsumes the Hollywood noir legacy within the broader project of antidetective cinema. Film noir's foregrounding of urban nightmares, its convoluted intermeshing of temporal and spatial coordinates, and its quick-witted and quick-fisted investigator form only one part of the antidetective impulse within *Epilog*. Indeed, *Epilog* questions noir's ultimate faith in the detective as the upholder of moral standards in a depraved society, most famously stated in this characterization of the hardboiled private eye: "But down these mean streets a man must go who is . . . neither tarnished nor afraid . . . a man of honor, by instinct, by inevitability" (Chandler 1946: 237). In contrast, Zabel is both tarnished and afraid. His status as a reader of malaise is foregrounded more than is his sense of honor, and even the former is proved to be ineffectual since his reading is overwhelmed by more powerful adversaries and marked by failure.

Although Zabel refuses to compromise the truth and insists on exposing all criminals, the film also highlights the fact that his detection is a quest not only for truth but also for profit. In fact, the journalistic report "Epilog" becomes a commodity that Zabel attempts to sell to the publisher. Perhaps it is the incommensurability of the investigative and moneymaking projects that dooms Zabel's endeavors to failure. Zabel's potential publisher, Dr. Mannheim, is skeptical of his ambitions and wary of buying this radical text. Halfway through Zabel's reconstruction of the crime, Mannheim lauds him for having evaded political details in his narrative, and announces his magazine's explicitly apolitical nature: "My magazine contains nothing about politics. Politics is black and white—that leads to gray. I have a colorful magazine." This eschewal of politics is suggestive of postwar responses to coming to terms with the past and could be construed as Käutner's comment on a society that is indifferent to crime, especially to its political variant. Mannheim functions in Käutner's film as the representative of a postwar society that cannot bear to face the truth, and, by implication, one that does not care whodunit. At the same time, by placing this remark toward the end of a film that relies on gray tones and that refers to a problematic German past and present, Käutner posits *Epilog* as the antithesis to Mannheim's colorful magazine and puts forth his work as a severe political statement in the apolitical milieu of 1950s German detective cinema.

By doubling precedents from detective genres (e.g., the detective's insatiable search for truth) in order finally to undermine them (by revealing the unreliability of truth), *Epilog* becomes the first example of antidetection in West German cinema. The film signals a departure from the epistemological model of detection and undermines the traditional method of questioning sources in the pursuit of truth. Instead, it casts doubts on all certainties, affirming only the inescapable truth of death. The film does hope to achieve some degree of enlightenment, however, in two ways: first, by inviting viewers to reflect on the limitations of truth and the possible anachronism of an epistemological model of detection; and, second, by provoking viewers to become more active interpreters themselves and to reexamine clues on screen to become more subtle readers of signs, whether of guilt, innocence, or a more pervasive sense of ambivalence.

Antidetection continues to have a powerful presence in West German cinema, where it symptomatically registers the crises affecting society. Reémigré directors such as Robert Siodmak and Fritz Lang incorporate their Hollywood noir legacy into the antidetective films they make after returning to Germany, that is, in *Nachts, wenn der Teufel kam* (The Devil Came at Night, 1957) and *Tausend Augen des Dr. Mabuse* (The Thousand Eyes of Dr. Mabuse, 1960), respectively. From the mid-1960s on, the New German Cinema relies on antidetection in works like *Mord und Totschlag* (A Degree of Murder, 1967), *Detektive* (Detectives, 1968), *Götter der Pest* (Gods of the Plague, 1970), and *Messer im Kopf* (Knife in the Head, 1978).

Like *Epilog*, New German antidetective films clearly depart from the formulaic detective movies of the 1960s and 1970s, such as the Johannes Mario Simmel or Jerry Cotton series and the post-Lang Mabuse films. They also explicitly address the political context of sixties radicalism and its escalation into terrorism and state violence. Finally, noir elements surface in these New German antidetective films, but the directors are conscious of quoting a tradition that precedes them and their use of noir becomes the imitation of an imitation—Hollywood noir read through the French New Wave, then quoted in the German context.

Epilog's aesthetic and political choices set forth the West German detective film beyond its zero–hour languor. Käutner's film carries dead ends as well as new beginnings within itself—both the negation of traditional detective cinema's faith in closure and the refreshing possibilities of antidetective cinema—sustaining his epilogue through and beyond the 1950s.

Notes

1. This number is not insignificant when compared to production rates of other genres of the time: adventure films form 10 percent of total West German film production during the period; melodramas such as rubble films account for 30 percent, whereas comedies account for 45 percent of total film production (Schuster 1999: 133).
2. Similar sentiments are expressed in *Der Kurier*, 8 September 1950; *Die Rheinpfalz*, 17 December 1957; and *Filmblätter*, 5 December 1959. When not otherwise noted, all translations are by the author.
3. Observations on German detective film have normally occupied only a small part of book chapters or articles, for instance in Klaus Kreimeier's article on 1950s German cinema (1985). Norbert Grob's essay is restricted to the years 1959–60 (1993), addressing a limited array of pre-New German Cinema films, including *Das Mädchen Rosemarie* (The

Girl Rosemarie, 1958), *Am Tag, als der Regen kam* (The Day It Rained, 1959), and *Schwarzer Kies* (Black Gravel, 1960). More recently, Tim Bergfelder's essay on the Edgar Wallace films treats the West German detective genre in some detail (2003).

4. An extensive discussion of antidetection has blossomed in Anglo-American criticism, especially since the 1990s, started by critics such as John Irwin (1994) and Patricia Merivale (1999), and revolving around authors such as Umberto Eco, Jorge Luis Borges, Paul Auster, George Simenon, and Friedrich Dürrenmatt. The German film scholar Norbert Grob uses the term *Super Krimi* to refer to 1960s German detective film as "post-naive" detective cinema (1993: 216). I use the term "antidetective film" because it signifies a questioning of, and occasionally a movement antithetical to, the conventions set up by traditional detective cinema, a point on which I rely in my reading of German film of the 1950s.

5. The Third Reich and World War II, the main reasons behind the filmmakers' exile, formed the backdrop to noir films such as *Hangmen Also Die* (1943) and *Lifeboat* (1944).

6. Other crime thrillers included in the German Film Week were *Wer fuhr den grauen Ford?*, *Der Mann, der sich selber sucht* (The Man in Search of Himself, 1950), and *Der Fall Rabanser* (The Rabanser Case, 1950).

7. *Epilog's* use of the boat as an allegory of postwar Germany forges interesting connections with other films in which ships are used as privileged locations, including *Das Totenschiff* (The Ship of the Dead, 1959), the boat romance *Unter den Brücken* (Under the Bridges, 1944), and the crime film *Dr. Crippen an Bord* (Dr. Crippen Onboard, 1942). The self-contained space of *Epilog's* ship highlights the film's message about the ship's self-destruction, and its "no exit" imagery connects to film noir's hopelessness and doom.

Chapter 5

LOCATION *HEIMAT*: TRACKING REFUGEE IMAGES, FROM DEFA TO THE *HEIMATFILM*

Johannes von Moltke

Taking Refuge in *Heimat*: Expellees in the Homeland Film

Picture a long trek of people moving slowly across a vast, snow-covered plain, filmed at an angle so as to maximize the length of the trek and to exploit the formal dynamic of the diagonal cutting across the rectangular frame. Picture this image spliced together with other similar ones, cut to the sound of shuffling feet. This, according to the permanent exhibition at the *Haus der Geschichte* (Historical Museum) in Bonn, is the founding moment of the Federal Republic of Germany (FRG). Before we even enter the first section of the exhibit, entitled *Last der Vergangenheit und die Spaltung Deutschlands* (The Burden of the Past and the Division of Germany) we are confronted with the audiovisual representation of the westward trek on a monitor mounted in the museum foyer. The Federal Republic on display at the *Haus der Geschichte* is a nation born from the experience of defeat, flight, and expulsion.

Whatever the dubious historiographical merits of this foundational narrative, the images with which the exhibit begins are part of a visual repertoire that has accompanied German history since the end of World War II. As Robert Moeller has recently shown, discourses on postwar flight and expulsion and on the integration of expellees into the newly constituted West German state have formed a *basso continuo* to political and historiographical debates throughout the history of the Federal Republic (2001).[1] While this discourse reverberated differently in private and public spheres, I think Moeller is right in criticizing a prominent contributor to these debates like Günter Grass for misrepresenting the history of (how Germans have talked about) expulsion. In his celebrated novel *Im Krebsgang* (Crabwalk, 2002), Grass deliberately sketches a repression hypothesis around issues of flight and expulsion as the backdrop for his own intervention, which memorializes the sinking of the *Wilhelm Gustloff*, a ship carrying thousands of refugees across the Baltic in early 1945. Moeller argues, however, that "those who praised Grass for breaking a taboo" with the publication of *Im Krebsgang* "seemed uncritically to accept Grass's account of postwar memory" (2003: 179). Far from taboo, these questions have simmered *at* the surface of cultural and political discourse in the Federal Republic, not below it. As Joschka Fischer bluntly put it in an interview, these questions were "nowhere near taboo. My entire childhood and adolescence consists of these stories of expulsion, occupation, bomb nights and the expellee conventions" (2003). But despite its continuous presence, there is arguably a renewed urgency to the matter in recent years, as the witness generation begins to die out, as ethnic conflict in the Balkans brought new images of flight and expulsion during the 1990s, and as Germans, Poles, and Czechs engage in heated debates about whether, how, and where to "musealize" the history of expulsion (Franzen 2003; Krzeminski and Michnik 2002). Consequently, Germans have seen images of refugees recirculate on television, in accompanying book publications, and in glossy newsprint; public debates and a wide range of literary treatments have likewise drawn on this repertoire of images.[2]

The images in question are pictures of treks, of haggard women carrying their bundled babies westward, or of decimated families pulling carts piled high with their last possessions. As icons of public memory that have been endlessly circulated, copied, and reframed over the past half century, they constitute part of what Cornelia Brink calls the *soziale Bildgedächtnis* (social visual memory) of an event (1998: 8). This visual memory was first formulated during the immediate postwar years and gained clear contours during the long decade of the 1950s. Along with other emblematic images of the war and postwar years, visual representations of expellees and refugees began circulating early on in photojournalism; they were invoked in parliamentary debates about repatriation and about the recent past. In addition, refugees figured prominently in West German sociology of the 1950s, which regarded them as "prototypes" for the far-reaching changes that faced postwar society. In his influential study of the refugee family, for example, the conservative sociologist Helmut Schelsky repeatedly insisted that the transformations he observed were "not the exception, or opposite, to any constant family structure in German society, but appear[ed] to be instead the most advanced and pronounced form of a wholesale transformation in the contemporary German family" (1953: 50; see also Pfeil 1948).

But it was arguably the visual medium of cinema that contributed most lastingly to the construction of the postwar image of refugees. Here, I have in mind not only early *Trümmerfilme* (rubble films) such as *Die Mörder sind unter uns* (The Murderers Are among Us, 1946) and *Film ohne Titel* (Film Without a Name, 1948), or individual titles devoted explicitly to refugee stories, such as Frank Wisbar's *Nacht fiel über Gotenhafen* (Darkness Fell on Gotenhafen, 1959), which offers an early treatment of the events that Grass chronicles in *Im Krebsgang*. After World War II, familiarity with the topic of expulsion was soon not just a matter of historical experience or sociological research—it rapidly became a generic convention as images of refugees found their way into the narratives and iconographies of West Germany's favorite genre, the *Heimatfilm*. Beginning with *Grün ist die Heide* (Green Is the Heather, 1951), scores of *Flüchtlinge* (refugees) and *Vertriebene* (expellees) made regular appearances in these films. Not always were these appearances staged as blatantly as in Paul May's *Heimat, Deine Lieder* (Heimat, Your Songs, 1959), which incorporates a choir of orphaned expellees singing the *Heimatlied* at a screening of the documentary *Schlesien wie es war* (Silesia as It Used to Be) before a fictional audience of expelled Silesians in a local inn.[3] Other films wrote the motif of expulsion into their protagonists' biographies, as in *Der Förster vom Silberwald* (The Game Warden of the Silver Forest, 1955), where we learn that a local hunter—the incarnation of moral virtue, a cultured lover of nature played by Rudolf Prack—learned to play the organ on "our estate in my lost *Heimat*." A recurring screenwriting practice that also suggests the topical force of the issue involved introducing the motif of expulsion in remakes of old films, thus bringing them "up to date"—as, for example, in *Wenn am Sonntagabend die Dorfmusik spielt* (When the Village Music Plays on Sunday Nights, 1953 [1933]) or Wolfgang Staudte's version of *Rose Bernd* (1957 [1919]). Films like *Grün ist die Heide* or Wolfgang Liebeneiner's version of *Waldwinter* (Forest Winter, 1956 [1936]) were similarly "updated" remakes of older films into which writers and producers now introduced images of refugees as "topical-modern motifs" (Lüthge 1951). In the resulting films, expellees figured centrally in the plot while also providing much of the visual spectacle characteristic of the *Heimatfilm*. In some cases, this spectacular function of the expellee could be dissociated from the narrative altogether, serving instead to charge the films with a wistful tone of loss. Thus, in Hans Deppe's *Wenn die Heide blüht* (When the Heath Is in Blossom, 1960) one sequence shows a group of *Vertriebene* singing a *Heimat* song and celebrating an old man's seventy-fifth wedding anniversary as evening falls. The only connection of this group of characters to the principal cast is that they live on the farm where the action takes place. Without contributing to that action, they clearly "flavor" it with a dual sense of nostalgia and of topicality.

Given the prominence of refugees and expellees in these films, it is inadequate to dismiss them as escapist fare. To claim that the concrete problems of integrating expellees into the Federal Republic "did not find their way into the world of the *Heimatfilm*" (Trimborn 1998: 116) is to espouse a literal, reflectionist approach to the films at best. Such a claim misses the significant role of these films in offering imaginary solutions to real social problems. A more allegorical reading can show how these films engage in a sustained way with the logic, if not with the letter, of the refugee phenomenon (and of its economic dimension in particular). In this article, I should therefore like to look at how the generic framework of the *Heimatfilm* affects the construction of expulsion as social memory.

There are several explanations for the prominence of refugees in the *Heimatfilm*. Generally speaking, the genre's concern with questions of home provided a popular framework in which to negotiate both the refugee experience of homelessness and the pressing question of how to integrate the refugees as a social group into postwar German society. However, in taking up the issue of refugee migrations, the *Heimatfilm* would not only aim to defuse its potentially explosive social and political ramifications. In a remarkable turn, the genre also managed, in films like *Waldwinter*, to fold a whole village of Silesian expellees into its ongoing project of modernizing the provinces. As I hope to show, *Waldwinter* does not simply imagine refugee populations either as pining for a lost home or as an added burden on a suffering population; instead, it pictures refugees as the vanguard of postwar modernization, clad in provincial dress.

But in revisiting the image of refugees in the cinema of the 1950s, I have a second objective in mind; for the issues raised by the *Heimatfilm* of the Adenauer era are not confined entirely to the West. As I have argued elsewhere (von Moltke 2005), there are also a number of DEFA (Deutsche Film-Aktiengesellschaft, or German Film Corporation) productions that need to be reintroduced into this debate. Films such as Konrad Wolf's directorial debut *Einmal ist keinmal* (Once is Never, 1955), Martin Hellwig's *Das verurteilte Dorf* (The Condemned Village, 1952), or Kurt Maetzig's epic *Schlösser und Katen* (Palaces and Huts, 1957) often exhibit surprising affinities with the West German *Heimatfilm*, even as they contribute to the socialist resignification of the genre's provincial spaces. The same, I now want to suggest, applies in the case of the images of *Vertriebene*, named *Umsiedler* (resettlers) in the GDR. Here,

I will focus on Artur Pohl's directorial debut, *Die Brücke* (The Bridge, 1949), which centers explicitly on the issue of resettlement. *Die Brücke* is a remarkable document in that its narrative about the integration of displaced Germans from the eastern provinces into the fabric of local society predates by several years the corresponding preoccupation in Western *Heimatfilme*. More striking still, Pohl's film exhibits a number of affinities with a film like *Waldwinter* regarding the mise-en-scène of the refugee. Though neither *Die Brücke* nor *Waldwinter* stand out as masterworks of German cinema, their very "ordinariness" allows us to retrace an iconography and a discourse that positions the millions of postwar refugees at the heart of two distinct foundational narratives, in which they do structurally similar work.

Relocating the Economic Miracle: *Waldwinter* (1956)

In 1938, as a result of the Munich Accords that allowed Hitler to annex parts of Czechoslovakia, the Bohemian town of Gablonz (today, Jablonec in the Czech Republic) was incorporated into the German Reich. As part of the annexed areas, Gablonz was subject to Nazi population policies, which drove Czech nationals out of the Sudetenland and replaced them with ethnic Germans. This administered displacement of an entire population was reversed after 1945. After the defeat of Nazi Germany, the Czech government issued the notorious Benes Decrees, forcing the remaining German population to leave Gablonz (cf. Franzen 2001: 212–21). Some 18,000 of these expellees eventually made their way to the Bavarian city of Kaufbeuren and settled on its outskirts. This unique resettling process—in which an entire community was displaced, virtually intact, from its origin to a new destination—was accompanied by a far-reaching business plan, promoted by a particularly enterprising refugee named Erich Huschka.

Against the initial resistance of both the local population and the American occupation forces, he managed to secure a lease for a former explosives factory that had been largely demolished by the Americans in November of 1945. Bringing the dominant trade of Gablonz to Bavaria, the refugees founded an entire glassblowing and jewelry industry in their new hometown, making a significant contribution to the economic recovery of Kaufbeuren. By 1947, the settlement already boasted 92 registered businesses employing a total workforce of 811. As a result, and in recognition of the geographic and economic transformation it had undergone, on 8 August 1952, the city of Kaufbeuren renamed the area in which the Gablonzer population had settled "Kaufbeuren-Neugablonz."

Around the time of its incorporation, Neugablonz published an advertising flyer entitled "Which Is the Shortest Route to New-Gablonz?" The flyer takes the form of a map whose graphic design conflates multiple political, economic, and cultural messages in a single image. In its effort to help potential visitors locate the small town of Neu-Gablonz, the map is dominated by two large arrows. One arrow points out "Rhine-Main Airport," Germany's largest port of air-bound entry, located in the American zone of occupation.[4] Accessible by land, by sea, but especially by air, Germany is represented as a relay in the circuits of (Western) economic exchange. The second arrow, pointing directly at Neu-Gablonz from the original Gablonz in a black area to the northeast is more difficult to read without some knowledge of the town's "displaced" history. If the arrow to Frankfurt connects to an economic network, then the arrow to Neu-Gablonz represents a historical migration, as the date "1945" would suggest.

Centered at the bottom of the map, Kaufbeuren—Neu-Gablonz appears as a historical destination for the expelled population of Gablonz, but even more prominently as an economic destination for foreign trade from the West. The example of Neu-Gablonz illustrates how the reactionary politics and values associated with expellees as a social group were absorbed into their crucial role as modernizers in the process of economic reconstruction. Without in any way discounting the substantial and lasting political impact of eight million new citizens or the many intractable social, political, and cultural problems this raised, the integration of expellees during the 1950s also needs to be considered as a driving factor in West Germany's postwar recovery. For these new populations supplied much of the labor force for the "economic miracle." Entire so-called *Flüchtlingsindustrien*, industries run by expellees, contributed to the transformation of agrarian states like Bavaria into industrial *Standorte* (centers or locations). The massive population increase represented by the refugees both accelerated and intensified the process of industrialization. As the sociological "prototypes" of postwar displacement, expellees illustrate the degree to which even forced mobility sustained a broader project of modernization.

But the map adds at least one further dimension to this project by situating Neu-Gablonz as a tourist destination, itself a point of departure for daytrips to the various sites in the lower Alps, listed at the bottom of the image. Here, the graphic register shifts from a geographic map to a topographical panorama. While the design appears even more disjointed as a result, the added "message" is decipherable nonetheless: as a historically charged economic *Standort*, Neu-Gablonz is worth a trip not only for the goods it has to offer (thanks to the hard work of its refugee population) but also for its geographic location. In answering the question "how do I travel to Neu-Gablonz," the map thus also makes a threefold argument as to "why" anyone should undertake this journey in the first place: a unique *Standort* in the new Germany, Neu-Gablonz promises a blend of economic modernity, artisan tradition, and Alpine nature.

This mix defines the place of *Heimat* in postwar Germany, and its mise-en-scène in the *Heimatfilm* in particular. Nowhere is this more evident than in Wolfgang Liebeneiner's 1957 remake of *Waldwinter*, based on the novel by Paul Keller and also released under the title *Glocken der Heimat* (Bells of the Homeland). As the director put it, the film addressed "the fate of refugees in our time." Liebeneiner's synopsis would have been an irresistible pitch to any producer riding the so-called *Heimatfilmwelle* (wave of *Heimatfilme*) at the time: "after many trials and tribulations, [a] Silesian family regains its old *Heimat* in the Bavarian forest, its new *Heimat*."[5] Accordingly, the distributor urged theater owners to advertise *Waldwinter* to local groupings of the more than two million Silesians living in the Federal Republic who ("so we have been assured by well-placed sources") were "'starved' for a film like this one."[6]

But advertising copy for the film might also have read, "How do I travel to Falkenstein?" as Liebeneiner's film takes up the threefold project encoded in the Neu-Gablonz poster. Like so many other *Heimatfilme*, *Waldwinter* showcases its location—in this case, the Bavarian Forest—as a tourist destination. Here, the village of Silesian refugees that has relocated completely to the local baron's old hunting estate, "regains its old *Heimat* in the new *Heimat*" by marketing the traditional skill of its native glassblowers. By the time a new generator arrives to power the newly minted glass factory at the end of the film, the picturesque community of Falkenstein is fully connected to the grid of the Economic Miracle.

The small-scale economic miracle that unfolds in Falkenstein is predicated on the historical displacement of the Silesians from their "old *Heimat*." This becomes obvious in the film's opening sequence, which takes place in Silesia and ends with the image of the villagers walking off in a long line into the distance. Significantly, however, this generic and easily recognizable image is evoked only to be buried in the fabric of the film an instant later. As the villagers depart, the camera tilts down for a close-up of a snow-covered embankment, but when it tilts back up, we have skipped westward in space and forward in time. The parallelism established by the match cut is so strong, however, that it takes the viewers some time before they notice that this is no longer the Eastern front during the last winter of World War II. Instead we find ourselves on the Silesian baron's hunting estate in the Bavarian Forest.

This equivalence between the old and the new *Heimat*, articulated here through a simple editing device, emblematizes the narrative logic of the film. *Waldwinter* stages the baron's Bavarian estate as *Ersatz* for Silesia. As such, however, Falkenstein also becomes a "local metaphor" for the West German nation under reconstruction (see Confino 1997). Having established the similarity of old and new *Heimat*, the film turns to the central question of how to inhabit that space—that is, of how to reestablish *Heimat* for a refugee community in West Germany during the 1950s. The answer, it turns out, lies in joining the productivist ethos of the *Wirtschaftswunder*. The film's visual spectacle celebrates *Heimat* as a pristine refuge as well as an attractive tourist patrimony; its central narrative intrigue, however, is socioeconomic: how to provide for—and ultimately "integrate"—a whole village of refugees into the postwar West

German economy. Two answers are proposed over the course of the narrative, only to be dismissed: first, the baron's grandson Martin counsels his grandfather to sell the estate, move to Munich, and let the villagers fend for themselves in the Federal Republic's labor market. This solution is unacceptable to the baron, whose quasi-feudal values include a sense of responsibility for the people he calls *meine Schlesier* (my Silesians). Second, the baron's manager, prodded by his scheming wife, plots to turn the estate into a hotel. While this would bring in line the story with the profilmic space under the sign of tourism, the hotel solution again fails to provide for, and integrate, the refugees as a whole. Consequently, the manager is exposed, and a third plan, championed by the baron's adoptive granddaughter Marianne, carries the day. Marianne shares with her grandfather the sense of "responsibility" and "community," but the feudal ring of these values is tempered by her youth, by her "naturalness" (in a stock image of the *Heimat* genre, we see her feeding a deer in the winter forest), and by the film's romance plot.

Early in the film we learn that Marianne has come up with the idea to transform the hunting estate into a glassworks. Marianne has remained faithfully at her adoptive grandparents' side throughout the decade after their flight from Silesia; in Falkenstein, she tends to the household and works toward transforming the estate from a feudal hunting castle into a site for the production of consumer goods. More than any other figure in the film, Marianne combines two qualities that will ensure the survival of Falkenstein and, by extension, of *Heimat*. Mindful of her own Silesian traditions and dedicated to the preservation of nature, she is also the representative of a forward-looking, enterprising "new" generation that embraces postwar modernization. In this respect, Marianne personifies the construction of femininity in the *Heimat* genre as described by Georg Seeßlen: "a driving force of modernization, she recognizes and accepts the signs of the times much faster than the men"; simultaneously, however, she is semiotically aligned with nature and with tradition. "The ideal woman of the *Heimatfilm*," Seeßlen suggests, "facilitates both economic modernization and ideological restoration" (1990: 350).

The human face that Marianne puts on modernization is precisely the face of *Heimat*. This becomes evident in the encounters between Marianne and Martin, whose business acumen needs to be *heimatified* by Marianne before he can set things right. A prodigal son of sorts, Martin is the latter-day incarnation of sociologist Helmut Schelsky's refugee: his materialist pursuits have led him to forsake his family for a life in Paris; he is conspicuously mobile, and associated with a "new" (and foreign) woman who has an independent social and business life. Martin has arrived in the leveled-off middle-class society that his displacement helped to bring about. But then again, the film noticeably displaces that social transformation from Germany to France, marking its consequences as "foreign" and in need of reintegration. The completion of Martin's *Bildungsroman* (educational novel) as a refugee, then, requires the prodigal son to return home and to place his business acumen in the service of *Heimat*.

When Martin is called in for help by his grandfather, he arrives from Paris in a car that seems as misplaced in Falkenstein as does his business attire and his suggestion that the baron and his wife move to Munich. For the baron, this suggestion is unacceptable not only because it seems unlikely that he and his wife would survive for very long in the enclosed space of a petit-bourgeois urban home, but also because such a plan disregards the needs of the larger community in Falkenstein. But Martin, the unsentimental businessman, ridicules his father's appeal to the value of responsibility: "Every responsibility ends somewhere," he asserts— implying that this is precisely where a healthy business sense begins. Confronted with the baron's concrete responsibility for "his Silesians," Martin coldly reminds him of the mobility of labor under capitalism: as skilled workers, they will easily find jobs elsewhere.

Martin's grandfather is scandalized: "the times may have changed, but morality? For my part, I can observe no change." This view, which the film ultimately endorses by transferring the baron's values to Marianne (who always already possessed them) and to Martin (who has yet to learn them), neatly articulates the film's politics in the context of the *Heimatfilm*. In the 1950s, this genre routinely offered imaginary compromises between radical change and radical conservatism (see von Moltke 2005). In adjusting to the "changing times" of the Economic Miracle in which one mode of production has irreversibly replaced another, *Heimat* becomes a mobile signifier that can be transported from Silesia to Bavaria, from a feudal past to a Fordist present, from *Gemeinschaft* (community) to *Gesellschaft* (society). At the same time, the ideological value of *Heimat*, its "morality," remains intact and serves to mask the very transition that it facilitates. It tempers aspects of modernization (e.g., displacement and increased mobility, increases in production and the threat of alienation, or social "fragmentation") with the promise of stability, tradition, and nature. *Waldwinter*'s ideological work consists of letting its viewers have the cake of tradition and eat it too—a goal that still resonates with the *Heimat* idea from the nineteenth century, when the *Heimat* movement "attempted to reconcile tenderness with worldliness, looking backward to the past with looking forward to an age of progress" (Confino 1997: 112). The same strategy resurfaces in the distributor's publicity materials for the film: providing graphics, headlines, and billboard designs, the company asked theater owners to advertise *Waldwinter* not only as "an experience of true love for the *Heimat* and for nature," but also as "a great, gripping film about the power of our hearts to preserve the old and give shape to the new."

When Marianne casts doubt on the soundness of Martin's judgment, she questions not his calculations but his values and lack of feeling. As a woman who "sees everything through the lens of sentiment," Marianne accuses Martin precisely of lacking such a view. His business advice "has nothing to do with feeling," she comments angrily, "let alone with such outdated concepts as *Heimat*, obligation, and responsibility." In a word, this traveling businessman from Paris is *heimatlos* (homeless): he "doesn't even know what that is: *Heimat*, being at home," explains his grandmother. And Marianne caustically remarks that he "has never managed to stay in one place for more than a few days. Why should he make an exception now?" The film will ultimately endorse Marianne's view that the lack of *Heimat* makes for poor economics. Consequently, Martin has to find reasons to "make an exception" and to remain in Falkenstein in order to acquire the values of *Heimat*. Only then will he be able to make the "right" decision.

Having set up the sparing couple of Keller's novel and the 1936 adaptation of *Waldwinter*, Liebeneiner's film unfolds a romantic plot that closely parallels Martin's education in the values of *Heimat*. Two further types of experience contribute to that education. First, his walks in the local woods convince Martin (and the viewer) of Falkenstein's natural beauty as something in need of preservation. Second, as Martin repeatedly looks in on the local families who have brought their skills from one *Heimat* to the next, he gradually appreciates the value of Silesian craftsmanship and heritage. We see children gathered around the kitchen table producing nutcrackers, and three generations of past, present, and future glassblowers preserving the tradition of the so-called *Tränenglass* (glass of tears). These delicate glasses symbolically contain the tears of Hedwig, the Silesian patron saint who "weeps for all those who have lost their homes." As he looks on together with Marianne, Martin realizes that, in their combination of tradition and highly qualified artisanal labor, these cottage industries are poised to take the souvenir market by storm. When the director of a glassworks in a nearby town tells him that his factory is running three shifts and still unable to meet demand, Martin can finally reconcile business sense with *Heimat* sense. As Robert Moeller suggests in his insightful reading of the film, Martin "slowly comes to understand that in the *Heimat*, more than the bottom line is at stake" (2001: 139).

Indeed, in this film's political economy, learning the lessons of *Heimat* is the only way to ensure the survival of Falkenstein. *Heimat is* the bottom line in the new economic order, its basic exchange value. Untouched by Marianne's "feeling" and by his own insight into the hardly outmoded values of "*Heimat*, obligation, and responsibility," Martin's imported ways of doing business would have spelled the end of Falkenstein. His views need to be "localized" for production to begin. As Moeller rightly puts it, "once restored to the *Heimat*, he, too, grasps how to wed tradition and modernity" (2001: 139). With demand exceeding supply, all of the refugees are guaranteed work that requires their traditional skills, and the community becomes an exemplar of the *Wirtschaftswunder* ethos. For the refugees to "regain their old *Heimat* in the new," it turns out, is to take up their jobs as producers in the emergent tourist industry. Extolling tradition and stability in a rural setting, *Waldwinter* works to negotiate the transformation of postwar West German society in the wake of increased social and economic mobility; as a result, the baron's hunting estate in Bavaria is transformed from a picturesque refugee camp into a cottage industry, whose location and whose product—artisanal Bohemian glass—beckons the film's audience as potential tourists in the *Reisewelle* (travel wave) of the late 1950s.

Bridging toward the New Collective: *Die Brücke* (1949)

Significantly, *Waldwinter*'s cast of refugees remains relatively self-contained. That is to say, the obstacles that arise in their path toward regaining the old *Heimat* in the new generally come from "inside"—whether from the grandson, the scheming manager couple, or the jealous Hartwig, played by a brooding, young Klaus Kinski. This suggests that, unlike the afflicted baron Lüder Lüdersen who has trouble controlling his poaching habit in *Grün ist die Heide*, the main task facing the Silesians in *Waldwinter* is not that of integration into a foreign society but of managing internal strife on the road to economic recovery. Liebeneiner's narrative, in other words, is less an allegory of integration than of reconstruction, and the refugees are cast not as aliens who need to adapt to their new surroundings but as prototypes for a new West German identity.

Some years earlier in the East, by contrast, Artur Pohl had focused precisely on the question of integration and its attendant conflicts in his *Die Brücke*. Direct confrontation between the locals and the expellees furnishes the central tension of the narrative from the moment the opening credits divide the cast into *Einheimische* (locals) featuring DEFA notables such as Ilse Steppat and Arno Paulsen, and *Umsiedler* (resettlers). But this dramaturgic difference only serves to highlight a number of striking parallels between the two films. As in *Waldwinter*, the narration of *Die Brücke* deliberately elicits the spectator's sympathy for the group of expellees. If anything, Pohl's film further reinforces this sympathy through its Manichaean structure: all but demonizing the locals as self-serving and insensitive, *Die Brücke* extols the endurance and collective spirit of the resettlers, invoking the topos of "one single great family" to emphasize the group's organic social cohesion. For just as in *Waldwinter*—and contrary to historical verisimilitude—this is a group that has been displaced intact from its origins to the East. The film begins with the arrival of their trek as it takes up lodging in an old factory building that is connected to the village only by the eponymous bridge across the river. This makeshift residence (which is certainly more credibly dilapidated than the baron's hunting estate in *Waldwinter*) prefigures a further narrative parallel on the level of the mise-en-scène: here, too, the refugees will work their way into the fabric of the local community by virtue of their manufacturing skill. Like the Silesians in *Waldwinter*, the resettlers of *Die Brücke* are led in this quest by a benign patriarchal figure (if we adjust for the fact that here, the aristocrat is replaced by the aging worker Michaelis, who can carry the socialist realist function of the "positive hero"). And the gender logics of the two films offer further parallels as well: the intrigue that threatens the survival and integration of the displaced group in the new *Heimat* is directed in both films by a garishly costumed and made-up scheming woman, whose excesses (whether consumerist, as in *Waldwinter*, or sexual, as in *Die Brücke*) mark her as "dangerous." The reconciliation, on the other hand, falls to the "girlish femininity" (Fehrenbach 1995: 159) of a radiant daughter figure and her promise of renewal in both cases: just as Marianne had reconciled the prodigal son with the values of *Heimat* in *Waldwinter*, so does Michaelis's daughter Hanne manage to "bridge" the warring factions of locals and displaced persons in *Die Brücke*.

Indeed, Hanne's conciliatory function emblematizes the programmatic stance of *Die Brücke*. The film's title is symbolic to the point of heavy-handedness, as the breakdown and eventual mending of a bridge parallels the gradual recognition of the need to build physical and social bridges between the two groups. When we first see the newly arrived trek of refugees entering the village from their camp across the river, the bridge is in a dangerous state of disrepair. As the resettlers pick their way across the gaping holes, the gossiping locals associate them with gypsies and vermin. Although the film's narration never leaves any doubt about its sympathy for the resettlers, here the editing, the sound track, and a number of high-angle shots depict their collective stroll through the village in vaguely disquieting terms as a barrage that floods the empty streets. Faced with the onslaught, the "locals" hurriedly take in their laundry, close their gates, and peer out of their windows through observational mirrors. The visual impact of this early sequence was strong enough to lead a contemporary reviewer to speak of one of the "most impressive aesthetic attempts in postwar German cinema" (Lud., "Aus der Kraft des Schlichten: *Die Brücke*, ein neuer Gegenwartsfilm der DEFA," *Berliner Zeitung*, 1 February 1949).

In the symbolic logic that governs this film, the sequence as a whole suggests that the social fabric of the village is no stronger than the rotting wooden construction of the bridge. Both are portrayed as in need of repair. On the other hand, in the film's somewhat formulaic construction, the refugees are portrayed as essentially well-intentioned, kind, gentle folk entitled to help from the local population. "I'm sure we'll get along," suggests Michaelis, the film's intended positive hero: "We just have to get to know each other first." Michaelis shows the way toward this humanist reconciliation by engaging the townsfolk in discussion over a drink and lobbying for permission to start up a pottery collective in the camp that was initially meant to provide temporary housing for the refugees. Michaelis's potentially incendiary insistence that "we deserve some reparation" is defused by his gentle demeanor: both the screenplay and the acting serve to portray Michaelis as a figure incapable of harboring feelings of revenge or of wanting to reclaim lost territory to the East. As he puts it in a conversation in which refugees and villagers mark out their competing ideological positions, "our *Heimat* is far behind us." In a remarkable moment of new nationalist sentiment, he adds that his people bear no grudge for their resettlement since their destination was, after all, *Deutschland*.

Moeller suggests that, according to the official East German accounts, resettlers "had no one to blame for their fate but Hitler and the National Socialist regime. If they had wished to stay in their homes in Eastern Europe, they should have done something about it before 1939." Although other individual memories doubtless circulated in East Germany, Moeller argues, "there was little space in which they could percolate to the surface" (2003: 152). To a certain extent, *Die Brücke* might be read as one such space, and, thanks to the nature of the medium, a collective one at that. The film allows the refugees to articulate feelings of loss and oppression, portraying them primarily as victims and casting the villagers as the Nazis and soldiers who bear the blame for the army's excesses in the East.[7] In an extended sequence that stands out for its expressionist treatment of character and setting, Pohl imbues the central figure of Michaelis with an air that is at once wistful and forward-looking, nostalgic and resolute. After a night at the local bar, he ends up at the coffin maker's shop where he explains the refugee's privileged vantage point to his two newfound companions over a bottle of homemade schnapps. Having suffered more from the war than the unscathed local population, he suggests, the refugees are better positioned to protect the peace. Though he has seen much and is prepared to die, Michaelis explains that "our time will come," pointing out that soon his people will gain the right to vote and help direct affairs in the town council.

But the symbolic setting for this exchange also foreshadows the next sequence. As he heads home drunk, Michaelis dies at the hand of saboteurs (instigated once again by a scheming woman as in *Waldwinter*) who have booby-trapped the bridge. And yet, in keeping with the dual tone of loss and progress established in the previous sequence, the film imbues this murder with meaning, linking Michaelis's untimely death with the dawn of a new era in a single shot: after following a group of men carrying the corpse up the embankment on a stretcher, the camera pans past his grieving wife to reveal a sign that reads *Genossenschaft der Töpfer* (potters' cooperative) and then comes to rest on the smokestack of the new pottery. Thanks to Michaelis's tireless organizational efforts, the refugees have turned their camp into a factory and collectively organized an economic structure that allows them to exercise their traditional skills as potters. More important than the survival of the individual, this shot suggests, is his contribution to the establishment of a new *Flüchtlingsindustrie* (refuge-based industry), based on collective labor.

Directed by an experienced lighting technician and set designer who had worked for the theater during the Weimar years and who numbered the architect Hans Poelzig among his friends, Pohl's film earned praise for its expressionist lighting design and mise-en-scène. However, it was also widely criticized in contemporary reviews for its heavy-handedness, and for its formulaic treatment of the good *Umsiedler* and the bad villagers in particular (Gehler 1983). But criticism of Pohl's simplistic dramaturgy or humanist worldview may miss the film's argument about the structural function of *Umsiedler* in the new society. That function anticipates the role of the refugees as new social prototypes in *Waldwinter,* as well as in much of the decade's sociological literature on *Flüchtlinge* and *Vertriebene.* Both *Die Brücke* and Liebeneiner's film propose solutions to the problem of relocating *Heimat* that center on the initiative of the refugees. Where the baron ultimately sets up a glassworks, Michaelis and his compatriots (and *not* the locals) succeed in founding the village's first *Genossenschaft* (cooperative). In both cases, the traditional cohesion of the refugee group—ostensibly rooted in the common loss of *Heimat,* and defined as *Gemeinschaft* (community) in the West and as *Kollektiv* (collective) in the East—facilitates the move into new production, even as the locals still struggle to make ends meet.

What the *Umsiedler* teach the *Einheimische* in Pohl's film, then, is not so much integration as it is the importance of the collective. This is a flexible idea of the collective, to be sure—one that encompasses the economic unit of the cooperative as much as the ideological unit of the *Opfergemeinschaft* (community of victims): at the close of the film, we find the resettlers wading through the river that separates them from the village to help the locals put out a fire that threatens to engulf the entire town. The film's final images elide the opposition between *Einheimische* and *Umsiedler* in favor of a new/old *Opfergemeinschaft* that brings the community together as they put out burning buildings.

This conflation of various collectives, however, is central to the film's politics of the refugee which, like its Western counterparts, imagines the migrant as the prototype for a new order. Above and beyond indisputable East-West differences in nomenclature and official politics, both *Die Brücke* and *Waldwinter* construct foundational narratives around the figure of the refugee. These were, among others, narratives about Germans as a nation of victims—a pattern that Moeller (2001) has traced through ample material in the postwar period for the West. But they were not only that. In these films, refugees are also cast as the engines of postwar recovery. This, I believe, is a dimension of refugee representation all too often overlooked in the heated debates that frame the images I have been discussing—debates about the right to *Heimat*, the denial of suffering, or the relativization of Nazi atrocities.

Indeed, we might even read this dimension of refugee images back into the architectural logic of the permanent exhibit at the *Haus der Geschichte*. Its spiraling path leads us inexorably from the shuffling trek on the monitor up toward the institutions of the new democracy, past the signal achievements and consumer products of the *Wirtschaftswunder* and, via a half-ironic ramp about *Fortschrittsglaube* (belief in progress), it even takes us to the moon. In this mise-en-scène, the refugees at the beginning are undoubtedly victims upon whom to write the revisionist history of guiltless perpetrators. But perhaps we should now also see in those black-and-white images a foundation for the upward economic momentum of the spiral upon which we, as visitors, are about to embark. Victims of expulsion, these refugees also represent a vast labor force marching to regain the old *Heimat* in the new by contributing to the *Wiederaufbau* (reconstruction) on both sides of the intra-German border.

Nor has the last chapter in this foundational narrative of the refugee been written. The current debate about the *Bund der Vertriebenen*'s (Federation of Expellees) proposed *Zentrum gegen Vertreibungen* (Center against Expulsions) has inscribed rhetoric about (images of) refugees in a new framework that pits the "renationalization of memory" against its "Europeanization" (Hofmann 2003). In the heated and occasionally acrimonious exchanges, both sides are claiming the enlightened "European" angle as their own, even as they continue to disagree about the venue and even about the necessity for musealizing the history of expulsion. Far less explicit, but readily apparent in a more in-depth view of the matter, is the fact that the refugee figures once again in a foundational debate—only this time, that debate concerns not just Germany but the future shape of the European Union as it prepares to expand to the East.

Notes

1. A note on terminology: distinctions between flight and de facto expulsion are often difficult to draw and tend to serve political ends rather than contribute to historical accuracy. Clearly, the term *Vertriebene* (expellees) underlines the victimization that defines postwar displacement more than does the broader term *Flüchtlinge* (refugees). Both entered official discourse in the FRG with the foundation of a Ministry for Expellees, Refugees, and the War Damaged (Ministerium für Vertriebene, Flüchtlinge, und Kriegsgeschädigte), which was disbanded in 1969. Early GDR nomenclature attempted to deflate the issue by insisting on the official appellation *Umsiedler* (resettlers); while this term's connotation of unbroken agency works against easy notions of victimization, it remains a euphemism that does not reflect the real physical and political pressures that characterized postwar displacement.

2. In 2001, both the ZDF (Zweites Deutsches Fernsehen) and the ARD (Arbeitsgemeinschaft der öffentlich-rechtlichen Rundfunkanstalten der Bundesrepublik Deutschland) aired highly publicized documentations on *Die große Flucht* (ZDF) and *Die Vertriebenen* (ARD), respectively. Both are available on video and were accompanied by copiously illustrated book publications (Knopp 2001; Franzen 2001). A special issue of *Der Spiegel* was devoted to the topic of *Die Flucht der Deutschen* (*Spiegel Spezial*, no. 2, 2002). Recent literary works devoted to the topic of postwar flight and expulsion include texts as diverse as Rachel Seiffert's debut novel *The Dark Room* (2001), Reinhard Jirgl's *Die Unvollendeten* (2003), Walter Kempowski's massive compilation *Das Echolot* (1999), and Günter Grass's much-discussed novella *Im Krebsgang* (2002).

3. The credits acknowledge the *Bundesministerium für Vertriebene* as the source for these "Städte in Schlesien" (Silesian cities).

4. Indeed, it appears that West Germany (centered on the map in white) and Berlin (isolated behind the Iron Curtain in the prison-striped wasteland of the German Democratic Republic and Poland to the East) are represented as agglomerations of airports, which provide so many points of entry to the territory.

5. Quoted in press clipping from Bufa file, dated 1955 by hand.

6. See the DLF distributor's kit in DIF file on *Waldwinter*. Of all Germans fleeing westward from the territories East of the Oder and Neisse rivers, 40 percent were Silesians, making this a particularly appealing demographic group for the marketers of Liebeneiner's film (Schieder 1954: 51E).

7. Asked why the refugees have not yet elected an ombudsman to represent them to the camp authorities, Michaelis puns that the refugees are not yet used to elections (*Wahlen*) because until now they had no choice (*Wahl*), but were victims of some higher force: "You know, we aren't quite used to elections, because until now we had no choice. We always just had to."

Chapter 6

"Great Truths and Minor Truths": Kurt Maetzig's *Ernst Thälmann* Films, the Antifascism Myth, and the Politics of Biography in the German Democratic Republic

Russel Lemmons

From its inception in 1949, the German Democratic Republic (GDR) faced a crisis of legitimacy. Created only a short time after the Federal Republic of Germany (FRG), its leaders had to justify the existence of a second Germany, one monopolized by a Marxist-Leninist political party—the Socialist Unity Party (SED)—and allied with the Soviet Union. This effort gained increasing importance as the FRG experienced dramatic economic success during the 1950s, and the Cold War made it clear that Germany would remain divided for the foreseeable future. In response, the GDR developed an ever-expanding propaganda apparatus, the goal of which was to legitimize a separate socialist East German state.

Among the most important themes of this propaganda was antifascism, presented as a dramatic narrative that took the form of myth, one all the more compelling because it was based on fact. According to this account, the GDR was established and governed by those who had fought most heroically against the fascists (National Socialists). The leaders of the governing SED had opposed Hitler or were the heirs of those who had, and socialist East Germany was the result of this "legacy." Furthermore, the FRG, since it had embraced the institutions of the capitalist West, was connected to Germany's fascist heritage. GDR propaganda thus made its neighbor to the west representative of all the injustice in German history—capitalist exploitation, fascism, and mass murder. In contrast, East Germany was the product of all that was moral—humanism, socialism, and antifascism. Because its people understood their historical legacy, fascism could never develop there. Hence, it was the legitimate German state and embodied the hopes and dreams of all those who opposed capitalist exploitation and fascism (Grunenberg: 1993: 120–45).

Marxist-Leninist historians insisted that the working classes had made the history at the heart of the antifascism myth and tended to downplay the necessity of "great men." After all, the ultimate victory of socialism was inevitable, and no individual determined the course of historical developments. Nevertheless, biography played an important role in antifascist propaganda. Great figures from the socialist past— such as Karl Marx, Friedrich Engels, Vladimir Ilyich Lenin, Rosa Luxemburg, and Karl Liebknecht—could serve as models of the proper way to organize and lead the masses, the true creators of history. These figures represented the socialist archetype, and elaborate mythologies developed about them. As a result, written accounts of their lives often depicted them as one-dimensional figures, devoid of private lives, completely imbued with the ideology of revolutionary socialism. In the hands of their biographers they became immortal symbols, rather than flesh-and-blood individuals. These socialist heroes were simultaneously exceptional, in that they fought so steadfastly for their cause, and typical, because their daily lives were like anyone else's and of little interest. Such an approach to biography facilitated efforts to depict the GDR as the embodiment of their ideas and actions, providing further legitimization for the East German state (Dorpalen 1988: 43–44).

The most important historical figure in the GDR's antifascism myth was the communist leader Ernst Thälmann. Born in 1886 in Hamburg, Thälmann was a dockworker and member of the Social Democratic Party (SPD). After fighting in the trenches during World War I, he joined the left-wing Independent Socialist Party (USPD) and later the German Communist Party (KPD). A brilliant organizer and charismatic leader, Thälmann became an important party functionary. By 1925 he was chairman of the KPD's Central Committee and his party's candidate for president of the Weimar Republic. Under his leadership, the KPD became a vibrant revolutionary force and the most vociferous opponent of the emerging Nazi movement. In 1932, Thälmann ran for president again, Hitler being one of his opponents, further cementing the KPD chief's antifascist credentials. Hitler's "seizure of power" on 30 January 1933 forced him underground, but he was arrested in March. Accused of planning the February 1933 Reichstag fire, Thälmann spent the next eleven years in prison, only to be murdered in Buchenwald Concentration Camp in August 1944 (Hortzschansky et al. 1985).

From the point of view of the SED's leadership, Thälmann had an impeccable ideological pedigree, and he became the most important personality in the GDR's antifascism myth. The product of a humble background, he became the chairman of the KPD's Central Committee, a true proletarian leader. Recognizing the danger of the fascist menace, he led the working-class struggle against National Socialism. In the end, he had made the ultimate sacrifice for the cause, giving his life in the fight against fascism. If, as the regime's leadership asserted, East Germany was the fulfillment of Thälmann's legacy, no progressive could question its antifascist credentials or its legitimacy.

For this reason, an elaborate legend developed around the proletarian leader. The myth employed all of the media available to a modern industrialized state. In addition to the scholarship produced by professional historians, popular works with a similar agenda also appeared. Irma, the slain party leader's daughter, wrote a biography of her father intended for children. Max Zimmering wrote one of several children's novels about Thälmann, and East German poets lionized the martyred communist leader. The legend exploited other media as well. Thälmann memorials were built, and membership in the SED's youth organization, the Free German Youth (FDJ), began with the Thälmann Pioneers. Finally, Thälmann's life was the topic of several films and television movies, the most important being the two features, *Ernst Thälmann—Sohn seiner Klasse* (Ernst Thälmann—Son of His Class, 1954) and *Ernst Thälmann—Führer seiner Klasse* (Ernst Thälmann—Leader of His Class, 1955). Both of these motion pictures played a vital role in sustaining the Thälmann myth and securing its place in the legitimizing narrative of the GDR (Kannapin 2000).

In a 1996 interview, the director Kurt Maetzig recalled his experiences while making the films, providing an interesting example of the difficulties inherit in the creation of Marxist-Leninist biography:

> I didn't know him [Thälmann] personally, and I felt it would be a difficult task, but I also thought it was an honor to make a film about a workers' politician who, unlike all of the other politicians, had alerted everyone to the danger of fascism. . . . He was a victim, a martyr killed by the Nazis, and so I thought it would be an honor to make a film about him. But after I had accepted I discovered very soon that they didn't want to make the sort of film I had in mind, a film of a worker who despite great difficulties finds his personal path in political life. The leaders of the GDR wanted something totally different. They had young people in mind who during the fascist period had not heard anything about Thälmann, except the worst possible things–that he was a criminal and so on. And so they wanted to build a kind of monument for these young

people. Accordingly they put this sympathetic and simple man Thälmann on a pedestal and corrected the scenario all the time. They eliminated anything that was personal and not affirmative in the most obvious sense of the word; they wanted a film of an idealized person. (Brady 1999: 84)[1]

While it is easy to conclude that Maetzig's recollections were influenced by hindsight—he also confessed to being embarrassed by the propagandistic nature of the films–the documentary evidence supports his account. Furthermore, the director was not the only one of the epics' creators to encounter a political elite determined to make films very different from what he or she originally had in mind. The result was a spirited discussion among filmmakers and party officials concerning the direction of the films. Hence, a closer examination of the making of *Sohn seiner Klasse* and *Führer seiner Klasse* provides interesting insight into the creative process at DEFA (Deutsche Film-Aktiengesellschaft), especially at a time when, as Maetzig put it, "A Stalinist cultural policy was applied to us" (Brady 1999: 83). In addition, since the importance of depicting Thälmann as a complex, three-dimensional person was often the central issue at stake, such an investigation affords an invaluable avenue to understand better the politics of biography in the GDR.

As a first step in making the two features, DEFA created a "Thälmann Collective," which met for the first time on 8 October 1949. Among those present was Willi Bredel, who had published the first postwar biography of the martyred communist leader a year earlier. Others attending the meeting included Michael Tschesno-Hell, who would coauthor the two film scripts with Bredel; Rosa Thälmann, Ernst's widow, who would provide insight into her husband's personality; and various party functionaries and DEFA administrators. In accordance with a protocol issued by the Politburo, this group set about planning to make a film recording of the life of the slain communist leader. It would be an "historically accurate . . . political and humanistic feature film" linking Thälmann's struggle against fascism with the "great peace movement" under way in the new Germany. While everyone recognized that the project had far-reaching political implications, the collective saw the film as primarily biographical in focus. Not only was Rosa supposed to play an important role in the undertaking, but also a concerted effort would be made to accumulate as much information about Thälmann as possible. Many of the fallen KPD leader's comrades would be interviewed, with Bredel making a trip to Hamburg, which would also provide an opportunity for the screenwriter to visit some of the locations he would have to depict, further contributing to the project's historical accuracy. Only then would Bredel begin work on the screenplay (NY4219: file 9).

While the collective's second gathering on 15 October was relatively uneventful and concerned primarily with administrative matters, the third meeting, on 27 October, turned to one of the most difficult problems to be confronted, namely, the historical scope of the film. All agreed that Thälmann's life was too eventful to be recorded completely in a motion picture. Concentrating upon important historical incidents would give more focus to the film. A "pure biographical" structure would have to be abandoned on practical grounds. This was not to suggest that the screenwriters jettisoned efforts to portray Thälmann's humanity. The film's narrative, the committee determined, should revolve around the KPD chief's interaction with small groups of people, circumstances in which "the radiance of Thälmann's personality" would win others to the proletarian cause (NY4219: file 9).

There were also important developments at the fourth, and final, meeting of the collective. Tschesno-Hell agreed to coauthor the script, and the group further discussed the historical breadth of the film, giving the screenwriters advice on plot line and developing the overall direction of the project. One suggestion would have had the film begin with the "crisis of 1930–31," but concentrate on the November 1932 Berlin Transport Workers' strike, an event demonstrating the unity of the working class behind Thälmann's leadership. Otto Winzer, speaking on behalf of the Politburo, suggested alternatively that the film incorporate events from Thälmann's "youth and early years." Undoubtedly, Winzer wanted to ensure that it appealed not only to the "old fighters" of the Weimar period, but also to the youth of the GDR, who were so important to the new Germany's future (NY4219: file 9).

With these somewhat ambiguous parameters in mind, Bredel and Tschesno-Hell set about writing a screenplay for a film to be called *Ein Sohn des Volkes* (A Son of the People). Originally, the authors planned to take Winzer's advice and begin with events from Thälmann's youth. The first "treatment" for the film, written in late 1949 or early 1950, begins in Jan Thälmann's "workers' tavern" in 1890 Hamburg, the four-year-old Ernst standing at his father's side. Numerous harbor workers reading socialist literature are present; it is an "illegal meeting of Social Democrats." The police burst into the room, and the workers stuff their outlawed newspapers and pamphlets down young Ernst's pants. The boy flees to his mother, who removes the papers from his trousers. "She praises her son and says, laughing, [that] now the cops have found nothing." Ernst has received his first lesson in proletarian politics. Thälmann's parents play a pivotal role in this early scenario, providing their son with an ideal proletarian upbringing. They love him dearly and seek to instill in him the proper class consciousness. Later, when the teenaged Ernst, now employed as a seaman, returns to Hamburg after a stay of several months in the United States, "Mother Thälmann, hugs and kisses her son and is beside herself with joy." In short, the treatment shows Thälmann engaged not only in political activity such as a harbor strike, but also in the events of everyday life. He interacts with his loving parents, he goes to work—in the harbor, at his father's delivery business, and at an industrial laundry—and falls in love with his future wife, Rosa Engbrecht (Bredel Papers: file 190). At this point, Bredel and Tschesno-Hell sought to depict the proletarian leader as a three-dimensional character, a real person rather than a symbol. While clearly the film would have political overtones, its focus remained largely biographical. But this scenario presented practical problems from the outset. If the authors began with Thälmann's childhood, as they planned, there would be too much material for a single feature. Tschesno-Hell would later record that he and Bredel found themselves with enough material for three films, and to open with Thälmann's youth was simply impractical (*Neues Deutschland*, 5 January 1954). In response to this problem, in January 1951 DEFA decided to make two parts, *Sohn des Volkes* (Son of the People) and *Führer des Volkes* (Leader of the People), the first beginning in the final months of World War I and concluding in 1930. The second film would encompass the period from March 1932 to October 1949, concluding with the founding of the GDR (Bredel Papers: file 1091). While the sources do not record the reasons behind the abandoning of the original titles in favor of "Son of His Class" and "Leader of His Class," the change was probably inspired by political considerations. Apparently, the SED leadership—no one else would have made such an important decision–chose to alter the films' ideological focus, decreasing the importance of relating Thälmann's humanity in favor of another type of film, one whose primary goal was not to tell the story of the proletarian leader but to recreate the entire history of the twentieth-century German workers' movement. As subsequent scenarios and versions of the screenplay show, telling the communist leader's story had become secondary to relating a SED-approved version of recent German history.

Under these circumstances it is not surprising that Bredel and Tschesno-Hell faced other obstacles as well. Another problem was constant interference from members of the Politburo and other political figures concerning the ideological direction of the screenplay. The Politburo regularly discussed the progress of the project, and several of its members edited drafts of the screenplay for political and ideological content. In August 1951, for example, Walter Ulbricht wrote a letter regarding the first draft to the members of the Politburo as well as to the screenwriters. The SED chief insisted that Joseph Stalin did not play a large enough role in the film. Thälmann must meet with the Soviet leader in his Moscow office and have a private talk with him. Furthermore, he recommended the addition of a scene, "where Thälmann analyzes the general crisis in capitalism" (NY4182: file 1369). In the SED chief's eyes, the film's ultimate purpose was to promote the legitimacy of the GDR. Ulbricht's demands were in line with changes in SED cultural policy. During the early 1950s, many in the party leadership were increasingly critical of East German filmmakers, accusing them of "formalism," or creating art for its own sake. The party leadership demanded more socialist-realist films showing the inevitable victory of socialism and rendering "positive heroes" who could serve as role models for average people (Feinstein 2002: 30–31). Under the circumstances, it was not surprising that Ulbricht and other party leaders sought to create an icon whose every thought, word, and action promoted proletarian revolution. The politics of biography had evolved, and Bredel and Tschesno-Hell's ideas would have to be revised in keeping with the new ideological climate.

Hermann Axen was among the DEFA officials most eager to implement the new SED directives concerning film policy. Commenting on a 1951 scenario of *Sohn seiner Klasse*, Axen, a member of the DEFA Commission, reflected on the dominant position in the party: "The comrades on the Commission are of the opinion that the scenario does not fulfill the primary goal of depicting comrade Thälmann as leader of the working class in the struggle for peace and democracy and as leader of the party which has instituted justice and is today rebuilding Germany" (Schittly 2002: 65).

At a July 1952 DEFA Commission meeting, Axen maintained that the "main shortcoming" of the screenplay lay "with the authors in the old primitive depiction of Thälmann," which failed to exhibit his "most important characteristics," including "proletarian class consciousness, grand revolutionary instinct, rapid growth, [and] quick understanding of the teachings of Lenin and Stalin." In other words, Axen wished to create a cinematic history of the twentieth-century German workers' movement, with a "positive hero" at its nexus (DR1: file 4352).

Axen was not alone in believing that more emphasis had to be placed upon the historical context of the communist leader's actions. Hermann Lauter, another member of the DEFA Commission, maintained that certain events were of such importance to the history of the German proletariat that they must be shown in the films, even if Thälmann did not participate in them. Lauter insisted, for example, that Russia's October Revolution and the founding of the KPD be shown. After all, "the great historical importance of Thälmann is based upon the fact that he properly comprehended [these] developments." Another commission member agreed, holding that the main weakness of the script lay in the fact that there was "no connection with the October Revolution and its influence upon 1918 Germany" (DR1: file 4352).

By this point, Bredel and Tschesno-Hell were willing to accommodate the party's demands. At a 13 March 1953 meeting of the State Committee for Film Issues, the successor organization to the DEFA Commission, Lauter gave his stamp of approval to the revised script of *Sohn seiner Klasse.* "I have the impression," he affirmed, "that the comrade authors and comrade Dr. Maetzig have carried out all essential recommendations, especially those of comrade Ulbricht." Lauter's conclusion did not make the screenplay immune to criticism, however, and at least one member of the committee believed that the authors had gone too far in their effort to accommodate the demands of the party leadership. Sepp Schwab, the director general of DEFA, was highly critical of the opening scenes of the script, which take place during World War I. In the screenplay, Thälmann, the leader of a small band of soldiers on the western front, receives word that German sailors in Kiel had revolted against the imperial government. Overjoyed at the news, the future communist leader leads a successful revolt against the officers of his unit. Schwab pointed out that this scene was "historically inaccurate" because "in 1918 revolutionary soldiers' groups could only be found on the home front." And this was not the only falsification of history in the work. Another scene showed future GDR president Wilhelm Pieck in Berlin, fighting alongside Luxemburg and Liebknecht during the failed revolution of 9 November 1918. As Schwab pointed out, neither Luxemburg nor Pieck "were in Berlin at that time." Indeed, Schwab concluded, the first nineteen scenes of the screenplay were so full of historical fictions that they should be completely scrapped, and the action should open with the twentieth scene, which shows daily life in the Hamburg dockyards (DR1: file 4851).

Schwab's criticisms did not go unchallenged, and DEFA director Hans Rodenberg, while conceding that the opening scenes were the "weakness" of the film, insisted that they must remain in order to provide the historical background needed to help the audience understand subsequent events. Tschesno-Hell, who along with Bredel was attending the meeting as a "guest," defended the screenplay's version of developments on the western front even more doggedly. After all, he pointed out, one of the main goals of the film was to show Thälmann "as soldier, then as worker, then as leader. . . . War and peace is therefore important." While the committee agreed that the scenes from World War I should remain, it chose to scrap scenes showing Wilhelm Pieck, Liebknecht, and Luxemburg together on 9 November (DR1: file 4581).

In spite of these script problems, *Ernst Thälmann—Sohn seiner Klasse* began shooting in the spring of 1953 and premiered on 9 March 1954 in Berlin's Friedrichstadt-Palast. The 127-minute long feature depicts important events during the years 1918–23, and while none of the major incidents represented in the feature was entirely fabricated, the filmmakers clearly took a great deal of dramatic license, embellishing incidents to make an ideological point. As a result, there are numerous historical inaccuracies in the film, far too many to be recounted here (see Wollenberg 2000:115–18). The film begins with the controversial scenes depicting the closing days of the Great War, Thälmann leading a revolt of his comrades in the spirit of the Bolshevik Revolution, establishing from the outset the link between his activities and those of the great Russian leaders. It ends with the famous Hamburg Rebellion, in which Thälmann leads the city's workers in a revolt against the fascist leaders of the Weimar Republic.

While the message of *Sohn seiner Klasse* is anything but subtle, DEFA refused to leave viewers to their own devices. The leaders of the GDR had simply invested too much money, time, and effort in the project to risk the possibility that moviegoers might miss the message of the film, and the media made a concerted effort to orchestrate audience response. All of the resources at the state's disposal praised the film as a superb example of socialist cinematic art. In a toast delivered at the premier party, Pieck lauded the film as a message to "all peace loving Germans, especially our youth, to struggle for peace, democracy and socialism in the spirit of Thälmann (NY4036: file 464)." Moreover, DEFA issued a press packet in conjunction with the release of the film. It opens with a statement, written by Pieck, pointing out that "The contemplation of Ernst Thälmann is . . . for every decent German holy, his life and struggle a model for everyone." The GDR president concludes that "This film will not only be for German workers, but also for peace loving people of all countries, who honor and love Ernst Thälmann" and fight to fulfill his legacy (NY4219: file 10).

In light of Pieck's ringing endorsement, it is not surprising that the East German press praised the film. In an article appearing in the *Tägliche Rundschau* on 28 March 1954, Minister of Culture Johannes R. Becher presented his views on the film, which he called a "national heroic epic." All who labored on the film had accomplished "a great national deed in the interests of the preservation of peace and the reunification of Germany." *Sohn seiner Klasse* was, in Becher's words, "a masterful depiction of one of the most glorious chapters in the history of the German workers' movement." Other reviewers heaped praise upon the film as well, eagerly anticipating the upcoming release of *Führer seiner Klasse* (Maetzig Papers: file 1).

Bredel and Tschesno-Hell began work on the second screenplay in the late summer of 1953. By now, they knew what the party leadership and DEFA's State Committee expected, and the original treatment, completed on 8 September, remained largely unchanged as the authors developed it into a screenplay. The sole significant change involved reducing the scope of the film, scrapping several scenes showing events in 1929 (DR1: file 4418). Ultimately, the action would begin with the crisis facing Germany in 1930. While there is no indication in the documentary evidence, most likely the decision to eliminate these scenes was the product of practical considerations, and they were probably sacrificed in favor of others viewed as more important.

The second feature debuted on 7 October 1955 in Berlin's Volksbühne (Schenk 1994: 371). Dramatically, it opens in 1930 with Thälmann's struggle against the specter of fascism and concludes, anachronistically, with the Red Army's defeat of Germany and Thälmann's murder in 1944. As in the case of *Sohn seiner Klasse*, the leaders of the regime took an active interest in the political message of the film: *Führer seiner Klasse* is permeated from start to finish with images designed to link the socialist present with the antifascist past, and Thälmann's KPD is portrayed as the sole significant opposition to the unholy alliance of fascism and capitalism.

Once again, DEFA left nothing to chance when it came to the proper interpretation of the film, and it issued a press packet designed to inform critics of its significance. Reviews of the film uniformly lauded it as a significant contribution to the development of socialism in the GDR. In addition, the regime went to extensive lengths to ensure that the message of both films reached as wide an audience as possible. Millions saw them in theaters during the 1950s and even more in schools and at FDJ and SED meetings over the next decades. The party also sponsored meetings at which workers and intellectuals were asked if they understood the message of the films, and apparently they did. A student in Halle, for example, stated that "the special thing about the Thälmann film is that it shows us German men, heroic fighters from the German working class, who remained unbroken in the face of setbacks, and can serve as our models." Another worker recognized the implicit link between past and present, saying that "Today we fight in our workplace, I, for example, at my lathe" (NY4219: file 10). While it was clear that viewers grasped the meaning of Maetzig's epics, the sincerity of such statements is open to question. Whether the audiences actually believed the interpretation of historical events presented in the films is simply impossible to determine. It was, however, important to the party leadership that moviegoers voice their approval, and they did.

This is not to suggest that no one dared criticize several components of *Sohn seiner Klasse* and *Führer seiner Klasse*, and, as the discussions surrounding the screenplay of the first Thälmann film show, even the Stalinization of the film industry did not bring about the complete end of the debate. Indeed, there was some surprisingly open disagreement concerning the two films among the GDR's cultural elite. Interestingly, much of this debate surrounded the central issue confronting the makers of the two films: how to resolve the tension between the individual's role in events and the forces of history. In other words, how much should the films focus upon Thälmann's life and how much upon the history of the working classes? As a 1955 meeting of the Filmmakers' Club, an organization created to encourage discussion of issues concerning film among the country's leading cinematic figures, shows, these questions remained contentious (NY4219: file 10).

While *Führer seiner Klasse* was the subject of the gathering, held in East Berlin's Academy of Sciences on 17 November, the participants repeatedly referred to the first feature, generally agreeing that it was inferior to the second. Those taking part in the meeting included critics and filmmakers from both the GDR and other, mostly Eastern European, nations. Among those attending were Maetzig and Tschesno-Hell, who would speak on behalf of the films' creators. While all present praised the epics for their contribution to the construction of socialism, some participants criticized important components of the story. Several, for example, questioned the historical accuracy of specific scenes, the way in which Thälmann's personality was portrayed, and the narrative structure of the last third of *Führer seiner Klasse*, all of which led to a lively discussion concerning the politics of biography and the role of "truth" in socialist film (NY4219: file 10).

Among the scenes criticized for their lack of historical accuracy were those in *Sohn seiner Klasse* recreating the 1923 Hamburg revolt. The film assigns the failure of the uprising to the machinations of Thälmann's political rivals, who supposedly refused to send the insurgents in Hamburg the weapons they needed. In reality, as more than one viewer pointed out, the German army had used force to stop the planned shipment of weapons to Hamburg, and the failure of the revolt was not the product of sectarianism in the KPD. In addition, a Western film critic, Klaus Norbert Schäffer from Hamburg, criticized the second film for ignoring the fact that "the Social Democrats [had] fought together with the Communists, and not only the Communists, but also the Christians and who knows how many other people." Furthermore, Schäffer pointed out, scenes in the film showing life in "Buchenwald and other concentration camps" failed to portray the solidarity that developed between communist and noncommunist prisoners. Also, *Führer seiner Klasse* neglected to show that Thälmann was incarcerated in three different prisons, all of the jail scenes being shot on the same set. Finally, Schäffer and several other participants were quite critical of the last third of the sequel, which turned completely away from Thälmann's experiences in order to concentrate upon the Soviet invasion of Germany. These final scenes, they insisted, were incongruous with the rest of the project because they turned away completely from the subject of the film, the KPD's antifascist resistance (NY4219: file 10).

Tschesno-Hell responded by maintaining that these inaccuracies were inconsequential when compared with the "great truths" related in the films. "What you say is not entirely correct. There are great truths and minor truths. In art it is absolutely legitimate to permit the great truths to have precedence. And the great artistic truth is always in agreement with reality." In other words, the "great truth" of the antifascist myth was more important than "minor" inaccuracies introduced in order to make that myth come alive. Complete historical accuracy had been abandoned in order to foster much more important political truths: that Thälmann "under the most difficult circumstances" had led the KPD, the only German political movement to challenge Hitler-fascism; that Thälmann was an "example to millions"; and that the communist movement was the only political force that "the Nazis feared." Finally, the detailed depiction of the Soviet invasion, the screenwriter asserted, assured *Führer seiner Klasse*'s historical accuracy. The undeniable fact was that, in spite of Thälmann and the KPD's efforts, the German people had not liberated themselves from fascism, and the people of the GDR were only free because of the glorious accomplishments of the Red Army. Tschesno-Hell concluded that the film had to relate this fact in the name of a "greater truth" (NY4219: file 10).

Another criticism raised at the meeting held that the films portrayed Thälmann as a "cardboard hero," devoid of any personality. Several of those present responded to this charge. A Bulgarian journalist, for example, pointed out that "Thälmann's personal life is the life of the German working classes." Another participant, Peter Edel, agreed, stating that "Thälmann really had no personal life, it was the life of the German working class." In other words, he lived his life imbued with revolution, his every thought and action for the benefit of the proletariat. All of those refuting the contention that the films portrayed their central character as soulless and void of emotion pointed to the same brief scene: that showing the imprisoned Thälmann crying in response to the execution of one of his closest comrades (NY4219: file 10).

It is interesting that all three responses cited the same short scene in their argument. Ironically, the fact that three people could provide only a single counterexample ultimately supports the contention that the films portray Thälmann as a "cardboard hero." In order to make him representative of the entire working classes, an example for everyone, the screenwriters, director, and actors had to abandon any effort to depict his distinct characteristics. The Thälmann of Maetzig's films is not a human being but a symbol of "one of the most glorious chapters in the history of the German workers' movement." As Tschesno-Hell put it: "The Thälmann Film is therefore a historical-biographical film. The historical events are depicted not to illustrate the development of Thälmann, but rather the opposite: Thälmann's development is representative of . . . historical events" (*Neues Deutschland*, 5 January 1954).

The KPD leader had become, in the hands of East German filmmakers, an icon linking the glorious past with the socialist present and with the promise of a better tomorrow. The final scene of *Führer seiner Klasse* recreates Thälmann's fate at the hands of Nazi thugs, but it does not show his death. Rather, Thälmann marches on, red flag in the background, into the glorious socialist future. Speaking at the November 1955 meeting of the Filmmaker's Club, Tschesno-Hell explained why the film does not show the KPD leader's death: "He was certainly murdered! How should one show that ? Would it be best to end the film with the massacre, with the murder? That just would not work. . . . We did not want to show it that way. We wanted the great truth, the great truth that lies in the first part [of the films] and with Thälmann in the second part. Thälmann's function and struggle [today]. And in the German Democratic Republic there are thousands of Thälmanns. Who function and struggle. That is historical unity and that is artistic unity" (NY4219: file 10). He was not dead, but rather Thälmann's legacy lived on in the accomplishments of the German Democratic Republic.

The Thälmann portrayed in Maetzig's two epics is a far cry from the original intention of the filmmakers, who as the director put it, sought to create "a film of a worker who despite great difficulties finds his personal path in political life." Early treatments and scenarios for *Sohn seiner Klasse* sought to depict Thälmann in precisely this fashion, as a three-dimensional individual, not only with strengths, but also with weaknesses to be overcome. Anecdotes from the KPD chief's life were collected in order to flesh out his character. In short, Maetzig, Bredel, and Tschesno-Hell sought to create a film biography in which a mortal human being overcomes overwhelming odds to become the leader of the German working class. DEFA and party officials wanted a very different sort of film, one that was ultimately a history of the twentieth-century German communist movement. As a result, none of the anecdotes collected from those who knew the KPD chief worked their way into the films. Furthermore, Rosa, the martyred communist leader's widow, the person who knew him best, ultimately had little influence upon the composition of the films. Following the fourth and final meeting of the Thälmann Collective at the end of 1949, she disappears from the documentary record, participating in none of the meetings at which scenarios and scripts were discussed. Rosa only reemerged after the features were completed, serving as an active participant in efforts to encourage the East German people to view them (NY4003: file 72). Hence, it is not surprising that Thälmann's uniqueness, his childhood experiences, his personal development, and his innermost thoughts are all absent from the films. Party and DEFA officials had rejected everything that was "not affirmative in the most obvious sense of the word," that did not portray an "idealized person." Many DEFA and SED officials were willing to go to extensive lengths to create this ideal proletarian leader, even to falsifying events in the name of a "greater truth." The Thälmann of *Sohn seiner Klasse* and *Führer seiner Klasse* was a far cry from that of Bredel and Tschesno-Hell's original vision of the four-year-old boy with socialist literature hidden in his pants. It is impossible to envision the Thälmann of Maetzig's epics getting hugged by his mother or falling in love; rather his personal existence was "the life of the German working class."

The differences between those who tried to create a three-dimensional Thälmann and those who sought to forge a proletarian icon are reflective of the tensions inherent in the concept of Marxist-Leninist biography. Biography relates the life of an individual. Yet Marxism-Leninism teaches that individuals do not make history—social classes do. Hence, in the eyes of much of the GDR leadership, portraying Thälmann as a person became secondary to recreating the revolutionary history of the German proletariat. As a result, the films are not biographies but renditions of an idealized working class led by an infallible hero. In their efforts to create a communist "everyman" who could serve as a model for all East Germans, DEFA and party officials created an ideal to which no one could realistically aspire.

Finally, as the debate surrounding the features shows, opinion concerning artistic matters was never uniform in the GDR. Even at the height of Stalinization, artists and politicians often disagreed. A frequently lively discussion concerning the character of the films preceded their production, and many of the same issues reemerged after they opened. It is important, however, to keep in mind that there were limitations placed upon discussions about Maetzig's films. While some felt free to criticize certain components of the films, all agreed that *Sohn seiner Klasse* and *Führer seiner Klasse* were important films making a vital contribution to the building of socialism in the GDR. Ultimately, these features would reflect the official party version of Thälmann's life. As a result, Bredel and Tschesno-Hell had to alter their screenplays in accordance with the vision of Ulbricht, the Politburo, and DEFA officials. In the end, the screenwriters and director even went so far as publicly to defend this metamorphosis. But such were the limitations upon artistic freedom imposed by Stalinism.

Notes

I would like to thank the German Academic Exchange Service (DAAD), the National Endowment for the Humanities, and Jacksonville State University for the financial support needed to complete the research for this essay.

1. This passage was translated by Martin Brady. All other translations are the author's.

Chapter 7

THE FIRST DEFA FAIRY TALES:
COLD WAR FANTASIES OF THE 1950s

Marc Silberman

During its forty-five-year history the DEFA film studios of the German Democratic Republic developed an international reputation for high-quality children's entertainment. As in other socialist countries, films for children and youth were understood to be a vehicle of moral concepts and as such, subject to the broader political and ideological dictates of educating young people. In general, they were seen as specially structured fictions aimed at socializing youth by showing people to be capable of learning new ways and by producing acceptable heroes as models for a socialist society. From the outset, the DEFA *Spielfilmstudio* (feature film studio) produced entertainment oriented toward young people. Indeed, its third feature-length production was Gerhard Lamprecht's *Irgendwo in Berlin* (Somewhere in Berlin, 1946). Set among the ruins of the occupied city, the film focuses on typical postwar dilemmas of young people: absent or war-traumatized fathers, child impoverishment, and the temptation to survive by means of petty criminality. The name Lamprecht, who had directed the most popular children's film of the Weimar Republic, *Emil und die Detektive* (Emil and the Detectives, 1931), based on Erich Kästner's bestselling novel, is a good index for DEFA's early attempt to connect to the progressive tradition of children's film entertainment of the late Weimar Republic.[1]

Two of the most popular DEFA films were adaptations of fairy tales by Wilhelm Hauff, the beloved nineteenth-century author of three volumes of *Kunstmärchen* (literary fairy tales): Paul Verhoeven's 1950 *Das kalte Herz* (The Cold Heart) and Wolfgang Staudte's 1953 *Die Geschichte vom kleinen Muck* (The Story of Little Mook). Measured both in number of viewers and in export sales, these two films ranked among the all-time top DEFA successes with 13 million and 11 million viewers, respectively, in the GDR (Wiedemann 1998: 11). This striking circumstance suggests that they deserve close attention both as successful visual narratives but also as stories that captured in a particularly imaginative way the difficult adjustments in postwar Germany. This essay will briefly examine first the historical context of fairy tales as a genre of children's cinema entertainment, and then offer readings of both films within the context of emerging Cold War tensions in early 1950s Germany when questions of social renewal and national identity were not only discussed by intellectuals and politicians but also inscribed in popular culture, such as fairy tales.

Tales and sagas were, from the cinema's beginning, a popular source of narrative material, and the Brothers Grimm tales were among the first to be drawn on, as evidenced by Georges Méliès's *Cendrillon* (Cinderella, 1899). Grimm's fairy tales offered fantastic elements that cinematic techniques could translate into attractive visual stories. The early adaptations of fairy tales up to the 1920s usually featured real actors and location shooting in natural settings combined with elaborate trick photography. Only gradually did the view come to dominate that the more radical the stylization of the material, the more successful the adaptation would be. Thus, by the mid-1920s, fairy-tale films with animation, hand puppets, marionettes, silhouettes, and cutouts were preferred, while *Realfilme* (realistic adaptations) were viewed as less imaginative, especially for children. Yet none of these movies were distributed as children's entertainment. Rather, they were usually screened during the afternoons for young people and then again in the evenings for adults. Neither did the category of films for children or youth exist in the early decades of the cinema, nor was there any kind of protective legislation to exclude them from screenings. Moreover, fairy-tale films constituted only a fraction of the actual film entertainment aimed at children during afternoon screenings. Already in the 1910s, exhibitors were offering a variety of primarily American shorts to entertain them (e.g., Keystone Cops, Charlie Chaplin, Laurel and Hardy), and when Hollywood productions once again began streaming into Germany after the war boycott was lifted in 1921, films with child-oriented stars like Mary Pickford and Jacky Coogan as well as *Tom Mix* and *Rin Tin Tin* serials captured the children's imaginations. It is no wonder, then, that already before World War I, and quite vocally during the 1920s, "morally sanitized" fairy-tale films were being called for as part of the cinema reform movement in Germany. Children had to be protected from what were considered "trash" movies, and pedagogically more acceptable entertainment became a rallying cry of the educational reform movement as well as of conservative politicians (Heidtmann 1992: 38).[2] By the end of the 1920s the production of self-defined children's films that aimed at a children's audience with child actors had been established, and the first full-length features for children appeared, including the aforementioned *Emil und die Detektive*. Usually, however, children's films consisted of short tales, most frequently pedagogically altered stories by the Brothers Grimm, which were not shown in the cinemas but made available to schools by state agencies. Indeed, children's cinema was identified by this point almost exclusively with fairy-tale films, whether adapted from classical folktales or from literary fairy tales. This situation remained more or less constant during the Third Reich as well, when fairy-tale films were screened for children both in cinemas and in programming for the new television medium (Hickethier 1991: 93–99).[3]

After 1945 two different concepts of the fairy-tale film arose with the division of Germany and its media landscape. In the Federal Republic it came almost exclusively under the purview of noncommercial distributors and exhibitors (e.g., public television, schools, churches, and youth centers), while commercial cinemas at the most would program "family film entertainment." Not only financing problems and inadequate film projection facilities, but also conservative views about age-appropriate entertainment pushed the genre into a shadow zone of visual, technical, and artistic incompetence. Thus, there was a certain logic in the 1957 decision of the federal government to change the consumer-oriented *Jugendschutzgesetz* (Law to Protect Young People) to exclude children under six years of age from the cinema entirely in order to protect them from, among other things, the "premature" introduction to the visual violence and fantasies of fairy tales. Yet the result was to discourage commercial activity in the area of children's entertainment and to shift responsibility for its production to television programming, which fulfilled the task of substitute babysitter with narrowly conceived ideas about children's needs. At first, West German television simply adapted children's content and presentational forms of older media such as theater and radio broadcasting as well as reruns of 1930s and 1940s film material, but it created little or no new content of its own.[4] Apparently, television was simply not in a position to present for children imaginative scenarios that were in some way connected to the postwar physical and psychological reality. With its kitsch images of an intact world where violence and evil disappear and conflicts always take a turn for the better, the TV fairy tale became the quintessential model of child-oriented programming that aimed to please the "naive" imaginative capacities of young viewers by means of reductive, simplifying narratives, and visual strategies. Not until the 1970s did the production of fairy-tale films in the Federal Republic of Germany (FRG) take a quantitative and qualitative turn for the better.[5] And as preschool

and children's TV programming increased in general, international folktales and modern fairy tales replaced those of the Grimm Brothers, Hans
Christian Andersen, Hauff, and the *Arabian Nights* as the most popular
source material.

In the GDR, where the DEFA *Spielfilmstudio* was established from the
outset as a noncommercial, exclusive state cinema enterprise, the trajectory of children's film entertainment gave rise to an alternative story. As
in many other cultural domains, the Soviet model quickly dominated,
and very early on special Sunday matinee programs were arranged for
children. Here the first DEFA films featuring young people (see note 1)
as well as older Soviet youth features were screened. Beginning in 1952,
DEFA documentaries and cultural films aiming specifically at children
and young people became part of the programming mix. Soviet fairy-tale
films were also screened for children, and Aleksandr Ptushko's impressive
Kamennyy tsvetok (The Stone Flower, 1946) influenced DEFA's decision to
produce its own first fairy-tale film, *Das kalte Herz*. Typical for the fairy-
tale features that emerged from the East European socialist countries,
DEFA's fairy tales were constructed around smart and stupid rather than
good and evil characters, and class antagonisms between the poor people
and the power holders dominated the conflict situations (Giera 1982: 2–4).
Thus, familiar folktales by the Grimm Brothers, but also the more realistic tales of Hauff and Andersen, were adapted to demonstrate how the
simple folk used intelligence and courage to make kings, princesses, and
haughty bourgeoisie look foolish, or to show how a hero of the people
saved a benevolent king or paternalistic leader from the treacherous courtiers who surrounded him.

In April 1953, the SED's Central Committee passed an official resolution to develop specialized studios, including one devoted to children's
films. While this specialized studio was in fact never established and in its
stead a "children's film group" was created within DEFA's *Spielfilmstudio*,
the resolution recognized that cinema entertainment needed to attend to
the socialist educational needs of children and young people.[6] Moreover,
when television broadcasting began the next year in the GDR, children's
programming was part of the mix from the outset. Nonetheless, there
were strong reservations about fairy tales expressed in the 1950s, also
in response to *Das kalte Herz* and *Die Geschichte vom kleinen Muck*. A narrow view of realism among cultural ideologues relegated fantasy tales to
the sphere of idealistic, romantic, and mystical folk culture. Their bloody
details and violent plots seemed related to negative behavior and thought
patterns, which in the wake of fascism were seen as major targets for ideological critique (Richter-de Vroe 1990: 19; see also Bathrick 1995: 167–77).
From this perspective, folktales and the Romantic *Kunstmärchen* belonged

to the German cultural heritage, but they were not necessarily appropriate for young children. During the second half of the 1950s and in part as a result of the success of DEFA's first two Hauff adaptations, the studio went on to develop a continuous production of fairy-tale films aimed specifically at children and employing fantasy and magical elements as a means for demonstrating how conflicts and contradictions could be resolved.[7] Concurrently, a more differentiated view of audience needs emerged at the DEFA studios, in particular, following the children's film conferences at the Dresden *Trickfilmstudio* (animation studio) in November 1958 and at the Babelsberg *Spielfilmstudio* in December 1959.[8] In the course of the 1960s, children's films (usually under sixty minutes in length) for the youngest segment of five- to ten-year-olds largely migrated from cinema to television programming, and the *Spielfilmstudio* assumed primary responsibility for the youth film aimed at the age group of ten- to fifteen-year-olds.

The historical status of the fairy-tale film forms the background for the first two DEFA fairy-tale productions, both of which were *Realfilme* (i.e., not animated films) and based on anticapitalistic *Kunstmärchen* by Wilhelm Hauff. Significantly, Hauff in the 1820s contributed to a genre shift in which the fairy tale evolved from a poetic form for adult reading into a popular genre of children's literature. This led to hierarchical differentiations between "sophisticated" literary tales (e.g., by Novalis and Goethe) and entertaining, folksy tales such as those by Hauff (Mayer and Tismar 1997: 98). Hauff's three anthologies of fairy tales were explicitly aimed at the "sons and daughters of the educated classes," but he conceived them not only or primarily for children but also for the middle-class parents who purchased or borrowed the books from lending libraries to read to their children (Hinz 1989: 110–11). In other words, Hauff developed narrative strategies that explicitly addressed children as well as implicitly engaged alert adults who could understand his irony and indirectness. Moreover, and this is especially pertinent for the two DEFA adaptations under consideration here, children's stories, often masked as adventure tales, can make social structures transparent. From this perspective, Hauff's tales of personal transformation were relevant not only during the 1820s restoration in post-Napoleonic Germany but also in post-World War II Germany.

Verhoeven's *Das Kalte Herz*

Das Kalte Herz is a parable about a prodigal son, who, seeking wealth and respect, sells his soul (i.e., his heart) to the devil. After years of travel away from home, after becoming satiated and bored with his self-indulgent lifestyle, and after shunning both mother and wife, the imprudent Peter returns home and finds real happiness where he had first strayed from the path of wisdom and humility. The plot is structured by dualities, by warring socioeconomic principles identified with the independent craftsmen who manufacture glass objects and the profit-oriented capitalism of the lumber barons. The stern but obliging *Glasmännlein* (little glass man) reminds Peter of the virtues of modesty, devotion, and rootedness, while the cunning, destructive Dutchman Michael, who changes size at will, embodies the spirit of money, speed, and mobility. The film script adopted Hauff's plot with relatively minor changes made by eliminating descriptive passages, condensing peripheral episodes, strengthening characters' motivations, and expanding some of the fairy-tale motifs. Moreover, it emphasized the characters' social perspective and class differences. The design of interior spaces as well as the props and costumes clearly distinguish the evil wealthy characters from the honest and ambitious craftspeople and exploited workers. Also, in contrast to the literary source, the film dwells on the protagonist's heartless business ethics and deceptive commercial practices. Finally, many visual and structural details independent of the plot stress the lesson that avarice—but not money as such—undermines the interests both of the individual and the community.

Verhoeven's only DEFA production, *Das kalte Herz*, was planned from the outset as a big-budget film with a large technical team and well-known actors.[9] Because it was to be DEFA's very first color film, a special laboratory was outfitted on the Babelsberg studio lot for the cameraman Bruno Mondi, who developed a nuanced color dramaturgy for the visually opulent film. Announced as an "adult fairy tale," Verhoeven employed elaborate historical costumes and sets as well as amazingly sophisticated trick photography for the time, credited to Ernst Kunstmann here as well as in Staudte's *Muck* film. Thus, the contrasting landscapes identified with the elfin *Glasmännlein* and Dutchman Michael create a wonderful fairy-tale atmosphere. From the perspective of film aesthetics, however, *Das kalte Herz* reflects for the most part Ufa cinematography of the 1940s. Image construction and editing are rather conventional, for instance, in the outdoor festival scene at the beginning that harks back to Ufa revue films; and the superficial polish of the acting, especially among the younger actors, harks back to character role-playing of the 1940s cinema (König et al. 1996: 78).

The main character, the charcoal maker Peter Munk, is introduced as a social outsider in a rural community. His dream to be free, the yearning to escape his marginalized position, is conveyed in the introductory sequence by the cliché image of a bird soaring in the sky or in a later image of Peter dreamily staring out a window at the bright moon. Subsequently Dutchman Michael, in the form of a giant, will tempt him to leave the Black Forest and to enter the beckoning world of capitalism by addressing his sense of male identity:

> Peter: I have never been away from here.
>
> Dutchman Michael: That's no life for a real man.

He promises the dream world of capitalism with its incessant circulation of commodities, represented in the following scenes as ruthless, vulgar, sexualized, and egotistic. The price for this world is conscience: with a stone heart in his breast Peter is no longer afflicted with (feminine) feelings of fear, love, and devotion. He can forget "home" and throw himself into the tempting pleasures that can be bought with money. Dutchman Michael's counterpart is the *Glasmännlein*, a tiny, patient leprechaun who lives in the forest surrounded by gentle nature and friendly, little animals. Valuing reason, productive labor, and love, he tries to convince Peter to embrace these qualities. At the end of the film story the chastened protagonist realizes the merit of this ethic. Reunited with his wife, he discovers in the very home he had left as a young social climber the (idealized) community of apparently like-minded workers who can assure his future happiness. The gender-specific import of worldly, potent, male capitalism and protective, feminine security at home constructs a message for those distressed individuals who appreciate the magical leprechaun as an invisible authority with the power to bring about a happy end after all the turmoil. In addition, conventional shots of beautifully forested hills and valleys with happy rural folk engaged in productive labor—familiar visual topoi from the classical *Heimatfilm* genre—frame the entire story and intensify the message of security and happiness in the familiar circle of one's own family and neighbors.

There is as well another perspective for audience identification inscribed in the film. In the last fifteen minutes Peter engages in two dialogues that strongly motivate his remorse and contrition. In the first dialogue with the wealthy, cynical Ezekiel, who as it turns out is also one of Dutchman Michael's heartless clients, Peter expresses his fear of death:

> Peter: How do you feel about dying?
>
> Ezekiel: You'll be buried.
>
> Peter: And those who are hanged?
>
> Ezekiel: They rot in the noose.

Peter: And their hearts?

Ezekiel: Eaten by the ravens . . .

Peter: What do you think will happen to our hearts?

Ezekiel: I once asked my school teacher. He said that dead people's hearts are weighed. The light ones rise, the heavy ones sink. I think our stones will be pretty heavy. But we've got lots of time 'til then.

Peter: Not I. Not I. I want to live! Do you hear me? I want to live!

Peter decides, as in the literary source, to reclaim his heart by playing a trick on the giant. He succeeds, and the struggle provides a good opportunity for cinematographic fireworks and trick photography. Reawakened as a sensitive person with a beating heart, he now faces the consequences of his former inhumanity: his debtors thrown into misery, his neglected mother impoverished, his wife killed by a blow from his very own hand. He laments his fate to the *Glasmännlein* in the forest:

Peter: I no longer want to live. Strike me dead so that my miserable life will simply end.

Glasmännlein: It's not that easy, dear boy. You think you can die and everything is over. Who dries the tears? Who eases the distress you have brought to others?

Peter: How can I once again begin another life?

Glasmännlein: Give it a try!

Peter: What must I do so that they will love me again?

Glasmännlein: Live with your own kind! You'll succeed. Stand up! Look, trees are growing here, and there is your old axe. Begin! Swing the axe and everything will be erased.

Here the script deviates from Hauff's tale, where—in response to Peter's desperate plea for death—the leprechaun presents to him his wife and mother: "'They want to forgive you,' spoke the *Glasmännlein*, 'because you feel true regret, and everything will be forgotten . . . '" The film script expands this exchange before presenting the happy end. Referring to guilt feelings caused by past crimes, the *Glasmännlein* expresses the hope that, by taking up hard work again, a new beginning is really possible. Indeed, work can even erase the bad past. By means of a magical metamorphosis, Peter suddenly appears in his old work clothes with a traditional worker's cap in his hand, and, as if awakening from a bad dream, he discovers the wife he believes he killed standing behind him with outstretched arms.

Traumatic experiences being transformed into happy memories through goodwill and dependable labor indicates an early, wishful pattern of "coming to terms with the past" in German postwar popular culture.

Staudte's *Die Geschichte vom kleinen Muck*

If *Das kalte Herz* articulates through the protagonist's magical metamorphosis the promise of a new beginning in a not-yet-realized community, three years later Staudte's *Die Geschichte vom kleinen Muck* confronts some of the obstacles on the way to this new society.[10] Hauff's tale shows how a naive, physically deformed boy grows into a lonely, embittered but wise adult. After his parents' death the innocent Little Mook is on his own, with no inherited wealth or wisdom. Full of illusions, he embarks on the classical path of self-knowledge, a journey from home into the unknown world beyond the horizon where he expects to find happiness. Outfitted with magical slippers that carry him at dizzying speeds and with a magic cane that can find buried gold, Little Mook time and again encounters the sober realities of a heartless court society full of malicious, greedy people. Condemned to death but sent into exile instead, he is able to take revenge on the obsequious courtiers and then retreats entirely from society to become a hermit. In contrast to the realistic tendency of the historical costume film pursued by Verhoeven, Staudte drew on the literary source's "Arabian Nights" exoticism. Oriental sets and musical motifs, fantastic costumes and interiors, a playful buoyancy and elegance on the part of the actors, and astonishing special effects create the magic of a fairy-tale world. The various stages on the sobering path to self-knowledge are faithfully adapted from the literary source, but this Little Mook does not become Hauff's wealthy misanthrope who at the end lives far removed from the uninviting world; rather, he learns that honest work and community respect are at the root of real happiness.

Staudte, whose films frequently are structured by retrospective narratives, must have been attracted to this material. Hauff's tale is one of six embedded in a framing device in which business travelers in a caravan tell each other stories during their rest stops. The group of traveling companions represents for Hauff a utopian model of intellectual sociability in which an arbitrary group of individuals comes together through the very activity of reciprocal narration. In this case, Hauff's narrator Muley tells his listeners not only the story of Little Mook but also a second, additionally "distancing" story to frame this plot: his father told him the remarkable adventure story because the young Muley had insulted and mistreated the old hunchback Mook. At the end of the story, he assures his captivated audience that he contritely accepted his father's pedagogical lesson and that, ever since, he as well as his friends, to whom he repeated the story, admired old Mook. Oral narration is, of course, never neutral but rather a constructed relationship of speaker and listener situated in a social context marked by reciprocity. The film version anticipates the emphatic narrative gesture of the source by, for example, listing the introductory film credits in the form of a printed story that unfolds on screen. More important than this signal of the narrational process, however, are the subsequent changes to the frame story. Here it is not an angry father who metes out the punishment to his impudent son by forcing him to listen to the story of Little Mook, nor is it a voluntary, arbitrary group of travelers entertaining one another. Rather, the old Mook himself now addresses a gang of children and their leader Mustapha, who together have subjected him to a wild, humiliating (and cinematically impressive) chase through the village. The cunning, hunchbacked midget succeeds in trapping the children in his pottery shop and insists that they listen to the story of the evil old man they consider him to be until the clock winds down. Thus, the old Mook begins to speak in the conventional fairy-tale style, but interrupts himself immediately in order to present his tale of suffering and misery precisely not through the distancing perspective of a fantastic story but rather as his own, historically verifiable experience: "Once upon a time . . . no, I simply cannot begin that way! I was once just like you, Mustapha."

On the one hand, the arbitrarily limited time of narration ("until the clock winds down") functions to meld the "prisoners" gradually into a solid but voluntary narrative community. For the interior film plot is twice interrupted by the clock (Little Mook's story is divided into three sections), which creates such curiosity on the part of the children that they themselves decide each time on the continuation of the narration. In the final sequence the children celebrate the old Mook, carry him triumphantly on their shoulders through the city, and even protect him now from the scorn of ignorant citizens. In other words, this becomes a story about the enthusiastic acceptance of an outsider and the admiration he enjoys from the newly formed (narrative) community of young people. On the other hand, the decision to shift the narrator's voice brings to the fore an internal social conflict that suggests parallels to existing tensions during these formative years of the GDR society. Instead of the spatially and temporally distanced narrator of the Hauff tale (i.e., the traveler Muley), the film presents the story through the voice of old Mook himself, to whom the children as well as the film audience listen in rapt attention. The protagonist of his narrated story learns lessons through his own mistakes and false decisions until at the end the adult Mook, the physically deformed but kind and helpful eccentric, stands before his audience. The gain in wisdom on the part of the children and the film audience is based on the identificatory potential of the compassionately portrayed Mook figure and his narrated struggle against a narrow-minded, hierarchically organized society. Thus, the oral/visual narration includes the listener/audience within a community and cements the bond between social life and narrated tale.

With the exception of the young, intelligent Princess Amarza and her friendly lover Hassan (both inventions of the scriptwriters), the adult characters in the film are all portrayed as ignorant (Mook's father), cranky and domineering (Mrs. Ahazvi), impoverished and exploited (the runner Murad), or power-hungry and egotistic (the sultan). In other words, none of them functions as an identificatory figure. Typical for the socially critical irony of Staudte's DEFA films are episodes of exaggerated situational comedy that reveal the general corruption of the sultan's court and his subservient advisers through careful dramaturgy, camera work, and editing. Little Mook is especially challenged when he comes into contact with the caricature of a closed society dominated by underlings. He is threatened from two directions: by intrigues and arrogance on the one hand and by the war-profit economy on the other hand. The latter threat represents disaster, alluding to palpable, contemporary Cold War fears of an East-West German split. The Sultan is planning a war against his eastern neighbor because "the sun rises earlier there," and his greedy war advisers encourage him because they smell a lucrative business opportunity in a potential war. Mook, whose magic slippers make him the speediest runner in the land, is able to prevent the debacle by means of a smart, decisive move to intercept the declaration of war. Peace is assured, and Little Mook is able to bring together Princess Amarza with her star-crossed lover Hassan from the neighboring country, anticipating a reunion of the conflicted neighbors. Staudte employed his entire range of satiric film techniques to criticize polemically and with malicious joy the other threat, the personality cult around the sultan. The drastic caricature shows a self-important "leader" who never leaves his palace and who is convinced of his own charisma but who is obsessed with rituals of subjugation. Meanwhile, the courtiers around him alternate between slavish attentiveness and competition for their own positions of power. These burlesque, slapstick set pieces reveal subaltern behavior patterns and narrow-minded beliefs that must have resonated among a GDR film audience regularly subjected to the public theater of power staged by the party elite in the early 1950s.

With the constellation of the youthful group of rapt listeners Staudte was projecting the utopian vision of a free, self-determined people.[11] For the DEFA press office, the film represented a positive image of the future for those who had suffered and survived World War II: "Its ethical message is just as relevant today as one hundred years ago, in fact, even more so after the mistakes of fascism, whose consequences make it so difficult for us to build a new, better, humane society based on decency and friendliness" (quoted in Orbanz 1977: 27). More relevant actually during the time of upheavals in 1953, when Staudte was shooting the film, was the appeal to an audience for whom the learned lessons and resolute behavior of Little Mook might have suggested a pertinent message: those who speak of injustice and do something about it should not be treated as outsiders deserving contempt, but rather precisely the nonconformists deserve the trust of the citizens.[12] Truly a fairy-tale vision!

Fairy Tales as Social Renewal

The ongoing and repeated adaptation of popular tales in various media suggests that they contribute to the actualization of changing social norms and value systems, enriching them with sociohistorically determined imagination. In the case of cinema adaptations, media-specific techniques—visual stylization, trick photography, animation, and so forth—are able to negotiate the very ambiguities of fairy tales that balance fiction and historical reality, and fantasy and fact. Just as symptomatic for fairy tales is the frequent temporal or spatial plot shift to a faraway time or place that we found in Hauff's source tales, a conscious strategy of avoiding the reality principle in order to nurture the hope of changing that very reality. The two cinematic tales discussed here each seeks a new community of trust against the backdrop of the social collapse after World War II, and each accommodates in its own way the hopes tempered by shame and the limits set by guilt in postwar Germany. It should come as no surprise, then, that the obvious tendencies toward German partition emerging with Cold War political tensions and inscribed in the establishment of two German states in the fall of 1949 found a correspondence in the dualistically imagined fantasy world of Hauff's tales. Other plot details similarly resonated with contemporary challenges of motivating a war-weary population and impoverished refugees to contribute to, and identify with, the project of a socialist society envisioned by the government. DEFA's first two fairy tales were transitional: in their address to children and adults, in their sophisticated but restrained use of fantasy elements, and in compromises they imagined for the characters' conflicts. DEFA's ongoing experiments with this genre deserve further examination, for they undoubtedly represent a rich field for investigating the ambiguities, tensions, and contradictions in East Germany's attempts to mold identification among its youngest citizens with its project of social(ist) renewal.

Notes

This article is a revised, shortened version of a 2002 conference presentation in Marbach that has appeared in German (Silberman 2005).

1. Other topical DEFA features from the early years in which children and young people play a major role in stories about economic need, youth criminality, and lack of parental guidance include: *1–2-3 Corona* (1948), *Und wenn's nur einer wär* (And If Only It Were So, 1949), *Die Kuckucks* (The Cuckoo Family, 1949), *Die Jungen vom Kranichsee* (The Boys of Crane Lake, 1950), and *Saure Wochen—Frohe Feste* (Hard Days—Happy Days, 1950).

2. While leftist organizations and parties did become involved in documentary and feature-film productions after the mid 1920s, they never focused their limited resources on movies for children or youths. (On left-wing film production in the Weimar Republic, see Murray 1990.) Left-wing intellectuals, however, were interested in addressing the cultural needs especially of working-class young people, as reflected in their contributions to school music and school opera in the late 1920s (see, e.g., Brecht's learning plays).

3. Beginning after the mid-1930s, the earliest programming in German television included shows for children such as physical exercises (body discipline) and stories (fairy tales and puppet shows). Although children's films were not produced during the Third Reich for economic and political reasons, the category of youth films was expanded. According to Hickethier, between 1933 and 1945 about thirty films for young people (especially for boys) were distributed that featured model heroes and military themes, e.g. *Pour le Mérite* (Badge of Honor, 1938), *D III 88* (1939), *Kampfgeschwader Lützow* (Lutzow Bomber Squadron, 1941), and *Junge Adler* (Young Eagles, 1944).

4. In the FRG, an average 48.67 percent of TV programming for children in the 1950s consisted of fairy tales, fables, and stories, dominated by marionette and puppet shows (see Merkelbach and Stötzel 1990: 25).

5. A not unlikely impetus behind this turn was the publication of Bruno Bettelheim's influential book *The Uses of Enchantment* in 1976 (translated into German in 1977), in which the author argued that fairy tales have an important psychological function in the development of the childhood personality because they take children's anxieties seriously and help to explain them.

6. See Odenwald (2001: 314–16 [Section X]) for details about the confusion concerning plans for an independent children's film studio, which—unmentioned by Odenwald—were exacerbated by the political instability around the government's New Course in 1953. Odenwald does not mention that the *Trickfilmstudio* (animated film studio), also included in the plans of that April 1953 resolution, was in fact created in 1955 and was devoted almost exclusively to the production of short films for children. On the beginnings of the animated film in the GDR see Häntzsche (1980: 72–76), including brief mention of the first fairy-tale shorts using animation and puppets.

7. These feature-length fairy tales include *Der Teufel vom Mühlenberg* (The Devil from Mill Mountain 1955, based on motifs from Harz Mountain tales); *Das tapfere Schneiderlein* (The Valiant Tailor, 1956, based on Grimm); *Das singende, klingende Bäumchen* (The Singing, Ringing Tree, 1957, based on Grimm); *Die Geschichte vom armen Hassan* (The Story of Poor Hassan, 1958, based on a Uighur folktale); *Das Feuerzeug* (The Tinder Box, 1959, based on a Hans Christian Andersen tale); and *Das Zaubermännchen* (Rumpelstiltskin, 1960, based on Grimm).

8. Documents and statements from these two film conferences, which led to increased production of shorts at the *Trickfilmstudio* and of feature-length films at the *Spielfilmstudio*

for children and youths, can be found in the journal *Deutsche Filmkunst* 12 (1958), 378–79, 389; 2 (1960), 38–47.

9. Paul Verhoeven (1901–75; not to be confused with the Dutch director of the same name, born in 1938, who now makes Hollywood action films) was a character actor and director of stage, film, and later television productions. He began to work for Ufa in 1937, and by 1945 had completed almost fifteen films, mostly romantic comedies and marriage farces. After the war he established himself in Munich and was hired by DEFA for *Das kalte Herz* because the originally scheduled director, Erich Engel, left the state film company, and Verhoeven was one of the few directors who had proven experience with color film stock, for instance, his 1945 Ufa color film *Das kleine Hofkonzert* (The Small Court Concert) was a romantic musical comedy.

10. Staudte (1906–84) was a stage actor in Berlin until his career ended in 1933 for political reasons. He then became a radio announcer, specializing in fairy-tale broadcasts, and later became the director of short films for advertising. Beginning in 1941 he began to make feature films. Staudte was responsible for producing the first German postwar narrative film, a DEFA production, *Die Mörder sind unter uns* (The Murderers Are among Us, 1946), and continued working for DEFA until 1955, when he emigrated to West Germany. For Staudte, who had developed a reputation for socially critical films, the adaptation of a Hauff tale was initially just a stop-gap solution to an embarrassing quandary when his plans to film Bertolt Brecht's *Mutter Courage und ihre Kinder* (Mother Courage and Her Children) were put on hold.

11. In a pre-opening studio report, Staudte's co-scriptwriter, Peter Podehl, pointed out that the earliest discussions about producing a Little Mook film (1951) after the success of Verhoeven's Hauff adaptation already assumed it would be aimed at an adult audience (1953: 16).

12. Location and studio shooting for Staudte's film lasted from 16 February until 31 July 1953. During this time Stalin died (March), and the most serious political crisis of the young GDR, the uprising of 17 June, swept through the country. It is typical that fairy-tale films, as holiday and family entertainment, open in December in the cinemas, and this was the case for both Staudte's and Verhoeven's Hauff adaptations.

Chapter 8

VISUALIZING THE ENEMY:
REPRESENTATIONS OF THE "OTHER GERMANY"
IN DOCUMENTARIES PRODUCED BY THE
FRG AND GDR IN THE 1950S

Matthias Steinle

"If they had not existed, they would have had to invent each other." That is how much the FRG's and GDR's images of each other were complementary in the confrontation of the Cold War. For the purpose of self-legitimization, the "other side" served as a negative foil identified as either "communist-totalitarian" or "capitalist-fascist"; together they were locked in a communicative space that was sustained by the heated Cold War polemics in the media. Several factors—the conditions in Berlin before the Wall, continuing familial ties, commerce between the zones, and above all the ability of broadcasts to reach across geographic borders—contributed to a situation in which FRG and GDR were connected to each other like a "system of communicating pipes" (Kleßmann 1997: 459).

In this context, the mutual perceptions of the FRG and the GDR in documentary films of the 1950s are interesting for many reasons. Given the limited opportunities for on-location shooting after the German-German division, the question naturally arises: what kind of documentary images could be produced and how were they dealt with discursively? Through a comparative perspective, a number of visual motifs and representational strategies can shed light on the function of these images as counterimages or, in some cases, of appropriated images from the other side (Zimmermann 1998; Heimann 2000; Steinle 2003). The documentary, with its promise of an unmediated representation of reality, came to play a central role in this process of self-legitimization. For their productions, the FRG and the GDR each claimed a monopoly on factuality and truthfulness but denied exactly this possibility to the other side by summarily denouncing their productions as propaganda. Accordingly, the discourse of documentary was influenced and determined by the ideological paradigms of the German division.[1]

This article examines how media constructions used the promise of documentary authenticity to present the other half of a previously unified country as part of an antagonistic system or as the enemy as such. In terms of available sources, the initial situation must be described as an asymmetrical relationship. In contrast to the FRG, the GDR used documentary film early in the struggle between the political systems, among others through the first full-length DEFA documentary, Andrew Thorndike's *Der Weg nach oben* (The Ascending Path, 1950); Thorndike and his wife Annelie subsequently directed prestige projects such as *Die Sieben vom Rhein* (The Seven from the Rhine, 1954) and *Du und mancher Kamerad* (You and Many a Comrade, 1956). Because the first West German documentary film about the Soviet Occupation Zone, also referred to as the *Ostzone* (Eastern Zone), was not made until 1952, this comparative analysis will begin with *Zwei Städte* (Two Cities), a 1949 production of the U.S. occupational forces directed by Stuart Schulberg. The Federal Republic entered into a direct confrontation with the GDR only around the middle of the decade, and then mainly through films from the Bundesministerium für gesamtdeutsche Fragen (Federal Ministry for German-German Concerns, BMG) with typical titles like *Sowjetzone ohne Zensur* (Soviet Zone Uncensored, 1954), to mention one film by Erhard Fitze. After the final integration in the two respective political blocs and military alliances in 1955, both sides developed fixed sets of stereotypes and subgenres such as DEFA's socalled *Sabogentenfilme* (saboteur-spy films) and *Archivfilme* (archive films) that in turn were countered by the FRG through films about Berlin and the *Zonengrenze* (zonal border). At the end of the decade, television emerged as a central player in a war on the airwaves that thenceforward dominated this media-based confrontation until the collapse of the GDR.

The Prehistory

In the Soviet Occupation Zone (SBZ), the licensing of DEFA laid the foundation for a company that, as a state monopoly, dominated film production until the end of the GDR (Schittly 2002). Already by February 1946, DEFA started showing the weekly newsreel *Der Augenzeuge* (The Eyewitness), which gave East German filmmakers the opportunity to document everyday life, but of course under the control of the Soviet Military Administration (SMAD)

(Krebs 1996: 28). Taking a more restrained approach at the beginning of the Cold War, *Der Augenzeuge* after 1948 became a sort of official bulletin for the SED (Sozialistische Einheitspartei Deutschland, Socialist Unity Party of Germany) (Jordan 1996b: 281). The newsreels provided the material for the first DEFA documentaries, which also modeled their dramaturgy and formal elements on *Der Augenzeuge*. The first attacks on the Western Allies and their "tendencies toward separatism and remilitarization" were launched by Ludwig Lober in the documentary film, *Brücke zur Zukunft* (Bridge to the Future, 1947) and by Bruno Kleberg in *Ein Weg–Ein Ziel* (One Path–One Purpose, 1948).

In the Western zones, such weekly newsreels made under German direction did not exist. Until the enactment of the occupational statutes of 1949, the Western Allies maintained a monopoly on audiovisual media. In contrast to *Der Augenzeuge*, which regularly reported from the Western parts of Germany, the American-British newsreel, *Welt im Film* (The World in Film) paid little attention to the Eastern Zone (see Bodensieck 1992: 47). Only after the founding of the GDR did *Welt im Film* direct its polemics against the "Soviet-East German State," as did the newly founded, government-friendly *Neue deutsche Wochenschau* (NDW; New German Weekly News) (Schwarz 2002: 406ff.).

The British and French military administrations had awarded the first film licenses to Germans by the late summer of 1946; only the Americans hesitated until the end of the year. With additional licenses in the American Zone being awarded at a slow pace, documentary film production took off only at the end of 1948, after the official approach to German-German relations had been decided (Hahn 1997: 412ff.). The concept of reeducation, according to which trustworthy Germans were in charge of the reorientation process, had little influence on documentary film practice. Internal disputes in the Office of Military Government for Germany, United States (OMGUS) over punitive or liberal approaches were primarily to blame for the delays; contributors factors were the continuities in terms of personnel and production method at Ufa (Universum Film-AG) and in the genre of the *Kulturfilm* (cultural film) with its aesthetic program of "Beauty above Everything" (Hahn 1997: 418).

U.S. and East German Images of the Other

In response to the East-West-conflict and General Clay's 1947 "Operation Talk Back," the Documentary Film Unit (DFU) within OMGUS added films to their program that could counteract communist propaganda and thus contain the Soviet influence. In this context, *Zwei Städte*, one of the most important productions under the direction of U.S. film officer Stuart Schulberg, was released shortly before the official end of the OMGUS government on 5 August 1949. This ten-minute film short was intended to show the Americans' occupation policies in a positive light and to promote their sociopolitical platform over and against "communism." The dramaturgical structure of *Zwei Städte* is very simple: In accordance with the black-and-white perspective of the Cold War, the cities of Dresden and Stuttgart are used to juxtapose the two opposing ideologies in the style of "Dresden in the rain, Stuttgart in the sun" (Jordan 1996a: 33). Already the opening credits with the tendentious tinting of a map showing West Germany as white and East Germany as gray foreshadows the view of both sides to be presented.

Dresden is the city of ruins, of propaganda, and of lack. In long traveling shots along mountains of rubble and destroyed houses, the city of 1948 appears in uniform gray tones. Several close-ups of official announcements and posters show the so-called *Ostzone* (Eastern Zone) as a place of ubiquitous propaganda. The camera focuses on haggard old people to reveal the poverty of the population. Empty store windows, mock-ups in glass cases, and lines of people in front of shops are supposed to convey the image of a system of deficiencies. Stuttgart, on the other hand, presents itself to the audience as a bustling city in the bright morning sun. Every motif of deprivation in Dresden is answered by its positive counterpart in Stuttgart. There images of stocked shelves and consumer goods dominate, with tiled roofs as well as construction sites and construction vehicles evoking the project of reconstruction.

The overtly polemical voiceover is illustrated by the film's montage effects. For example, fast wipes endow the East German propaganda posters with an aggressive character. By contrast, the slow dissolve from a bombed-out residential street in Stuttgart shortly after the war to its reconstructed appearance in 1948 conveys the sense of harmony restored. This scene also defines the time period of the American occupation: 1945 stands as a starting point for the reconstruction project in the West and its accompanying myths of a Zero Hour and a "new beginning." The future belongs to the Western Zone, whereas the Eastern Zone remains hopelessly tied to the past through the lingering traces of the war and the presence of propaganda.

In the dichotomous worldview of *Zwei Städte*, the other part of Germany remains just as abstract as its people. The film attacks their worldview without any serious examination of its content. The material aspect, the economic situation, remains the key point in the confrontation with the other system. The available images of self and other accommodated the West German audience in several ways. After all, the look forward distracts from the burdens of the past and the question of culpability. In relation to the message of salvation found in economic affluence, the images of poverty and oppression in the other part of Germany functions like an indulgence that seems all the easier to pay as East Germany remains an abstract entity controlled by hostile powers.

A film like *Zwei Städte* did not remain without an appropriate "response." Above all it was Andrew Thorndike at DEFA, aside from *Der Augenzeuge,* whose documentaries took on the "Adenauer state." After he had contrasted the dormant wharfs in Kiel and Hamburg to a blooming shipyard on the Baltic coast in *Von Hamburg bis Stralsund* (From Hamburg to Stralsund, 1950), Thorndike started working on *Der Weg nach oben* with Karl Gass. In this first feature-length DEFA documentary, the opposition between the two German states generates a similarly self-legitimating argument (Jordan 1996a: 30ff.).

Der Weg nach oben opened on the eve of the GDR's first anniversary on 7 October 1950. As the programmatic title suggests, the film describes the most important stations of the young GDR as a "chronicle of ascension," to quote the working title (Herlinghaus 1969:18). In contrast to this "canon of progressive historical stages" (Gries 1994: 17), the presentation of West Germany aims to place the FRG in line with National Socialism, and in that tradition, as a vassal of the Western powers and a servant of U.S. imperialist politics, respectively. The film's first minutes which, according to an intertitle, deal with "the liberation from Hitler fascism," show this very clearly. Over footage showing the Nazi elites at the Nuremburg Trials, the voiceover declares that their project is being continued by Konrad Adenauer, Winston Churchill, Harry Truman, and Kurt Schumacher.

The commentary describes U.S. policy toward the Federal Republic as an economic oppression that will end up paralyzing industries everywhere in the West. The images chosen to illustrate this point clearly reveal the problem with this method of compilation. For example, pipe-smoking boatmen and cutters languishing in a harbor could just as well stand for unemployment as for an idyllic evening after work. The filmmakers were aware of this methodological problem to the extent that they attempted to find the most symbolically rich newsreel footage. This is especially obvious in the sequences that aim to prove the dominance of the United States. Again and again the camera pans from military boots or West German flags to the "Stars and Stripes" flying above everything as metonymic evidence of American dominance.

Der Weg nach oben presents West Germany as a world of beautiful illusions. With two million unemployed, child labor is common and, lacking any public support, female students are forced to prostitute themselves. In this context the film also incites anti-American and nationalistic resentments, particularly when U.S. soldiers are shown holding hands with young women. The images from the FRG are of minor quality, and a dry journalistic style predominates. In a complete reversal of *Zwei Städte*, the aesthetic supports a rhetoric that associates everyday life in the FRG with a bleary gray while presenting similar scenes in the GDR through careful lighting. The only exception can be found in the discourse of cultural criticism used to denounce the moral and cultural degeneration of the West in the most graphic ways. Scenes from beauty, food, and dance contests and of wrestling women are cut rhythmically to produce a frenetic spectacle, with the shrill voice of the commentator wailing: "Carnival! Sensation! An American century!" It is not clear though whether the self-portrait created through the relentless but boring pathos of reconstruction—and in a medium as sensual as film!—did not, if anything, increase the fascination with the "golden West."

In contrast to the DFU production of *Zwei Städte*, which presents the other worldview only through an abstract and only geographically local-izable image of the enemy, *Der Weg nach oben* conjures up a highly pal-pable image of "Bonn's separatist state" in the form of Western politicians and American pop and entertainment culture. However, even in *Der Weg nach oben*, the subject of history remains a mere object both visually and conceptually. It remains left to the commentary to conjure the emotions of pathos that the images are not able to rouse on their own (Rülicke-Weiler 1979: 147). By reacting to the other German state through the medium of the documentary film, *Zwei Städte*, as well as *Der Weg nach oben*, developed aesthetic strategies for a limited spectrum of themes against which all sub-sequent developments can be measured.

Images of the Enemy in Early East and West German Documentaries

The founding of a separate DEFA studio in 1952 dedicated exclusively to documentary film and newsreel production took place under the condi-tions of a Stalinist ideological instrumentalization. Most of the films can be categorized as the kind of "straightforward propaganda" (Jordan 1996a: 43) found in films like *Ami go home* (1952). The main topics of the films that deal with the West include protests against the armament race, the threat of atomic warfare, and the American military presence, as well as calls for peace and national unity and appeals to all Germans to meet "at the same table" (Riedel 1993: 122). The aesthetic and rhetorical structure of these films follows a schema based on unambiguousness and compre-hensibility: the compiled newsreel material serves to illustrate in briskly cut sequences the main theses presented by the male commentator in indignant, solemn, and, sometimes, ironic tones.

The most ambitious project was initiated as part of the "Germans at the Same Table" campaign and realized by Andrew Thorndike in collaboration with his wife Annelie in the film *Die Sieben vom Rhein*. The film depicts the visit of West German workers to an East German steel factory. *Die Sieben von Rhein* was the first DEFA documentary to rely on original sound as a formative principle and, by extension, an important discursive function in the context of the German division. For the first time, visiting West Germans speak in their own words about the advantages of the GDR. Unfortunately, such technical innovations were hampered by the cumbersome 35-mm studio sound equipment, which made spontaneous recordings almost impossible and produced little more than "political layman's theater" (Opgenoorth 1984: 68).

In the beginning, the FRG did not have much with which to counter the documentary films of DEFA. Radio was still a massively effective medium, and the Berlin-based RIAS (Radio in the American Sector) was the most powerful weapon in the Cold War. In 1952, the BMG took up the visual confrontation with the "Soviet Zone" with *Blick hinter den Eisernen Vorhang* (A Look behind the Iron Curtain, 1952), the first known documentary about the GDR that presents its political system through film clips from Soviet and DEFA feature films as well as from news reports. Despite the satiric elements, there were concerns about the visual power of the original material; that is why the film could only be seen in the context of political education. The method of representing the other German state through its own media products was to become one of the most important visual strategies in the media war. After the closing of the German-German border, this method made it possible not only to show images "from over there," but also to appropriate these images through interpretation and commentary, a method perfected by television in the second half of the 1950s.

While the first BMG production had offered selected audiences a "look behind the iron curtain" by appropriating film clips, a later film from 1954 promised the representation of *Sowjetzone ohne Zensur* (Soviet Zone without Censorship) with a conscious gesture toward the documentary ethos. The tone of the film by Erhard Fitze is decidedly anticommunist. Already the hand-painted opening image, which dissolves into black leader, relies on the familiar light symbolism. In front of a pitch-black background, a watchtower stands, with its floodlight illuminating the barbed wire in the foreground and evoking associations with a prison camp. Using an eyewitness at the scene, *Sowjetzone ohne Zensur* relies on a similar persuasive strategy as *Die Sieben vom Rhein*. A West German, who was in the GDR with his camera, presents and comments on his images. His commentaries are supplemented by those of a county commissioner, who uses his federal authority to explain the political background, and a woman whose naive questions function as clues for the male specialist. Through the specific example of the city of Wittenberge and its surroundings, the Soviet Zone is presented as a system resting on three pillars: economic scarcity, political oppression, and communist propaganda. The approach of the director-author-cameraman, who relies on a film technique still considered unprofessional at the time, places these film images from the GDR within the genre of amateur film, even if the end product is a professionally produced work. In accordance with the amateur-film aesthetic, the image is often shaky and badly lit. Already the qualitative weaknesses of the images, with their prevailing gray tones, give a clear impression of the dreariness of everyday life in the GDR. Decaying houses, old cars, long lines in front of stores, and political propaganda dominate the cityscape in the same way shown for Dresden in *Zwei Städte*. After all, the superiority of one's own system seems so evident that it does not even have to be presented as a positive countermodel to the Soviet Zone.

Sowjetzone ohne Zensur is largely content with a description of the situation that avoids personalized images of the enemy. East German politicians are not identified by name and appear at most in photographs in store windows. Everything GDR-specific is presented as Soviet but without any reference to their connections or commonalities. Accordingly, there is no historical discourse that addresses the reasons for the division. The absence of any future perspective for a united Germany is underscored by the film's last images of abandoned train tracks at the border, leading nowhere. By adopting the patterns of interpretation and representation developed in *Zwei Städte, Sowjetzone ohne Zensur* thus completes the total integration in the West.

Berlin Films and *Sabogentenfilme*

Berlin occupied a special position in the documentary project, and its political and economical situation was thematized in numerous films. Because of its geographic location in the heart of the GDR, the city was both the West's bridgehead and Achilles' heel in the Cold War. This explains the intensity of the GDR-polemics against West Berlin as a center for black marketers and secret agents, a city whose open borders prompted hundreds of thousands to turn their backs on the GDR every year; the West German portraits of the city were correspondingly positive.

Already the DFU documentaries produced by OMGUS had built on the myth of the airlift and elevated the city to a symbol of the free world. The West German—which means the West Berlin films—saw themselves in this tradition. For the most part, the confrontation with the GDR took place through demarcation by means of positive self-representation. The main argument and leitmotif was the economic boom in West Berlin, which insured the enclave's independence and survival capability and that was alluded to in films such as *Berlin produziert* (Berlin Produces, 1950) or *Berlin kommt wieder* (Berlin Is Coming Back, 1951). The GDR or the eastern part of the city appeared in these films only on the margins or, *ex negativo*, through the refugees coming to the West. But the refugee problem also inspired other films that did not present the glowing self-image found in *Zwei Städte*. The NDW Production *Das neue Kapitel* (The New Chapter, 1954), for example, points out that more refugees came than could initially be integrated.

Self-critical overtones in the Berlin films disappeared at the very latest with the Berlin crisis as a result of Khrushchev's ultimatum in 1958. The 1959 Berlin Campaign by the federal government resulted in a series of films with such programmatic titles as *Berlin—Stadt der Freiheit* (Berlin—City of Freedom, 1959) and *Attentat auf die Freiheit—Berliner Dokumente* (Assault on Freedom—Berlin Documents, 1959) whose "anti-Soviet sledgehammer propaganda" turned out to be a double-edged sword for the regional representatives who showed them worldwide at the request of Bonn's Foreign Ministry (Buchwald 1992: 26).

Because of the geographic situation, West Berlin in the mid-1950s became a turnstile for news services from all kind of countries. Here the DEFA feature, *Der Fall Dr. Wagner* (The Case of Dr. Wagner, 1954), represents the end point of a series of films about sabotage and agents, ironically called *Sabogentenfilme* by their viewers (Mückenberger 1997: 58). Now documentaries contributed to the confrontation with *Feinde des Friedens* (Enemies of Peace, 1954), to cite the film by Helmut Schneider. *Protokoll Westberlin* (Film Proceedings West Berlin, 1959), made by the same director under the revealing working title "Cancer Sore West Berlin," rehearses almost all of the negative stereotypes from the Cold War and offers an exemplary selection of the main topoi of anti-Western espionage rhetoric: trials against spies and dissidents, leaflet balloons with inflammatory pamphlets, sabotage actions, military and industrial espionage, smut and trash literature aimed at GDR youth, and the corresponding neglect of youth in the West that made them susceptible for recruitment by the secret service. The approach of most of the films about this thematic was relatively simple. They usually relied on newsreel footage, which accounts for the frequent déjà-vu effects. An authoritative voiceover explains the images, sometimes supplemented by explanations from a Stasi officer. As a tactical instrument of the Cold War, the *Sabogentenfilme* had few aesthetic ambitions but a clear line of attack motivated directly by intra- and inter-German politics. Out of the construction of an external enemy who agitated from within resulted the demand both for an incessant vigilance aimed inward and an aggressive fortitude aimed outward, which in turn justified more state control and repression. West German organizations that participated actively as "instruments of the Cold War" were to be denounced openly and publicly (Nolte 1985: 358ff.). One of the groups targeted was the *Kampfgruppe gegen Unmenschlichkeit* (Brigade against Inhumanity), to whom DEFA dedicated a film with the slightly modified title *Kampfgruppe der Unmenschlichkeit* (KgU–Brigade of Inhumanity, 1956).[2]

The KgU film accused the West Berlin-based organization of acts of sabotage in the GDR and planning crimes like the poisoning of food. The film's sequences were either taken from archival material or restaged in the form of dramatic scenes. Thus the representation of an attempted explosion of a train bridge relies on the crudest clichés of the spy-film genre, with shots being fired and dark figures disappearing into the night. For documentary credibility, the film includes footage of the headquarters of the KgU in West Berlin complete with signs that show the name of the street for evidence. The film's director, Joachim Hadaschik, developed this strategy into a central propagandistic tool in his next work, *Agenten im Schatten einer Partei* (Agents in the Shadow of a Party, 1957) about the so-called *Ostbüro*, the GDR office, of the SPD.[3] The disclosure in the commentary of the street address of the conspiratorial SPD organization is made even more obvious by several shots of buildings and the corresponding street signs in close-up. In addition, multiple exposures show the heads of the leaders, while the commentator reveals their names and areas of expertise. The images thus serve the function of a concrete threat, in that they—supported by their documentary status—demonstrate knowledge and power in the antagonist's realm of influence. A (more) nuanced representation, such as found in the fictional Berlin films from the "thaw" period in the second half of 1950s (e.g., *Berlin—Ecke Schönhauser* [Berlin—Corner Schönhauser, 1957]), or in a few West German films like *Die Halbstarken* (The Hooligans, 1956), was very much the exception among feature films and a near impossibility in documentary films that were hellbent on "depicting reality."

The "Post-Stalinist Blockbuster": *Du und mancher Kamerad*

Unlike the multitude of crude images about the enemy that attracted no interest outside of day-to-day political propaganda, a film came into the movie houses in 1956 that played a central ideological, political, and aesthetic role for the GDR documentary film. Shot under the direction of the

Thorndikes in collaboration with Karl Eduard von Schnitzler, *Du und mancher Kamerad* became the most expensive DEFA documentary made up to that point. For almost two years they and countless colleagues worked on the project with support from the highest levels of government, an enormous effort that gave the film the character of a "post-Stalinist blockbuster" (Steinle 2003: 113ff.). In the course of their research, over one and a half million meters of archival footage were screened, from which scarcely three thousand meters were finally chosen. In the GDR four million viewers saw the film within half a year, a public reception that was encouraged through organized visits of entire school classes and production collectives. International audiences also took notice, and the film was exported to over fifty countries under the exhibition title *The German Story* (Mückenberger 2000: 47). In the FRG the *Interministerielle Ausschuß* (Inter-Ministerial Committee) labeled it a *Sperrfilm* (banned film) and prohibited its release.[4]

Du und mancher Kamerad builds upon the basic thesis that both world wars were instigated by economic interest groups in order to conquer new markets. Additionally, the film covers a great arc, reaching from the Wilhelmine Empire through the Weimar Republic and the Nazi dictatorship up to the year 1955, presenting the GDR as a result of an inevitable historical development. Hence the statement: "Here the lessons of history were learned"—in stark contrast to the FRG. Over there, reactionary shooting and heritage clubs make their presence felt everywhere. Even the old military and economic elites are in power again, represented by names like Krupp, Flick, and the former "Hitler generals." In order to prove this continuity, the film develops a highly efficient strategy. Historical film and photo documents are used to show some officers together with Hitler and other Nazi bigwigs and to identify them through white arrows in the freeze-frame. After a cut, they are then presented in contemporary newsreels as generals in Adenauer's *Bundeswehr*.

The film set standards for dealing with history—or, rather, with its instrumentalization—and for dealing with filmic source material (Heimann 1997: 213f.). *Du und mancher Kamerad* established the tradition of *Archivfilme* (archival films) and exerted a strong stylistic influence at DEFA, especially in the work of Karl Gass and Heynowski & Scheumann (Herlinghaus 1969: 30). Furthermore, it served as a model for European documentary filmmakers such as Paul Rotha and Erwin Leiser. Additional archival footage fueled the propaganda efforts in the confrontation with the FRG and was presented to the public as part of the series *Archive sagen aus* (The Archives Speak). The main topic in all of the films is the continued presence of Nazi elites in the FRG. *Urlaub auf Sylt* (Vacation on Sylt, 1957), the first contribution to the series by the Thorndikes, uncovers the activities of the mayor of the city of Westerland, Heinz Reinefarth, as an

SS officer during the war (Shaw 2001: 190).[5] In proving the identity of the Third Reich and FRG on the basis of personal continuities, specific filming techniques proved highly effective as did the occasional use of irony. *Urlaub auf Sylt* begins like an advertising film for the tourist office, with images of a beach promenade accompanied by soft music. Even the subsequent meeting with a smiling mayor reveals nothing unusual until the image freezes and the close-up of his head is superimposed by a portrait of Reinefarth in SS uniform. Through the filmic technique of multiple exposures, images from the present and the past are superimposed onto each other and become one in the filmic present. The congruency of the two systems is not just a political thesis and rhetorical metaphor but can be visually experienced by the audience through the device of pars pro toto, that is, of presenting parts as representative of the whole. At the end of the film an intertitle warns "People, be alert," but that did not prevent Reinefarth's reelection as mayor. However, the film did have consequences for the West German cameramen who had helped DEFA stage this coup. They were put in prison for several months on account of espionage (Leyda 1967: 112).

The *Enthüllungsfilme* (exposure films) that developed after *Du und mancher Kamerad* under the aegis of the Thorndikes defined the representational strategies of the documentary in the confrontation with the FRG within a historical context. A series of later films followed this pattern. The most well known include *Ein Tagebuch für Anne Frank* (A Diary for Anne Frank, 1959) and *So macht man Kanzler* (That's How Chancellors Are Made, 1961) by Thorndike student Joachim Hellwig, as well as the reports made by Heynowski for GDR television, *Mord in Lwow* (Murder in Lwow, 1959) and *Aktion J* (Action J, 1961). Despite their enlightened habitus, these films are less about imparting critical knowledge than about creating an emotionally based anti-West German attitude. Made according to the methods of *Archive sagen aus* as a part of the SED's political campaigns, these films are exemplary of the "instrumentalized antifascism" (Lemke 1995) with which the SED externalized National Socialism and discharged the encumbering responsibility for the past to the West (Vogel 1974: 169).

West German Depictions of a Militarized "Eastern Zone"

In terms of expenditures, nothing among the documentaries of the FRG is comparable to the grand narrative of *Du und mancher Kamerad*. Similarly, DEFA's aggressive attacks in historical matters remained without a direct response. West German productions that dealt with the Nazi period generally ended with 8 May 1945 and promoted the notion of a

Zero Hour. That year, or the year 1949, defined their historical horizon in the confrontation with the GDR.

The contributions of the BMG, which commissioned most of the films about the GDR, concentrated on depicting then-current conditions in the *Ostzone*. After the transformation of the Kasernierte Volkspolizei (Standing People's Police, KVP) into regular army units in 1955, the Nationale Volksarmee (National People's Army, NVA) used martial military parades to create the self-images of the GDR that the West perceived as threatening images of the enemy and appropriated eagerly for its own documentaries. The BMG production *Bilder aus der Sowjetzone 1955/56* (Images from the Soviet Zone 1955/56, 1956) built upon the same principle as *Sowjetzone ohne Zensur*. Substandard amateur film footage is used to show the West Germans how it really looked behind the "Iron Curtain"—and what they were being spared. Aesthetically, rhetorically, and thematically, the film followed the established Cold War patterns and, in the tradition of *Zwei Städte*, presented the GDR as a land of ruins, shortages, militarism, and omnipresent propaganda. The representation of the militarization of society and of the organizations responsible achieves new height when the film's second half features nothing but protest marches and parades for at least twenty minutes. Through such formal devices, *Bilder aus der Sowjetzone 1955/56* constructs a uniform, and uniformed, GDR society that marches threateningly in lockstep.

The next film commissioned by BMG, *Die Armee der SED* (The Army of the SED, 1957), chronicles the secret buildup of the NVA using GDR sources. The film footage thus appropriated is given a relatively sober and objective West German voiceover that provides background information. But the advantage of having qualitatively good images—primarily scenes taken from GDR newsreels and documentaries—brings with it the danger of ideologically dysfunctional effects. Thus, the producers of *Die Armee der SED* are not always successful in breaking the propagandistic perspective of the source material. This is especially the case when the verbal component added through the West German commentary falls behind the effects provided by the fascinating images of technology or by the exhilarating music. At the same time, it is precisely the low quality of amateurish images often shot by a candid camera which, as in *Bilder aus der Sowjetzone 1955/56* about a gray and out-of-focus GDR, accounts for their strength in the Cold War discourse.

The *Zonengrenzfilme* (zonal border films) avoided this discrepancy between quality and functionality. They used the look of the border to gain insights into the system of SED dictatorship. In *Zonengrenze* (Zone Border, 1959), Kurt Stefan was one of the first to present the border in the form of a journey alongside its fences. In the process, he mentions neither the political context nor the most recent past. The Germans on both sides remain anonymous ciphers for the unity of the people and its suffering. The film presents the zonal border through a number of recurring motifs: watchtowers, signs with the inscription "Beware, Zonal Border!" along the ten-meter-wide median strip, patrolling men in uniforms, blocked-off streets and railroad tracks, border crossings and barbed wire. Thus, the alignment of representational strategies and motifs inscribes the intended interpretation into the filmic image. The frequent pans from one side to the other side, from west to east, make possible a "crossing" of the border and a joining together of what now is separated. Similar landscapes and architectures underscore the unity of a historically defined *Kulturnation* (cultural nation), something the commentary continuously emphasizes. While some pans have a unifying function, others present the division as a wound in the landscape by organizing tracking shots along barbed-wire fences or median strips. Looking at the GDR through the barbed wire creates the impression of a large prison camp. The filmic rhetoric conjures up the horror vision of the zonal border through a synecdoche, with the narrow framing of a monstrous border standing in for the oppressive practices of the responsible regime. Associations with a prison open up the temporal horizon, and the films take advantage of the burden of the German past without actually entering the historical terrain. The GDR rhetoric about the fascist legacies of the FRG, which was exemplarily tested in the *Archivfilme*, thus finds its equivalent in the *Zonengrenzfilme* with their charges of totalitarianism against the "prison camp GDR." Both approaches depend on a visual argumentation that builds on the apparent self-evidence of the available documentary images through a limited number of strategies in the construction of meaning. Of greatest importance is the emotional address to the audience; intellectual engagement with the subject matter remains secondary. In addition, the *Archivfilme* and *Zonengrenzfilme* share the rhetorical pattern of pars pro toto mentioned above. To a large degree, the rhetorical and representational strategies developed in the *Zonengrenzfilme* could be easily incorporated into West German documentaries made after, and in response to, the building of the Berlin Wall.

Picture Wars on the Airwaves: Television

Generally there were few West German films about the GDR before television took up the topic at the end of the decade. In the middle of the 1950s, the young medium of television still found itself in the experimental phase in terms of program forms, structures, and categories, even though the trial phase had been completed and the West German ARD (after 1954) and the East German Deutsche Fernsehfunk, or DFF (after 1956) were already broadcasting regularly. With the exception of television news, the early years saw very little journalistic confrontation with the other side because of the strong influence of literary forms on both sides of the Iron Curtain (Hickethier 1998: 79).

SFB (Sender Freies Berlin) producer Günter Lincke, in August 1956, became one of the first on West German television to focus on the GDR in his monthly series, *Mitteldeutsches Tagebuch* (Diary from Middle Germany). The individual programs had different forms that corresponded with the experimental character of the early years: reports with magazine characteristics, broadcast interviews, and documentaries that were entirely preproduced. This last group included *Luther-Erinnerungsstätten* (Luther Memorials), which ARD aired on 31 October 1956. The images from the GDR came exclusively from amateur films, the only source for contemporaneous impressions of the GDR. The quality of much of the footage was correspondingly low, with shaky hand-held cameras showing tourist attractions. Confronted with the depressing political situation, Lincke, in *Luther-Erinnerungsstätten*, flees from the present into the past, into the age of Luther or some other timeless idyll. But apart from the staid culture-film aesthetics, one can still find elements of reportage and critical coverage. The filmmaker strikes for balance in the sense that positive things about the GDR, such as the exemplary renovation of the Wartburg, are mentioned as well. Soviet soldiers are shown but not in order to mobilize anti-Bolshevist fears; rather, they allow the commentator to observe that the Russian commandant must be thanked for the preservation of Wittenberg. After the increase in tensions over the Berlin question at the end of the 1950s, however, such subtle distinctions rarely appeared in that series.

Lincke became a protagonist in the German-German war on the airwaves, which intensified with the rise of television as the socially most important mass medium. This war was less defined by aesthetic questions than by political-ideological and pragmatic concerns. The *Mitteldeutsches Tagebuch* depended on what East German amateur filmmakers smuggled over the open borders into Berlin and was accordingly difficult to plan in advance. Getting up-to-date images was impossible under the conditions of the divisions, and amateur pictures could compensate for this dearth only to a degree. Thus, in many areas, using official GDR sources represented the only way of working with audiovisual material. The growing importance of television also increased the importance of television images from the other side, which were filmed off the screen in order then to be rebroadcast with "accurate" commentary. In FRG television, Thilo Koch in 1958 advanced this method as the guiding principle in his series,

Die Rote Optik (The Red Lens) (see Koch 1995). In the GDR, this West German program soon became the center of a countercampaign by the magazine series *Telestudio West* (TV-Studio West), which had been reckoning with FRG television programs since 1957. East German television had actually bought the required television recording studio for DM 100,000 in the Federal Republic (Hickethier 1998: 139). Eventually, Karl Eduard von Schnizler in 1960 institutionalized such polemics with his *Der Schwarze Kanal* (The Black Channel), which became a long-running weekly show (Gerlof 1999).[6] Koch screamed "plagiarism" and concluded that with *Der Schwarze Kanal*, the "inner-German television war" had gone on the full offensive (*Der Spiegel* 1960, no. 16: 90). Thereafter, a kind of "ping-pong of images" dominated the medium, with East and West representing the low-quality material of the other with their own commentary to an all-German public for their approval. The completion of Germany's physical division with the building of the Wall in 1961 only added to the lack of images for an adequate representation of the other side. This changed only after the signing of the Basic Treaty in 1972, which allowed for the exchange and accreditation of correspondents (Riedel 1993: 191ff.).

Summary and Outlook

In the first decade of the German division, the FRG and the GDR developed a media-based rhetoric in competing documentary film practices that followed the stereotyped patterns formed during the Cold War. A limited number of themes and motifs were available for the characterization of the other side, and specific representational strategies were established to convey them. The emerging subgenres in this "system debate" used the documentary's promise of access to reality in different ways. The *Archivfilme* of DEFA signaled historical authenticity through their use of found images. The more analytic West German films, on the other hand, explored GDR reality through amateur material whose qualitative weaknesses had the strategic strength of conveying a gray image of the GDR. The reports may have included "counterimages," though mostly not through a direct confrontation. The FRG countered the accusations of fascist continuity made by the GDR's *Archivfilme* with contemporary rather than historical material: films about the zonal border carried accusations of totalitarianism, which the viewer experienced sensually through close-ups of barbed wire.

In the course of the 1960s the established images and strategies on both sides were called into question. In the FRG, the images of the enemy were gradually supplemented by images that presented the GDR as something foreign and unknown. At times, the GDR was evoked as a corrective in order to demand social reforms; on rare occasions at the beginning of the 1970s, one could even find glimpses of a friend. The GDR maintained its ideologized images of the FRG as an enemy until the end but was able to endow them with greater authenticity and credibility through the formal innovations and new approaches developed by Heynowski & Scheumann in the 1960s and by Sabine Katins in the 1970s (Steinle 2003). Ironically, with reunification and the disillusionment that followed, many of these images of the enemy from the Cold War acquired new relevance, from the FRG as a source of individualistic isolation, social indifference, unemployment, and merciless capitalism, to the GDR as a generalized system of surveillance, propaganda, and lack. In the media images now produced from a (West) German perspective, the latter survive in the thematic and representational strategies adopted from the Cold War (Zimmermann 2002: 26) that have been described on the preceding pages.

Notes

1. Following recent theoretical discussions, the documentary film must be considered an aesthetic and rhetorical construction that conducts a discourse about reality built upon representational and cognitive conventions (Renov 1993; Hattendorf 1999; Odin 2000; Heller 2001).
2. The KgU was founded during the Berlin Blockade as a news service, which was financed by the CIC (Counterintelligence Corps) and then by the CIA (Central Intelligence Agency). Its task consisted of collecting information and helping refugees, as well as creating a resistance movement. After 1951, the KgU turned to sabotage actions.
3. Founded in 1946, the task of the East Office of the SPD (Sozialdemokratische Partei Deutschlands) consisted in aiding refugees, establishing contacts in the GDR, and supplying them with news. The East Office developed into an organization similar to the secret service which, like the other East Offices of the other parties, was financed by the BMG.
4. The Inter-Ministerial Committee was created in 1953 and consisted of representatives from various ministries. At first, stock and profit rights were the legal basis for this controversial censorship organ, which had determination over the import of products from the East Bloc.
5. Heinz Reinefarth (1903–79) participated as an SS-Brigade leader in the suppression of the Warsaw Ghetto uprising. He was elected as mayor of Westerland in 1951 and was a representative to the Schleswig-Holstein parliament after 1958.
6. The transcripts have been published by the Deutsches Rundfunkarchiv (DRA) on the web: http://dra.orb.de.

Chapter 9

THE TREATMENT OF THE PAST: GEZA VON RADVANYI'S *DER ARZT VON STALINGRAD* AND THE WEST GERMAN WAR FILM

Jennifer M. Kapczynski

Embattled Cinema

According to a 1960 report published by Werner Jungeblodt of the Catholic Film Commission for Germany, the number of war films screened in West Germany quadrupled between 1952 and 1958. Noting the difficulty of defining the war film genre, the author confined his remarks to those works concerning twentieth-century wars, whether combat films or those in which war merely provided the historical backdrop. While Jungeblodt offered some support for the genre, citing its potential to raise awareness about the horrors of battle, he also expressed concern about the impact of war films on the German public. In a segment entitled "Recapturing West Germany for the War Film," he argued that "the majority of these films signal an alarming relapse—a relapse into a spiritual condition that once characterized the Friedrich II films in Germany and that, after 1945, was chalked up to the Germans as militaristic" (Jungeblodt 1960: 9). Jungeblodt claimed that American war films had paved the way for this reversion, "making the German public receptive once more to themes of allegiance, manly pride, the duty of heroic death, blind obedience and battlefield glory" (9).

Jungeblodt's text, noteworthy as much for its anxiety regarding foreign influence as for its pursuit of the ethical and social implications of representing war, was responding to a genuine boom in war films. Despite efforts by some religious leaders to stem German attendance, such as

Werner Heß, film commissioner for the Protestant Church, who pressed audiences to cease all patronage of these films, the war film genre thrived throughout the 1950s (Barthel 1991: 262). Between 1954 and 1959, more than a dozen German productions appeared that treated the subject of military life during World War II. War films received not only popular support, but also critical acclaim. In 1959, Frank Wisbar's combat film *Hunde, wollt ihr ewig leben?* (Dogs, Do You Want to Live Forever?) won a *Bundesfilmpreis* (federal film prize) for the best film of 1958.

This body of films, far from forming a unified front, presented a variety of positions on the war and the armed forces. One finds favorable portrayals of soldierly camaraderie, like the *08/15* trilogy (1954–55) and *Der Stern von Afrika* (The Star of Africa, 1957); works emphasizing anti-Hitler resistance within the officer corps, like *Canaris* (Canaris: Master Spy, 1954) and *Fabrik der Offiziere* (The Officer Factory, 1960); treatments of the bitter conditions in both German and Soviet prison camps, including *Der Arzt von Stalingrad* (The Doctor of Stalingrad, 1958) and *Strafbataillon 999* (Punishment Battalion 999, 1959); and expressly antiwar films like *Die Brücke* (The Bridge, 1959).

Film historians have noted the rise of the genre and have argued that 1950s audiences, eager to move beyond the masculinity crisis of the immediate postwar years, were drawn to the patriarchal and heroic narratives typical of the war film. Thus, Sabine Hake observes that by the middle of the decade, postwar German audiences could look to their own national cinema "to indulge in their desire for images of male heroism unburdened by political ideologies" (2002: 97). Commenting on the rise of such unencumbered male figures, Manfred Barthel remarks that Adenauer-era cinema was generally preoccupied with "four articles of men's clothing. They were: the Catholic priest's frock; the doctor's white coat, the German soldier's uniform (type of weapon was immaterial); and the detective's trench coat" (1991: 247). Robert Moeller's study, *War Stories*, further illustrates that these films represented just one part of a larger West German trend during the 1950s to reshape (and generally render more palatable) the national narrative about the Nazi past (2001: 123–70).

While critics have discussed the prominence of the war film, to date they have devoted little attention to the individual films themselves. In part, this lack may stem from these films' status as unworthy objects for academic inquiry. As many contributions in this volume will attest, one enduring legacy of the Oberhausen Manifesto has been the view that "Papa's Cinema" offered little of interest for film studies. This is particularly true regarding the war film, which since the 1960s has been maligned for its conservative social and gender politics and for its selective recollection of the National Socialist past. In one typical account, the critic Joe Hembus argued in 1961 that postwar cinema employed a "dangerous process of mystification (*Benebelung*)" when it represented the Nazi past, with the result that the viewer could sit back comfortably in his theater seat in the knowledge that "his own declaration of innocence was being celebrated here" (134–35).

This article aims to reopen the war film genre as a subject for investigation. Although I agree that the war films of the 1950s generally played to German desires to rescue a positive concept of militarized masculinity, I believe that this idea bears further elaboration. Critical voices like Jungeblodt, Heß, and Hembus illustrate that even in its heyday, the genre remained hotly debated, as much for its glorification of militarism as for its tendency to spectacularize violence. I argue that the individual films of the genre are often more contradictory than has been recognized, and contain both visual and narrative tension about how to narrate the history of the war. Through a close reading of one war film, Geza von Radvanyi's *Der Arzt von Stalingrad*, I show how the genre openly stages a conversation about the relative value of German crimes and German suffering, and thereby foregrounds its own shaping of historical discourse. In this regard, my approach represents a departure from previous discussions of the genre, which have tended to view these films as monolithic expressions of a culture intent on revising or refuting its past.

I am particularly concerned with what *Der Arzt von Stalingrad* suggests about the limits of representing soldierly heroism after World War II. As Viktor Klemperer noted in 1946, the concept of heroism took on a special significance under the National Socialist regime, and "always appeared in uniform" (1976: 11). In order for Germany to move forward and to develop a "truly proper relationship to the essence of humanity, to culture, and democracy," the nation would have to discard that old definition (11). Following Klemperer, it seems important to investigate whether and how the war film attempts to redefine heroism according to humanist, rather than nationalist and militarist values. The question of heroism is closely bound up with suffering, and I also explore how von Radvanyi's film presents the issue of German war costs, and how this relates to the Cold War tensions surrounding the return of prisoners of war (POWs) in the 1950s. Lastly, I address the implications of the film's deployment of romance to represent German-Soviet relations. As I make clear, the film provides a contradictory picture of the eastern front experience, at once owning German responsibility for the invasion of the Soviet Union and literally romanticizing that enemy encounter.

A New Kind of Hero?

On 21 February 1958, *Der Arzt von Stalingrad* opened in West Germany. Von Radvanyi, who had begun directing in his native Hungary in the early 1940s, conceived of the film as the final work in a trilogy on the consequences of World War II. The series included *Valahol Európában* (It Happened in Europe, 1947), concerning the plight of children in postwar Europe, and *Donne senza nome* (Women Without Names, 1949), about women in a postwar relocation camp. Both films were well received and later earned von Radvanyi acknowledgment as a contributor to Italian neorealism. Critics have said that von Radvanyi never fulfilled this early postwar potential, however, because he preferred to create more popular fare (like his remake of *Mädchen in Uniform* [Girls in Uniform, 1958], starring Romy Schneider). When the director died in 1986 his name was more readily associated with entertainment than with art films.

For the final film of his war trilogy, von Radvanyi focused on the experiences of German POWs in a Soviet prison camp. *Der Arzt von Stalingrad* tells this story through the eyes of one such prisoner, Dr. Fritz Böhler. Significantly, von Radvanyi chose O. E. Hasse to play the lead. Audiences were familiar with Hasse not only from his stage and screen work during the Nazi era, but also from his more recent roles in war films like *Canaris* and the *08/15* series. Von Radvanyi's film, based on the 1956 eponymous novel by Heinz G. Konsalik (itself loosely based on a celebrated figure of the time, Dr. Ottmar Köhler, dubbed the "Angel of Stalingrad" for his work as a doctor in Soviet captivity), is not a combat film. It is a POW film and a "military biography," which, through the story of an individual soldier, emphasizes "personal sacrifice, a religious fervor, or a human crisis of some sort, . . . and presents [combat] as the basis of the problem, one section of a larger, noncombat story" (Basinger 2003: 12). While the film's grounding in biography lends it authenticity, the "biopic" format also provides the viewer with a single figure of identification. This is not an army film celebrating the diversity of the military population (a feature common to many wartime films both in the United States and Germany), or a combat film reveling in the drama of the trenches or the glories of new destructive technologies, but rather a movie structured around the experiences of a lone hero.

Through an extended flashback sequence that begins when Böhler finally returns to Germany, *Der Arzt von Stalingrad* narrates the doctor's struggle to maintain the health of his fellow inmates and to fulfill his professional duties. The arbitrary and often cruel Soviet camp commanders frequently hinder Böhler's efforts, forbidding him to conduct surgery and denying him basic medicines. Böhler's younger colleague, Dr. Sellnow (played by Walter Reyer), further complicates matters when he falls in love with one of the Russian officers, the capricious Alexandra Kasalinskaja (Eva Bartok). The relationship ends disastrously for both (earning them death and imprisonment, respectively). Now the sole remaining German physician, Böhler turns down an opportunity for early release. Sacrificing himself for the good of the community, he remains behind to continue his work until all of his compatriots are freed.

Der Arzt von Stalingrad opens with a sequence of archival footage documenting the homecoming of POWs. A church bell tolls, signaling a celebration, and the camera cuts from a long shot of onlookers joyously waving from the windows of a half-timbered house to several close shots of families embracing haggard returnees. One woman dejectedly searches the crowd, her loved one's photo in hand. In a seamless transition to the fiction film, the camera then cuts to a medium shot of a hotel entrance, and the film's central character makes his first appearance. The camera keeps pace with Böhler's slow progress across the lobby, and then tracks forward and beyond him, so that when the audience first hears the man's weary voice he is absent from the frame. He requests a room (implying that this former soldier has no home to which he might return). The camera pans down to reveal his hands as he fills out the registration, then swings up to reveal a framed photo of a ruin, with the caption: "This is what remained of the Hotel Anker in 1943."

The photograph prompts the beginning of a lengthy flashback episode. With a crackle, Hitler's oratory fills the airwaves. The radio address serves as an ironic voiceover, the dictator's bombast contrasting sharply with the accompanying sequences portraying the destruction of war. Von Radvanyi intersperses new footage with documentary material, and the camera cuts from a shot of gloomy bar patrons to images of conflagration, crashing planes, antiaircraft fire, and, finally, to a shot of injured soldiers in a barracks. A door bearing the word "field hospital" signals that these men are awaiting treatment, and the next shot cuts to their would-be healer, now facing the camera: Böhler, who performs surgery amid a full-scale assault. A medium shot reveals his steady manner. Although the operating lamp swings wildly and plaster streams from the ceiling, Böhler remains calm, even after the Russians have occupied the hospital. When the Soviets replace his German patient with one of their own wounded soldiers, Böhler simply calls for anesthetic—a physician to the last.

While the archival footage emphasizes the film's connection to contemporary events and confers an air of historical accuracy, the framing of Böhler against a larger mass of returning soldiers establishes him both as the film's main protagonist and as an "everyman." Böhler emerges as a sympathetic identification figure and as a strikingly modest hero. Böhler's initial appearance already hints at the humility and self-effacement that will characterize his actions in the POW camp; he is shot from behind, then excised from the shot altogether, only returning as a pair of hands. This is further underscored by his noticeably voiceless return. Böhler utters just one line before the onset of the flashback sequence, and he does not speak at all in the film's final scene, when the narrative returns to the present.

His silence suggests both that his war experiences are "unspeakable" and that they find no audience in the postwar moment of the frame story. In contrast to the Hitlerian "voiceover," which purports to tell the story of Stalingrad, Böhler never audibly assumes authorial control over the narrative. Although Böhler ultimately emerges as a dauntless warrior in white, tending to his patients even under the most difficult circumstances, the film stresses repeatedly that he is merely an ordinary man living in extraordinary circumstances. When a colleague later accuses Böhler of taking too much pleasure in his status as the camp's resident savior, the doctor contradicts him: "I'm no hero. I am Fritz Böhler from Würzburg."

Von Radvanyi's strategy of visual, aural, and narrative undercutting suggests an attempt to craft a new kind of postwar hero—one whose rejection of heroism renders him worthy of the designation. This is in stark opposition to the version of masculinity put forth in such 1930s films as *Morgenrot* (Dawn, 1933), in which soldiers happily die for the national cause, or *Wunder des Fliegens* (Miracle of Flight, 1935), which glorifies the death-defying devotion of German aviators. In fact, it is the doctor's consistent self-effacement that grants him a position of authority among the camp inhabitants and within the film as a whole.

Subsequent scenes further demonstrate that Böhler is avowedly apolitical, wedded to a profession rather than to a party, and more interested in sustaining the life of his community than in achieving personal glory. Despite a heart ailment, he chooses to remain in the camp to treat his fellow former soldiers, and Böhler avoids any mention of his own wartime travails. Another inmate reveals that the doctor lost his only daughter to Allied bombing. Böhler retains a progenitor's instincts, however. As Moeller has noted, "with no one waiting for him at home, [Böhler] is effectively positioned to be the caring father of the homosocial family of POWs" (2001: 151). In charting a course for German recovery, *Der Arzt von Stalingrad* substitutes a father for a *Führer* (i.e., Hitler) and stresses the importance of paternal guidance for national healing.

In creating an alternate model of postwar heroism, *Der Arzt von Stalingrad* effectively excises all references to the Wehrmacht military command. Although the central characters are all officers, the film presents them as doctors rather than as soldiers. This is in notable contrast to films like *08/15*, *Hunde wollt ihr ewig leben?*, or *Fabrik der Offiziere*, each of which features military leaders who are both inept and stubbornly devoted to the National Socialist cause. *Der Arzt von Stalingrad* sidesteps this issue—a move that accords with the film's general effort to represent the group of POWs as antiauthoritarian.

Paradoxically, this leads to a rather more complicated picture of responsibility than those provided by these contemporaneous works. Unlike May's and Wisbar's films, von Radvanyi's picture lacks a clearly identifiable scapegoat. Although the soldiers in *Der Arzt von Stalingrad* appear hapless victims in a war machine run amok, the film never names a guilty party. This is not to say that he averts the question of German culpability altogether. Compare von Radvanyi's film to *Der Stern von Afrika*, in which an anonymous voiceover describes the onset of hostilities as though the war itself were an agent (declaring "and so the war began"). In *Der Arzt von Stalingrad*, Böhler chides his fellow inmates when they chafe against the restrictions of camp life, reminding them that German aggression led to their plight: "You're forgetting that we're guests here . . . and if memory serves, we weren't even invited." Yet as I outline in the subsequent section, *Der Arzt von Stalingrad* often obscures this acknowledgment of responsibility through its portrayal of Soviet sadism, diluting the message that Germany caused its own suffering. The film thereby gives voice to two popular and conflicting 1950s positions on the recent past—that Germany must embrace its guilt, and that this guilt was tempered by German pain.

Competitive Suffering

In 1958, a spate of articles appeared in East German publications attacking *Der Arzt von Stalingrad* as an "inflammatory anti-Soviet film" (*Hetzfilm*). A reporter for *Neues Deutschland* accused the film of reviving fascist fantasies of the Soviet Other, and argued that "SS-types" could easily replace the Soviet figures in the film (ironically transforming them into the Soviet "Same"—7 August 1958). Citing statements by an East German doctor who knew the original "Doctor of Stalingrad," the writer further claimed that Dr. Köhler, "that current West German show pony," was a less-than-heroic liar. Striking a similar note, an article in *Berliner Zeitung* questioned the accuracy of both the literary and cinematic accounts, arguing that "Nazi concentration camp doctors," not Soviet physicians, provided the model for the narrative (2 August 1958). The controversy surrounding the film extended into the diplomatic ranks, as an article in the Berlin *National-Zeitung* reveals. In July 1958, the Soviet embassy representative I. Panasenko went before the Berlin Senate to protest the film's continued appearance in the cinemas of the Federal Republic, declaring that von

Radvanyi's work hindered efforts to bolster friendly relations between the two nations (*National-Zeitung*, 5 August 1958).

Although some West German critics disparaged the representation of the Soviet officers in *Der Arzt von Stalingrad* (like the reviewer for *Film-Dienst*, who noted that the film contained plentiful depictions of "Soviet malevolence and vigorous German nobility" [6 March 1958]), they took issue less with its characterization of the camp officials than with its treatment of the prisoners' existence. In one fairly typical review, Franziska Violet, writing for the *Süddeutsche Zeitung*, regretted that the film did not fulfill the promise of its opening sequence, and bemoaned the fashion in which "the tired clichés of German entertainment films inject themselves into the narrative and detract more and more from the seriousness of the theme" (29 April 1958). Along similar lines, Karl-Heinz Krüger complained that "the German film industry doesn't shy away from making even the most unspeakable catastrophe cinematically palatable," and labeled von Radvanyi's film a "tear-jerker behind barbed wire" (7 March 1958). Karl-friedrich Scherer took a more conciliatory tone. He praised the film for its treatment of a topic with such great potential "to reopen freshly-healed wounds," and argued that it successfully communicated the message that "those injuries that were struck by the powers of politics, war, and hate might only be healed through the understanding and goodwill of direct human relationships" (*Film-Echo*, 5 March 1958).

The reception of *Der Arzt von Stalingrad* illustrates the contested status of 1950s war films, both as aesthetic treatments of the recent past and as critical interventions in the Cold War politics of the day. At the heart of both the East and West German reviews lies a central issue: how should one represent the battle of Stalingrad and, more broadly, the German war experience? While the GDR critics took umbrage with the film's negative characterization of Soviet officers, many of the West German reviewers faulted the film for aestheticizing a historical moment which, in their view, was still more terrible than the narrative allowed. Despite some critics' positive assessment of the film as healing, the controversy surrounding von Radvanyi's work suggests that it did just as much to expose unresolved tensions surrounding the return of German POWs.

In 1958, those tensions were substantial. Following Konrad Adenauer's visit to the Soviet Union in 1956, Soviet authorities had announced the release of all remaining German soldiers from their POW camps. Countering this claim, West German veterans' groups insisted that thousands of German soldiers remained captive. Since the end of the war, these groups had worked to raise public awareness about the plight of those men still imprisoned, and had mounted numerous campaigns, including an exhibit about POW camps entitled *Wir mahnen* (We Admonish), which toured

Germany throughout the 1950s. According to a 1953 report in *Die neue Zeitung*, roughly three thousand visitors attended the exhibit in the first ten days alone (28 April 1953). In 1958, *Der Arzt von Stalingrad* easily played into West German concerns about the continued struggle for the release of German POWs and about the strained relations it caused between the FRG and the GDR.

Embodying the ambivalence regarding the Nazi past that prevailed in West Germany during the Adenauer era, *Der Arzt von Stalingrad* vacillates between acknowledgment of German responsibility and attention to this plight of the nation's former soldiers. As Moeller has argued, "one of the most powerful integrative myths of the 1950s emphasized not German well-being, but German suffering" (2001: 6). This is best illustrated by an early scene in the flashback narrative, in which Böhler and his assistant argue with their Soviet counterparts about the treatment of sick prisoners.

The episode begins with an exterior shot of the camp infirmary. The building's small onion-dome turrets hint that the space once served as a church. That suspicion is confirmed when, cutting to the initial interior shot, the camera pans down a brick wall inlaid with the three bars of a Russian Orthodox cross. It tracks down and back to reveal Böhler and his assistant, Dr. Sellnow, against a backdrop of religious frescoes. Two camp officials, Captain Alexandra Kasalinskaja and Captain Pjotr Markow (Hannes Messemer), accompany Böhler and Sellnow as they make their rounds.

After Böhler and Kasalinskaja square off over differences in their treatment strategies (Böhler simply wants to cure his patients, while the captain insists on following the prescribed Soviet "norm" of a three percent incidence of illness in prisoner populations), Sellnow enters the fray. More impassioned than his older and steadier colleague, Sellnow steps in and demands provocatively: "If you just want to kill the man you can inject him right here." Kasalinskaja's reply is swift and bitter, and clearly articulates the film's project to weigh German crimes against German suffering: "This is prison camp. Not German concentration camp." After a final exchange of barbs, the two Soviet officials turn to leave, and Böhler quickly moves to comfort the sick soldier whose treatment prompted the argument. A medium shot shows Böhler by the man's side, the frescoed figure of an angel hovering just behind them.

The religious iconography decorating the infirmary sanctifies the suffering of the wounded soldiers and frames it within a context of Christian martyrdom. In this context, Böhler becomes a saintly healer, and the film takes on hagiographic overtones. Subsequent scenes take up the concept of the miracle cure, and Böhler repeatedly stresses the importance of belief in the treatment process. Böhler's reliance on faith underscores the Soviet doctors' disregard for the sanctity of human life as well as for organized religion. At the same time, Böhler's invocation of divine power accentuates his distance from a National Socialist worldview—a particularly significant gesture in the 1950s, at a time when the church wielded enormous social and political influence, in part because of its reputation as an institution that had remained untainted in twelve years of Nazi rule.

The scene further emphasizes the soldiers' status as victims rather than as perpetrators. Eliding the actual Battle of Stalingrad, the film shows only the aftereffect of Germany's defeat, and the POWs never appear as architects of their own fate. Stalingrad is reworked, transformed from the place of Germany's greatest military defeat to the site of these soldiers' extended battle for survival. The concept of the perpetrator grows muddier still when, in this sequence, the film offers superficial acknowledgment of German atrocities. Kasalinskaja rejects any comparison of her methods with those of the concentration camps, but the scene's detailed portrayal of her disregard for her patients sharply undercuts the integrity of her words, and the audience is encouraged to entertain the very parallel that Kasalinskaja disputes. The equation draws further strength through Böhler and Sellnow's respective acts of defiance. In a stunning inversion, the German soldiers appear rebellious and antiauthoritarian—as if to underscore the fact that these men were never obedient followers of the *Führer*. Instead, fanaticism, once so highly praised by the Nazis, surfaces in the Soviet soldiers, who come across as unquestioning and even zealous in their execution of orders.

This scene stages one of many conversations in *Der Arzt von Stalingrad* about the war experience and about the comparative extent of German and Soviet victimization. The dialogues are striking, particularly because they originate in an era in which, according to the standard historical account, West Germany is supposed to have repressed discussion of war guilt altogether. Rather than eschewing mention of Nazi violence, the film employs a strategy of relativization. Although it makes numerous references to Soviet losses, *Der Arzt von Stalingrad* places primary narrative and visual emphasis on the tribulations of the German soldiers. The film's acknowledgment of German crimes ultimately falls flat, its brief mention of atrocities overwhelmed by the extent of German suffering onscreen. The film's portrayal of the Eastern Front as a space of romantic encounter, rather than as territorial aggression, further prompts the audience to perceive the soldiers as victims of fate. *Der Arzt von Stalingrad* characterizes the encounter with the East as a love affair, and casts the German man as the recipient, rather than as the initiator, of these ill-fated desires.

Romancing the East

Der Arzt von Stalingrad features two parallel romances, one that remains chaste and one whose passion destroys its participants. In the first case, Schultheiss, a German soldier (Paul Bösiger, who played the hapless Vierbein in *08/15*), falls in love with a female Soviet lieutenant (Vera Tschechowa). Their relationship never moves beyond mutual admiration, and when the young German receives his discharge from the camp, they part ways with only mournful glances. The second relationship takes a more prominent place in the narrative: the romance between Dr. Sellnow and Captain Kasalinskaja. Because the two give in to their desires, their relationship endangers them and the order of the camp. When Markow, Kasalinskaja's fellow officer and also her spurned lover, discovers the two together at the very moment in which Sellnow is supposed to be boarding his transport home, Markow provokes Sellnow to attack him and then shoots him on the spot. A moment later, a group of hulking guards arrives to take Kasalinskaja away, presumably to a Siberian prison camp.

The marketing materials for the film foreground the commercial appeal of this forbidden relationship. In an advertising poster produced by the Divina Film Company for German distribution, a photograph of Böhler's face occupies the central position. Counterbalancing the image, however, competing photographs, showing Kasalinskaja in the embrace of her two paramours, appear in the opposing upper right and bottom left corners. The Transozean-Film publicity brochure, which marketed the film internationally, similarly emphasizes Böhler's and Kasalinskaja's shared importance, and O. E. Hasse and Eva Bartok, the internationally known stars, receive dual billing on the first page.

The film's wavering between a war film and a "bodice ripper" is less curious than it initially might appear. Romance has long been featured in war narratives, and the pairing is not peculiar to German culture. Rainer Gansera has commented upon this phenomenon in cinema, and sees a semiotic interdependence between "armored bodies, designated for battle and destruction, and naked bodies, which exist for the sake of desire" (1989: 34). Most important for this analysis, one finds a proliferation of romantic attachments (ranging from flirtation to full-fledged affair) between German soldiers and Russian women in those war films produced in the Federal Republic during the 1950s.

In *Hunde wollt ihr ewig leben?*, sexual attraction leads one officer to help a Russian woman avoid deportation to a German labor camp. In his case, the gambit pays off: when they meet again in Soviet-controlled territory, she returns the favor and supplies him with food and instructions on how to rejoin his command. In the second film of the *08/15* trilogy, entitled "At the Front," a German soldier falls for a Russian woman living near the barracks. Only after the two have spent the night together is she unmasked as a spy. She betrays the German plans to retreat, and Red Army forces launch a deadly attack. If one accepts the fact that these German-Russian love affairs are a salient feature of war films set on the eastern front, the question remains how to understand the particular role that romance plays in rewriting the narrative of Germany's greatest military failure.

The reception of returning POWs affords some insight. The historian Frank Biess has shown that, during the 1950s, a substantial discussion took place in German medical and social welfare communities regarding the effects of Soviet imprisonment on former soldiers. Physicians diagnosed sickly returnees as suffering from "dystrophy," a broadly defined condition that included a "variety of physical symptoms such as water edema, liver damage, and loss of sexual instinct as well as a wide range of 'psycho-pathological behavior,' including apathy, depression, and loss of all moral inhibitions" (2001: 59). According to the prevailing discourse on dystrophy, the Eastern camp experience fundamentally altered the sexual identity of former soldiers, and "thus indicated that the unconditional surrender of the Wehrmacht was followed by a complete emasculation of its former soldiers in Soviet captivity" (61). Following Biess's work, these romantic encounters with the East appear as attempts to reconstruct, in a cinematic space, a normative sexual identity for the German soldier. The men in these war films do not suffer from impeded sex drives, and although they may make poor choices when it comes to their objects of desire, their masculinity remains intact.

In *Der Arzt von Stalingrad,* Sellnow represents a manly alternative to his rival, Markow. While Sellnow sports a beard and an athlete's physique, Markow is thin, clean-shaven, and comparatively effete. He has lost an arm in combat, and his empty sleeve indicates that he is, at best, "half" a man. The film also codes Markow's behavior as effeminate. On the one occasion that the audience sees him in a private setting, he sits in the domestic enclave of Kasalinskaja's room and strokes a cat that is perched on his lap. Prone to petty jealously, Markow prefers to manipulate matters from behind the scenes rather than engage in direct confrontation (as when he surreptitiously arranges for Sellnow's early departure).

Kasalinskaja, too, experiences some gender trouble. Sellnow emerges as the man who will reawaken her feminine side, which her experiences in the Soviet army, with its "unnatural" insistence on employing women in the military, presumably has suppressed. As the promotional materials for the international release explain, the captain, whose "heart has been hardened because of her hatred of all that is German, is now stirred by womanly feelings of love." Kasalinskaja must be *made* a woman.

Her conflict becomes most apparent when, after an argument, Sellnow presses her: "Is that the captain (*der* Kapitän) talking, or the woman (*die* Frau)?" In the same sense, she chooses between genders when she selects a partner. In favoring the manly Sellnow over the feminized Markow, she not only sides with the more conventional form of militarized masculinity, but also opts for a traditional gender role for herself—although in the context of the Soviet camp, her decision to follow her "womanly instincts" proves disastrous.

Significantly, while Sellnow's masculinity appears unharmed, the film implies that he bears little blame for their romance. Although Kasalinsskaja protests against Sellnow's advances, visual cues suggest that she plays the actual seducer. Perpetually posed before mirrors, Kasalinsskaja not only rediscovers her femininity, but also stages her desire to be desired, becoming a literal trap for the male gaze. This reaches a deadly conclusion in Markow's final confrontation with the lovers. At the scene's opening, Kasalinsskaja is the only figure whose reflection appears in the looking glass before her, but as the events progress, each of her partners is successively drawn into the frame, literally pulled in by her dangerous combination of lust and egotism. Her earlier resistance to Sellnow appears artificial, and the film suggests that she has engineered the entire affair. While this move again underscores the film's representation of German soldiers as victims—Sellnow is doubly captive when he falls prey to the captain's desire—it also plays into one of its more troubling discourses. Despite Böhler's comment that the Germans were "not invited," *Der Arzt von Stalingrad* juxtaposes military and sexual conquest and implies that the Soviet Union was a willing recipient of German "advances."

Looking Backward

Revisiting the war films of the 1950s, it becomes clear that the genre served a number of functions, not all of which were inherently reactionary. While these films allowed a reassessment of the past, this meant not simply mourning for a nation lost, but, in some cases, also addressing the more difficult questions of guilt and responsibility that were raised when the Nazi regime fell. The genre did not iterate a single cohesive statement about the German past, but rather included both positive recollections and highly critical assessments of the war years. And as in the case of *Der Arzt von Stalingrad*, a great many films offered ambivalent accounts of World War II. It is these works, with their confused desire to assume some of the burden of German guilt and simultaneously to revive an ideal of militarized heroism, which offer perhaps the greatest potential interest for film studies. Much work remains to be done in understanding how the individual war films of the 1950s engaged with contemporaneous debates about public memory.

In the final analysis, it must be said that *Der Arzt von Stalingrad* espouses a largely conservative view of the German experience in World War II. Von Radvanyi's film supports the 1950s West German discourse that privileged collective suffering over collective guilt. It portrays Böhler as a new, antiauthoritarian postwar hero, reads the prisoners of war as victims, and represents the Soviet officers as a group of hacks and sadists. In framing the Eastern campaign through the lens of a romantic encounter, the film further undercuts its own attempts to address German responsibility and depicts the Soviet Union as the primary aggressor. Although the film makes some acknowledgment of Nazi crimes, it places the greatest emphasis on German losses. Like many works of the 1950s, *Der Arzt von Stalingrad* also promotes a model of masculinity based on humble and apolitical paternalism.

And yet, as my examination of *Der Arzt von Stalingrad* demonstrates, these war films frequently provided a forum in which to rethink the costs of battle. Although von Radvanyi's film ultimately suggests that German suffering ameliorates the burden of German guilt, it also introduces contradictory arguments—and this, I contend, leaves room for alternate interpretations of the recent past. By staging a conversation about the aftermath of National Socialism, the film uncovers the work of retelling the nation's war stories. Far from offering a conclusive statement about the meaning of the combat experience, *Der Arzt von Stalingrad* closes with an open question, as Böhler, now back in Germany, encounters a military parade. A freeze-frame of his grim and resigned expression prompts the viewer to wonder what the world has learned from the horrors of the last war. The postwar documentary footage of marching soldiers from various nations, a clear reference to the Cold War, suggests that the lessons of the past remain, at best, obscure.

Chapter 10

FILM UND FRAU AND THE FEMALE SPECTATOR IN 1950S WEST GERMAN CINEMA

Hester Baer

The popular illustrated magazine *Film und Frau* (Film and Woman) began regular publication in 1949 and soon attained the second largest circulation among both women's magazines and film periodicals in the Federal Republic.[1] Describing itself as an entertainment magazine spotlighting fashion, film, and visual art, *Film und Frau* was the only women's magazine during the 1950s to focus primarily on film (I. Schwarz 1956). In a period when women comprised the majority of cinema spectators, *Film und Frau* was also the only film magazine to address a predominantly female readership.[2] Concomitant with the decline of the popular German cinema and the establishment of new cinema audiences in the 1960s, *Film und Frau* was ultimately subsumed into the magazine *Moderne Frau* (Modern Woman) in 1966.

Like other women's magazines of its time, *Film und Frau* addressed women as consumers, a fact reflected in the magazine's feature articles and photo reportages on film, fashion, and home decorating as well as in its substantial advertising component. Unlike other general interest women's magazines that overwhelmingly listed housewives as their ideal readers, *Film und Frau* sought to appeal especially to the "modern woman" (I. Schwarz 1956). This ideal modern reader was conceived as a working-class or middle-class *employed* woman who was interested in contemporary entertainment culture—a woman who presumably possessed her own disposable income and, not coincidently, a woman in roughly the same demographic as the West German film industry's ideal spectator during the 1950s, also known as *Lieschen Müller* (Wortig 1961).

In its features on art, its fashion spreads, and its film-related content, *Film und Frau* addressed issues of perception and representation in the context of women's experiences. Situating film spectatorship within the continuum of women's everyday lives, the magazine used film as a medium through which to tackle questions such as changing gender roles, balancing career and family, women in the new economy, and the organization of the postwar household. As such, the magazine sheds light on the context of film spectatorship for women in the 1950s. Not only does an analysis of *Film und Frau* help us to gain a sense of how female spectators in the 1950s learned how to find meaning in films, but the magazine itself was also instrumental in shaping modes of reception at the time.

Film historians have largely ignored *Film und Frau*.[3] In critical reevaluations of the 1950s where it is mentioned, it is often invoked as a signifier for: first, the feminization of mass culture and popular cinema in the postwar period (von Thüna 1989); second, the prominent role of consumer discourse in film production and reception in the 1950s (Carter 1997: 175); and third, the regulatory function played by the dominant culture in the attempt to redomesticate women and to control women's bodies in the Adenauer era (Brauerhoch 1983). Absent from these accounts, which focus particularly on the magazine's fashion spreads, is an evaluation of the larger appeal to the female reader-spectator in *Film und Frau* and its cultivation of a particularly female gaze. While the magazine was clearly instrumental in training the postwar female consumer and in establishing new models of femininity in the 1950s, its fashion spreads and other features did not uniformly commodify and objectify women. Rather, *Film und Frau* also provided a space of pleasure and fantasy for women; a site through which to navigate—not just as objects but also as agents—the new consumer landscape of the postwar period; and, finally, a forum for reformulating modes of representation and perception in "democratizing" Germany.

In what follows, I offer an overview of *Film und Frau* together with some preliminary conclusions about how it addressed female spectators and how it constructed a female audience for 1950s cinema. In researching *Film und Frau*, I looked at every issue of the magazine published between 1949 and 1962. Given the difficulties of working with *Film und Frau*—none of its contents has been indexed and few complete archived copies are available—I hope that my analysis will establish a more detailed understanding of the magazine and raise questions for future research.

When analyzing the contribution of women's magazines to the construction of the female spectator, feminist film theorists have focused on the ways in which illustrated magazines participate in the process of commodification that characterizes the relationship between women and film.

For Mary Ann Doane, illustrated magazines exemplify the connections among film, spectatorship, and consumption in at least three ways (1987: 24). First, the female spectator witnesses her own commodification in the pages of the fashion magazine (just as she does in the film) and "buys herself"; second, the commodity tie-in to the film is proffered; and third, the film itself is on display as a commodity. As Doane suggests, the Hollywood woman's film arose as a genre in large part as a result of the film industry's growing awareness of the power of the female consumer. Similarly, postwar Germany saw a proliferation of female-oriented cinematic genres that profited from women's economic power at the box office and that promoted consumerism by modeling products on screen and by selling commodity tie-ins, in part through women's magazines. Furthermore, and particularly salient for my argument, Doane proposes that "the much sought-after address to the female spectator often seems more readily accessible in the discursive apparatus surrounding the film than in the text itself" (26). Indeed, *Film und Frau* routinely addressed the female readers of its film features in a way that focused the female gaze on particular aspects of a film's narrative and visuals.

Writing about female spectators of Hollywood cinema in postwar Britain, Jackie Stacey argues for a less one-dimensional understanding of the relationship of women to film-related consumption. Stacey contests the model proposed by Doane—of women participating in their own domination and objectification through the processes of spectatorship and consumption—by highlighting women's agency as consumers and the contradictions that consumption poses for women. Drawing on feminist cultural studies, Stacey argues that "consumption is a site of negotiated meanings, of resistance and appropriation as well as of subjection and exploitation" (1994: 187). In her ethnographic research on female film fans, Stacey found that "female spectators are successfully constructed as consumers by Hollywood cinema *and* that they also used commodities connected with stars in ways that do not conform to the needs of the market" (189). Stacey emphasizes that spectatorship and consumer discourses were avenues through which female spectator-consumers negotiated gender identity as well as sites of pleasure and productive fantasy for women. Stacey's model is useful for an analysis of *Film und Frau*, a magazine that trained its readers in consumerism while also providing a site of negotiation, pleasure, and fantasy. Like the British viewers that Stacey studied, West German filmgoers in the 1950s likely used spectatorship, fandom, and consumerism for escapist purposes and as spaces through which to negotiate gender, class, and national identity in the aftermath of World War II, while they were simultaneously interpellated into new ideologies and social structures via these same channels.

In the German context, Patrice Petro has examined the connections between the address to the female spectator in Weimar illustrated magazines and cinema. Illustrated magazines and movies in the 1920s thematized issues of sexuality and gender identity in an attempt to appeal to female audiences. As Petro writes, "In the bourgeois cinema and press, these issues were fundamentally bound to economics and consumerism— to the need to address women's experiences and bind them to pleasurable forms of consumption" (1989: 90). The postwar Federal Republic saw a similar thematization of gender roles and identity in films and magazines that appealed to female audiences. While Petro's Weimar periodicals addressed changing modes of femininity in modernity—in particular the poles of androgyny and motherliness—*Film und Frau* addressed changing modes of femininity in the postwar period that departed from styles associated either with the New Woman of Weimar or with the feminine ideal of Nazism.

The few works to address *Film und Frau* explicitly have adopted a largely critical stance. Annette Brauerhoch argues that the magazine functioned as an organ of the patriarchal "Grandfather's Republic," enforcing a circumscribed version of femininity in the service of male economies (of desire, through the body images the magazine promoted, and of growing wealth and affluence, through the types of consumption the magazine encouraged) (1983). Erica Carter suggests that the housewife's spectatorial relation to the fashion spreads and luxury products in *Film und Frau* and in other magazines involved both narcissistic identification and disavowal brought about by the "evocation of the class divide that separated the fashionable lady from the female spectator" (1997: 224). Both Brauerhoch and Carter offer salient analyses that highlight the discursive function of the magazine in consolidating the patriarchal and capitalist structures of the postwar Federal Republic. Yet both readings, in focusing exclusively on fashion photography, neglect the interplay of image and text as well as the continuum of visual representation and spectatorial fantasy that permeates all of the elements of *Film und Frau*. Far from excluding the average reader—whether she was a housewife or a working woman—from the "scopophilic pleasures of active looking" (Carter 1997: 205), *Film und Frau* delineated an active female gaze throughout its articles and fashion spreads, a form of looking and perception attributed exclusively to women.

In 1956 Ingelene Schwarz completed a study of women's magazines in the Federal Republic that helps explain how these magazines were received in the postwar period. Schwarz isolates two primary characteristics of women's magazines in the 1950s. Most obviously, they devoted more space to issues that affected women than did magazines marketed to both sexes. Second, "One can name the timely effort to stick by female readers in the difficult postwar years and to encourage them again to seek a positive way into the future" (1956: 18). Schwarz suggests that women's magazines foregrounded these two unique functions in order to justify their continued existence at a time when the newly achieved "equal rights" of the sexes had fulfilled one goal of the women's press in Germany. In the nineteenth and early twentieth centuries, many women's magazines had devoted themselves to women's suffrage and explicitly addressed the goals of the women's movement through strong social and political platforms. While the large majority of postwar women's magazines was not explicitly political, the magazines did address key contemporary issues and provide practical tips for women during the difficult reconstruction years. Furthermore, women's magazines played an important role in exposing women to foreign cultures, from which they had been isolated during the Nazi period. As the program manifesto in the first issue of the magazine *Der Regenbogen* put it, "All (potential readers who were polled) wanted many practical things: recipes, useful tips, a fashion page. . . . In short, advice and help in the problems of everyday life. In addition, they wanted stimulation and entertainment: stories or a novel, good poems, a cultural page. Many said: 'Our horizons must be broadened again. We lived behind a wall for all those years, and now we want to know what the world looks like!'" (cited in Schwarz: 20).

According to Schwarz, who examined all sixty-eight women's magazines that appeared in the Federal Republic in 1955, they could be differentiated from the mainstream press not only by their content, but stylistically as well. A primary stylistic trait of the magazines was an "intimate" address to the female reader that constructed a "community of women" comprising the magazine's authors, producers, and readers. Diverse topics could be addressed in an "intimate," personalized fashion under the rubric "Hier sind wir ganz unter uns—unter uns Frauen" (We're among women here—it's just between us). For Schwarz, the most important stylistic marker of women's magazines was their striking emphasis on images, both in the magazines' content and in advertising. Advertising comprised a large portion of the magazines, and advertisements tended to work in dialogue with content, so that they became an essential part of the magazines. Like the feminist film theorists just discussed, Schwarz stresses the significant role of both visual images and consumer discourse in women's magazines.

In addition to fashion spreads, *Film und Frau* regularly published written features and photo reportages on the visual arts; in-depth coverage of the latest feature films, directors, and stars from Germany and abroad; and articles on contemporary women's issues such as work, housing, family life, and social and political topics. The magazine also included advice columns, serialized novels, poetry, recipes, patterns for sewing and knitting, book reviews, travel accounts, and advertising for a wide range of consumer products. On a formal level, a typical feature in *Film und Frau*—whatever its subject matter—addressed the reader-spectator with a diverse array of visual and narrative signifiers: photos, graphic art, editorial text, captions, and advertising. Often the line between areas of content was blurred, as a fashion spread became a lesson on visual art or an article about foreign ambassadors in Germany doubled as an advice column on home decorating. In addition to this image-oriented formal style, features and reportages on all subjects in *Film und Frau* generally displayed a focus on women's experiences and perspectives.

According to Schwarz, social and political articles in the 1950s commonly included reports on the so-called *Frauenüberschuß* (surplus of women) that discussed how disparaging and problematic this term was; editorials on the much-debated question of equal rights for women; and articles encouraging women to use their right to vote. Features for working women provided tips on how to find a good job and portraits of interesting careers. Following this model, *Film und Frau* did not publish explicitly political articles, but it consistently addressed the common concerns of modern, professional women in its features and advice columns.

In 1949, the column "Und Ihre Ansicht?" (And your opinion?) provided a forum for discussing controversial contemporary issues. Under this rubric, *Film und Frau* printed readers' letters and advice about changing postwar gender roles, women in the workplace, and marriages between older men and younger women (FF, no. 1 [1949]: 21; FF, no. 5 [1949]: 23; FF, no. 7 [1949]: 23).[4] The theme of the "surplus of women" was a common one. Not only did advice columns discuss the increasing age disparity in marriage that was one result of this "surplus," but articles enumerated the ways in which women could use the gender disparity to their advantage. Writers argued about the importance of equal rights for women in the workplace and in society at large. One article entitled "Das 'schwache' Geschlecht" (The "weak" sex), suggested that, given the current gender disparity, men were actually the weaker sex. This article went on to explain why women were equally well suited to perform traditionally male tasks (FF, no. 19 [1951]: 16–17). Many articles and columns focused on the difficulties of balancing career and family, often attempting to dispel the prejudices that blamed women's careers for the breakdown of the institution of marriage. Instead, these articles proposed that two-career marriages were more successful for both husband and wife than marriages defined by traditional roles (FF, no. 19 [1951]: 16–17).

Profiles of women abroad served a didactic function in postwar women's magazines because they sought to educate readers about the rest of the world after the isolation imposed by the Third Reich. Articles about foreign women in *Film und Frau* consisted primarily of portraits of famous women and celebrities. The magazine regularly featured articles on foreign artists, stars, and filmmakers, often sketching a broader picture of life in their native countries by displaying their homes and by providing a glimpse into their private lives. By the late 1950s, *Film und Frau* began to make its international focus more explicit. A new series entitled "Akkreditiert in Bonn" (Accredited in Bonn), about foreign ambassadors to West Germany, began in 1958. Personalized profiles of the ambassadors and their families provided a point of access for readers to learn about the customs and histories of the ambassadors' native cultures. Occasionally, the magazine also printed articles on the struggle for women's rights abroad (FF, no. 2 [1959]: 24–26).

In addition to articles on successful artists, actresses, and famous women at home and abroad, *Film und Frau* offered behind the scenes glimpses into women's careers, many of which were related to film or art. These articles not only reimagined the dominant culture as a place in which women played an essential role, but also encouraged female readers to view visual culture as a space into which they could intervene creatively and professionally. A 1949 photo essay and article on "Fräulein B.," a "script girl" for a major studio, portrayed this woman as the key to a given film's success, the woman who held the strings and who orchestrated the smooth running of the shoot (FF, no. 19 [1949]: 18–19). Even as it began to publish more pieces on motherhood and homemakers in 1953, *Film und Frau* increased its coverage of career life with a new regular column. "Interessante Frauenberufe" (Interesting Professions for Women) provided detailed information about the education necessary to embark on desirable career paths and explained the everyday work involved in such professions. Over the years, the column profiled careers as diverse as engineer, architect, beautician, graphic designer, photographer, film animator, medical technician, and optician.

Profiles of career women frequently situated these successful women within the private sphere of their homes. While this served on the one hand to redomesticate professional women, it also enabled the magazine to show its readers the material signs of their success (FF, no. 23 [1950]: 1–3; FF, no. 6 [1952]: 12–13; FF, no. 5 [1954]: 28–29).[5] As one photo essay put it, "It is the dream of all professional women to own their own home, even if it is very small. They have lived for too long in furnished rooms, between wardrobes and tables, pictures and drapes which others chose, and which surround them in a foreign and impersonal way. They are sick of the silent fight for the kitchen and the bathroom, and they would like finally to be able to have visitors who don't have to be registered by the landlady" (FF, no. 26 [1950]: 8). The 1950s ideal of owning one's own home is presented here with a twist: for women, it represents the dream of complete independence.

Features and photo essays on ideal homes and articles on home decorating were a consistent feature of *Film und Frau*. In 1949, practical articles like "Das ideale Einzimmerheim" (The ideal one-room home) provided tips on making the most of limited space during the period of housing shortages (FF, no. 8 [1949]: 8–9). There were also features on well-appointed homes that readers could only aspire to attaining one day (FF, no. 13 [1949]: 12–13; FF, no. 13 [1950]: 8–9; FF, no. 8 [1953]: 3–4). Over the course of the 1950s, it is possible to track the growing affluence of the ideal readers of *Film und Frau*, as articles on decorating small apartments give way to tips on furnishing newly built houses.

Similarly, advertisements in the magazine in 1949 and 1950 were largely limited to small items such as cigarettes, cosmetics, the omnipresent Nivea cream, tampons and sanitary napkins, and liquors. Cosmetic ads in the early years appealed to everyday, working women, highlighting the economic differences between the magazine's readers and the stars and models it routinely showcased in its photo and fashion spreads. In fact, *Film und Frau* often featured luxury items in its fashion spreads before they were regularly advertised in the magazine. By 1951, clothes appropriate for riding in cars were often included (FF, no. 14 [1951]: 12–13). In 1952 a special television dress was featured in the magazine (FF, no. 2 [1952]: 21), well over a year before a television would be advertised there. In 1953, a large fashion spread about televisions appeared in the same issue that included the first advertisement for a television (FF, no. 22 [1953]: 2–5). In keeping with the magazine's didactic tendencies regarding visual culture, the text of this piece includes a discussion of new forms of social interaction brought about by adding a television to one's living space.

By the mid-1950s, as the Economic Miracle moved into full swing, *Film und Frau* regularly included ads for large durable goods such as cars, televisions, kitchen and household appliances, furniture, and former luxury items such as nylon stockings. At this point, the economic gap between the magazine's readers and its stars was de-emphasized, and the everyday working woman was now often replaced by a famous star selling a product. Luxor soap, whose slogan was "Neun von zehn Stars benutzen Filmstars, Luxor Toiletteseife" (Nine out of ten film stars use Luxor toilet soap), debuted in West Germany in 1951, introducing the trope of the star as a commercial vehicle into the postwar press. The first Luxor ad, featuring the actress Joan Fontaine, appeared in *Film und Frau* in 1951; it was quickly followed by ads with the German stars Heidemarie Hatheyer and Hildegard Knef. Knef, a popular spokesmodel in the early 1950s, was also featured in *Film und Frau* ads promoting Happy End makeup and Ergee stockings.

The majority of ads in the magazine continued to make a specific appeal to working women, however. A 1956 advertisement for migraine tablets focused on the typical working woman's double burden: "Every second woman works double duty! Every second woman in the Federal Republic between the ages of fifteen and sixty-five has a profession. 'On the side' most of them are housewives as well, and often enough mothers too. Two jobs, year in, year out, from early in the morning until late at night. That doesn't leave much time for everyday pains" (FF, no. 8 [1956]: 40). Similarly, a famous Bosch ad campaign from the late 1950s that ran in many issues of *Film und Frau* featured the slogan "Gleichberechtigung für die Hausfrau" (Equality for the housewife) encouraging the rationalization of housework through the consumption of modern appliances to decrease this double burden.

While consumption of goods and services was the subtext of *Film und Frau*, the magazine's patent focus was the consumption of film, fashion, art, and culture. Cultural coverage in *Film und Frau* often included essays on literary topics, especially after the mid 1950s. In 1955, the magazine printed an essay on female characters in the works of Friedrich Schiller and a profile of Hermann Hesse written by Thomas Mann (FF, no. 16 [1955]: 22–23; FF, no. 18 [1955]: 2–4). A 1959 feature on "Frauendichtung heute" (Women's writing today) discussed works by Ingeborg Bachmann, Ina Seidel, and Marie-Luise Kaschnitz (FF, no. 10 [1959]: 48). The magazine also published a profile of Simone de Beauvoir (FF, no. 25 [1959]: 10). However, the large majority of cultural articles in *Film und Frau* focused on visual art, and most consisted of artist profiles. Famous male artists were occasionally featured in the magazine (FF, no. 1 [1950]: 10–11; FF, no. 15 [1953]: 15–16; FF, no. 15 [1954]: 18–21; FF, no. 9 [1957]: 41–43; FF, no. 12 [1957]: 18–20). Above all, though, these profiles presented a range of female artists: potters, painters, fashion designers, and sculptors, among others (FF, no. 2 [1952]: 5–6; FF, no. 18 [1952]: 9; FF, no. 11 [1953]: 26–27; FF, no. 19 [1954]: 16–18; FF, no. 19 [1954]: 24–27; FF, no. 8 [1955]: 16–18, 99; FF, no. 24 [1956]: 16–18, 100–101, 117).

According to Ingelene Schwarz, women's magazines used two strategies to represent cultural content in the 1950s: they discussed women's role as "guardians of culture" and they printed articles about cultural achievements that focused on female artists and artworks by women. Highlighting women's production and consumption of art and film, *Film und Frau* did not emphasize the idea that women must be "guardians of culture."

However, the magazine did conform to a different trope suggested by Schwarz: "Particular attention to feminine interests in the cultural sphere is characterized by frequent presentation and discussion of works that represent the figure of the woman artistically. In this regard, the artistic viewpoint of the modern woman stands at the center of attention" (1956: 57). Articles in *Film und Frau* about cinema implicitly addressed the representation of women on film by focusing on the aspects of the films that would appeal to female spectators, while its fashion spreads often placed models next to paintings and in frames, highlighting the objectification of women in art in ambivalent and striking ways.

Film und Frau devoted a substantial portion of each issue to film, with spreads on the latest releases and fan-oriented profiles of stars and directors. Occasionally the magazine printed essays on international cinema, film art, and new film technologies such as 3-D. From its inception, *Film und Frau* presented a balance of coverage that favored German cinema but that granted space in each issue to Hollywood films, with occasional contributions on French, English, and Swedish cinema.

Fashion content represented the other largest segment of each issue. Film and fashion content often overlapped, as fashion spreads revolved around new looks suggested by recent films, and features on film stars depicted the actresses sporting new fashions. Sometimes, film stars modeled for fashion spreads as well. The first few pages of *Film und Frau* were generally devoted to artistic fashion spreads, shot by some of the most well known fashion photographers of the era.[6] Each issue also contained standard features devoted to new trends and fashion advice.

Like the many *Film und Frau* articles that presented female fashion designers as artists, fashion spreads in the magazine introduced the latest dresses and accessories as works of art. The magazine sought to educate readers about the vocabulary of fashion's changing lines and colors, the materiality of its artistry. Again and again, fashion spreads explicitly appropriated the signifiers and settings of visual art and its exhibition practices in order to situate fashion within the wider field of visual culture, thus suggesting that fashion *is* art. Shot in museums, galleries, and artists' studios, the artistic fashion spreads showcased at the beginning of the magazine very often invoked historical art forms in their compositions, from the Old Masters to Pablo Picasso, Surrealism, and Expressionism.[7]

A 1950 cover portrayed a woman in a glittery evening dress, framed by the four sides of a window. Her fingers curl around one side of the frame, so that she appears to be moving out of the artwork. The same model, in the same dress, is pictured in the lead photograph of the issue's fashion spread, "Mode als Kunst" (Fashion as art). The rest of the spread portrays models posed against landscape paintings in evening gowns, which are described in the accompanying text as follows: "The evening dresses are shaped with a cultivated delicacy—dresses that are so charmingly womanly that they often remind one of old paintings by Watteau or of the era around 1920. . . . When looking at them, one almost forgets that the artist created these not only from a wonderful surplus of fantasy, but also in reference to a practical purpose: toward a creative stimulation of the whole textile sector of our economy, which gives work and bread to innumerable people" (FF, no. 14 [1950]: 3). Not only does this spread situate fashion in analogy to classic works of art, but it also positions fashion as a practical art form. Fashion attains its greatest artistry in clothing women's bodies, and it plays a key economic role as well: promoting growth in the textile industry, which employed many female workers. Fashion spreads like this one thus encouraged a female-oriented mode of perception attuned to the artistry of the clothes on display, while at the same time situating the production and consumption of fashion as an element in the economic reconstruction of the nation.

A fashion spread from 1959, entitled "Stilleben zwischen Sein und Schein" (Still life between reality and appearance) and photographed by Hubs Flöter, portrays a model posed in a variety of different outfits in front of a reproduction of Picasso's 1905 painting *The Absinthe Drinker*. The model's poses contrast with the poses of the woman and the clown in Picasso's painting. The text that accompanies the spread analyzes the effect of these contrasting images: "The fashion photographer has thoughtfully illuminated the strange interstitial space inhabited by the model. . . . The model obeys not her own, but another's mechanics. . . . The dress and the intentions of its creator are everything. . . . Thus the flesh and blood human being becomes merely function and illusion, like the figures in paintings who hardly portray themselves any longer, but rather represent color and compositional factors" (FF, no. 1 [1959]: 3). In this passage, fashion and painting are equated, both in terms of composition and in terms of their effects on the spectator. Comparing the model with the figures in the painting, the commentary continues: "Yet [the model's] corporeal presence is optically broken down and made questionable through the mirroring on the table top—the woman and the clown on the other hand, made lifelike precisely through this mirroring, step out of the painting's frame in a ghostly manner" (FF, no. 1 [1959]: 3). Here, ossified representations of women in painting and fashion photography are problematized in a self-reflexive fashion spread that provided readers with a framework for understanding the images in *Film und Frau*. Readers are encouraged to speculate on the cleft between real life, "corporeal presence," and the objectification of women in representation. Spreads like these sharpened readers' faculties of perception, encouraging a critical gaze trained to decode the blurred boundaries of the real and the illusory in the magazine and in visual culture at large.

While the haute couture featured in such fashion spreads would not have been affordable or accessible to the majority of female readers (Carter 1997: 212), the focus on art suggests that the spreads were more than advertisements for designers or spaces of consumer desire. Rather, they addressed questions of representation and perception: What are the important elements of a work of art? How should one view paintings, films, and designer clothing? How are women portrayed in visual art? By exploring such questions while creating a mode of address specifically aimed at a community of female readers and spectators, fashion spreads in *Film und Frau* participated in the magazine's larger project of training the female gaze, suggesting a specific mode of spectatorship through which women could or should look at art. At the same time, these artistic fashion spreads, by locating fashion within the art world, attempted to vest fashion with the legitimacy of high art.

This strategy bears many similarities to the magazine's attempts at legitimating film culture. Like film, fashion was portrayed both as high art that should be viewed for its own sake, and as a functional art form that could have an effect on the everyday lives of female consumers. Visual spreads on films were constructed almost like fashion spreads, with stills arranged artistically across several pages. Film spreads generally followed fashion spreads in the magazine, and the stylistic continuum of these spreads endowed film, as fashion, with the qualities of "high art." But, with film as with fashion, the texts accompanying these spreads often focused on training the gaze of readers toward specific visual and narrative signifiers. While *Film und Frau* thus legitimated fashion and film as viable art forms, it foregrounded their uniquely female-oriented status at the same time.

Articles on new films, for example, did not incorporate film reviews in the traditional sense. Rather, the magazine regularly featured pictorial retellings that combined several pages of film stills, reproduced in small-panel sequences, with short captions that narrated the films' plots. The stills sought to focus readers' attention on elements of composition and often included particularly unusual or unique shots. The captions often focused on female characters, or retold the film plots from a perspective that sought to reflect the interests of the female reader-spectator. Often, the magazine situated film narratives within the context of women's lives, suggesting issues that a given film might help women work through; sometimes these issues actually took precedence, and the authors barely referenced films ostensibly being presented.

In 1949, *Film und Frau* printed a spread on George Cukor's 1941 film *Two-Faced Woman*, Greta Garbo's last film, which had just been released in Germany. Stills from the film were accompanied by a lengthy article about the difficulties that professional women face in maintaining lasting and satisfying relationships. Cukor's film, which dealt peripherally with this issue, was only mentioned at the very end of the article, almost in passing (FF, no. 7 [1949]: 4–5). Here, as in many reviews of American films, *Film und Frau* suggested to spectators one way of viewing a glamorous Hollywood film whose world appeared very distant, presenting a set of meanings that applied to the viewers' lives.

German films, by contrast, were generally given more in-depth treatment, as they tended to thematize more explicitly the issues confronting German women in the postwar period. An article on Wolfgang Liebeneiner's 1948 film *Liebe 47* (Love '47) highlighted the film's attempt to appeal to female spectators: "*Liebe 47* is . . . an adaptation of Wolfgang Borchert's *Draußen vor der Tür* (The Man Outside)—and that is a man's play, aimed at decline and destruction from the first to the last scene. Liebeneiner added an extra component to the material that is so strong that it has become a woman's film: a woman outside, named Anna Gehrke" (FF, no. 9 [1949]: 4–5). As this article suggests, Liebeneiner, cognizant of his predominantly female audience, changed Borchert's play, creating a melodrama about infidelity, broken marriages, and the difficulties women at the home front faced during wartime.

A few issues later, the magazine printed a column by the same author, who had observed a group of men discussing Liebeneiner's film. Every man present expressed dismay over the infidelity of women during and after the war—none sympathized with the plight of the female character in the film. The *Film und Frau* author used this anecdote and Liebeneiner's film to provide a lengthy apologia for unfaithful women, praising the film for its fair treatment of the problem: "Almost worse than all the destroyed marriages and faithlessness of our times is the self-righteousness with which many of our contemporaries condemn such cases. To have paved the way for an unsentimental, fair understanding in this regard is one of the humane byproducts of that great experiment, *Liebe 47*" (FF, no. 18 [1949]: 8).

As these brief examples suggest, *Film und Frau* presented films within the framework of the "community of women" posited by Schwarz. Film narratives were retold from a female perspective that focused on aspects of a film salient to women, thus spotlighting the address to the female spectator. Not only were *Heimatfilme*, melodramas, and films about kings and queens given this sort of coverage, but also films such as Robert Siodmak's *Mein Vater, der Schauspieler* (My Father, the Actor, 1956); Ottomar

Domnick's *Jonas* (1957); and Herbert Vesely's *Das Brot der frühen Jahre* (The Bread of those Early Years, 1962)—films that would not necessarily be categorized as "women's films" (FF, no. 16 [1956]: 24–25; FF, no. 15 [1957]: 82–83; FF, no. 6 [1962]: 106–9).[8] As in the case of *Liebe 47*, the male reception of a film was sometimes discussed to demarcate the sphere of female spectatorship, the community of female viewers, which was established in the magazine.

Like its fashion spreads, the magazine's film coverage provided a model of female spectatorship. *Film und Frau* sought to inculcate in the female reader-spectator an active gaze that focused both on the artistic aspects of fashionable clothing or filmmaking and on their ties to everyday concerns. By investing a distinctly female mode of vision with links to consumer culture, *Film und Frau* not only helped shape individual identity construction through film spectatorship and the navigation of new styles, but also legitimated the consumption of film and fashion as art in the postwar period. As such, *Film und Frau* played a crucial role in establishing the female audience of 1950s German cinema.

Notes

1. *Film-Revue* had the widest circulation among film periodicals in 1958, with an average of 460,000, followed by *Film und Frau* (395,000), *Star Revue* (275,000) and *Filmjournal* (94,00) (von Thüna 1989: 249). *Constanze* was the biggest general interest women's magazine of the decade. In 1953, the circulation of *Film und Frau* was 266,171 copies, significantly less than *Constanze*'s 487,744, but greater than the third-place *Ihre Freundin*, whose circulation numbered 205,000. By 1955, *Film und Frau* had a circulation of 341, 500, while *Constanze*'s had risen to 588,730 (I. Schwarz 1956: 22). Between 1949 and 1954, *Film und Frau* cost 60 pfennigs; in 1955, its price went up to 70 pfennigs, concomitant with its shift from a predominantly black-and-white format to the inclusion of many more color pictures. Throughout the period of its publication, *Film und Frau* appeared biweekly.

2. Sources from the period suggest that women comprised approximately 70 percent of cinema audiences at the time (Wortig 1961:15). Women outnumbered men in West Germany well into the 1950s, due to the number of casualties and prisoners of war still being held after World War II.

3. For example, Hans Helmut Prinzler's exhaustive *Chronik des deutschen Films, 1895–1994* (1995) does not mention *Film und Frau*, nor does Fehrenbach include the magazine in her study of 1950s film culture (1995).

4. Throughout, references to *Film und Frau* will appear in the text under the abbreviation FF, followed by number of issue, year of publication, and page numbers. All translations are by the author.

5. This type of article was not limited to stories about women. Features on Jean Cocteau, Marc Chagall, and Oskar Kokoschka all showed these men at home, engaged in domestic activities (see FF, no. 9 [1951]: 5–6; FF, no. 12 [1957]: 18–20; FF, no. 9 [1957]: 41–43).

6. *Film und Frau* regularly published works by the photographers Regi Relang (1906–89); Hubs (Hubertus) Flöter (1910–74); and Charlotte Rohrbach (1902–81). Relang, who used her last name professionally, studied art and painting before turning to journalism and

photography. In 1938, she contracted with French *Vogue* and devoted herself to fashion photography. In the 1950s, she worked for *Constanze* and *Madame* as well as *Film und Frau*. Flöter had a brief stint as the director of the Ufa studios' photographic division before turning full time to fashion photography. He worked primarily for *Film und Frau* in the 1950s, becoming quite well known for his artistic fashion spreads. Rohrbach specialized in both fashion and architectural photography. In the 1930s, she had worked for *Die Dame*, the largest women's magazine at the time. During the Nazi period, she also produced advertising films. In the 1950s, she was employed full time by *Film und Frau* as the chief photographer for architecture and living.

7. Notably, the magazine rarely included the dominant form of contemporary visual art—abstraction—in its fashion spreads in the 1950s, although many of the clothes on display would have lent themselves to an abstract mode of representation. While it is outside of the scope of this chapter to address this issue in depth, it is interesting to note that any discussion of abstract art is wholly absent from the magazine after 1949, when abstraction was dismissed as a male-oriented style in a brief column on the subject (FF, no. 11 [1949]: 23).

8. For a reading of the retelling of *Das Brot der frühen Jahre*, that also focuses on female subjectivity and issues salient to female spectators, see Baer (2003: 174–75).

Chapter 11

RETERRITORIALIZING ENJOYMENT IN THE ADENAUER ERA: ROBERT A STEMMLE'S *TOXI*

Angelica Fenner

Former Ufa director Robert A. Stemmle's postwar film hit *Toxi* (1952) has gained a certain currency in academic circles in recent years as a visual artifact offering a point of entry for exploring discourses on race, consumer culture, national identity, and gender in the early years of the Federal Republic of Germany. The film was strategically released by Allianz Film GmbH in August 1952 to coincide with the school enrollment of the first wave of so-called occupation children born to German women variously involved with (primarily) U.S. occupational troops. Public officials and school administrators alike were aware of the fact that it was most especially the entry of children fathered by African-American soldiers that might create a stir. For, as a visible minority, these children not only represented the "trace" of Germany's defeat and ensuing occupation, the resulting transformation in the human landscape required a level of racial integration for which no precedent in the nascent republic existed.

Stemmle intervened in this historical moment with a didactic plot trajectory constructed around the choices a patrician Germany family must face when an Afro-German orphan is mysteriously deposited at their doorstep one winter evening. The extended three-generation household comes to metonymize the nation in its struggles to overcome entrenched racial perceptions and to master the new syntax of integration. Historians have thus found the film a useful source for situating social policy of the reconstruction era in relation to normativizing discourses of sexuality, race, and gender (Fehrenbach 2001). Cinematic approaches to the film (Brauerhoch 1997), on the other hand, have explored its visual iconography for continuities with, and divergences from, racialist discourses in the context of U.S. film history and thereby uncovered the specificity of integrationist discourse within postwar Germany.

This essay shifts the scholarly focus from the primary text itself to a critical evaluation of the status of historical spectatorship as evinced in *Toxi*'s reception in the media. In unpacking publicity brochures, film reviews, and early writings on the situation of Afro-German children, I will be foregrounding psychological processes of identification and positing the political nature of enjoyment in relationship to a pivotal film that established powerful resonances among West German viewers. According to the public survey published in *Filmblätter*, *Toxi* placed eighth among the top ten film hits (foreign and domestic) in West Germany upon its release during the third quarter of 1952 (8 August 1952). This is a matter of no small significance, given that *Toxi* was only one among 112 German films competing in 1952 with an even more sobering figure of 375 foreign films, of which 200 were American productions (Kalbus 1956: 66). As the film traveled from one exhibition venue to the next in the various federal states, Allianz-Film supplied movie houses with publicity photos and promotional cards for school distribution, as well as copies of Michael Jary's theme song, "Ich möchte so gern nach Hause geh'n" (I want to go home), which was passed on to music teachers at local kindergartens and orphanages. Exhibitors were encouraged to invite such choirs—stipulated as "needing to comprise a mixture of black and white children"—to perform at the film's opening at local venues. At some of these events, children could also look forward to pony rides, balloons, servings of cake and cocoa, and the child actress Elfie Fiegert's personal appearance. Accompanying adults were offered a subtext that disingenuously acknowledged how recent changes in the ethnic landscape dovetailed with the threat that offspring born out of wedlock generally posed to both bourgeois propriety and entrenched social and class divisions (Höhn 2002). The film acknowledged the legacy of racist attitudes within postwar society but offered collective catharsis to viewers by couching these concerns within a narrative trajectory and resolution that could leave viewers feeling assured that these internal symptoms were subsiding. Although *Toxi* was generally regarded in its time as a progressive intervention into the topic of racism, scholars today more readily concur that many of the discursive strategies employed in this benevolent endeavor stage racism anew. In the ensuing pages I will explore how racist tropes and spectatorial identification can operate in collusion to produce a historically conditioned form of enjoyment.

Historical Spectatorship, Visual Pleasure, and the Mise-en-Scène of Desire

My approach to spectatorship is indebted to a broader genealogy of psychoanalytic approaches to the cinema. While Christian Metz (1975) and Jean-Louis Baudry (1975) laid the groundwork for spectatorship studies by suggesting that the screen and exhibition space replicate psychological processes of projection, later theorists (Cowie 1984; Doane 1984; Penley 1985; Mayne 1993), in turn have shifted the focus to the relationship between discursive positions textually structured into the film and historically variable processes of identification that take place among viewers. Judith Mayne (1993) has identified two theoretical essays offering psychoanalytic definitions of fantasy that have been particularly helpful in elaborating the operation of identification. In "Fantasy and the Origins of Sexuality" Jean Laplanche and Jean-Bertrand Pontalis (1967) posit fantasy as essentially a form of mise-en-scène, stressing that it is about the "staging" of desire rather than about its linear pursuit. Their notion of staging delineates how particular subject positions are occupied within a tableau: "Fantasy . . . is not the object of desire, but its setting. In fantasy the subject does not pursue the object or its sign: he appears caught up himself in the sequence of images" (26). Freud's analysis in "A Child is Being Beaten" (1919), in turn, has been instrumental in the development of a definition of spectatorship that rejects unilateral paths of identification in favor of a triadic oscillation between the positions of voyeur, active subject, and passive object.

In Stemmle's film the trope of adoption constitutes the overarching mise-en-scène for the diegetic characters as well as for the media critiquing this allegorical drama. While the diegesis thematizes an orphaned child's petition for acceptance within a (Caucasian) family, what is under contestation in a broader sense is the extent to which children of visibly foreign patrimony should be understood to bear equal claim to citizenship in a nation still defining membership along ethnic lines. It is worth noting that, in reality, relatively few Afro-German children were actually available for adoption: less than 13 percent of German mothers of Afro-German children were willing to surrender custodial rights and put them up for adoption (Fehrenbach 2001: 184). Thus, the cinematic mise-en-scène of adoption ultimately served a more strategic function in the public eye, facilitating the historical repression of the origins of Afro-German children in the sexual fraternization between German women and occupation soldiers. By extension, the trope of adoption rendered all Afro-German children seemingly a priori exterior to German familial structures and, in turn, extracted a unique form of spectatorial pleasure from the drama positing their benevolent (re)incorporation into the national fold.

The fact that actress Elfie Fiegert was herself an adopted orphan unfortunately only reinforced this conflation of national phantasm and historical reality—so much so that the film's cast list presents the lead role of "Toxi" as performed by … Toxi. The opening paragraph of the film distributor's commercial newsletter offers evidence of the rhetoric at work in the film's strategic release: "With grace and charm she [Toxi, A. F.] breaks through the rampart of outdated conventions within a family and wins the hearts of everyone. It is not R. A. Stemmle's intention to tear open old wounds but rather to heal them. This is a call for understanding for all Toxis. Toxi is an appeal to our humanity, in an effort to prevent the living legacy of a turbulent postwar era from having to atone for something which is not their fault" (*Aktuelle Film Nachrichten*, 1 August 1952: 1).

These palliative lines reassure potential film exhibitors that the film would not alienate German viewers with overt invocations of guilt about the Nazi past implied in the term old wounds. The reference to "the rampart of outdated conventions" acknowledges that a complex condensation of moral issues, class biases, racial prejudices, and national loyalties comes to a head in this film, yet makes the shift in ideological stance—from passive witness or obliging accomplice within a fascist dictatorship to citizen of a democratic state—seem a matter of exchanging old conventions for more salubrious or utile codes of behavior. Furthermore, the distributor implies that the film will enable Germans to recover agency, situating them as spectators nobly bestowing sympathy upon a stigmatized group categorically neutralized of historical and political baggage by means of the affectionate label of "Toxis." While postwar Afro-German children did constitute a kind of social category by virtue of their historical uniqueness and their visibility, the collective labeling employed here collapses their individual biographies under one signifier, to imply that their appearance and, indeed, their fates were indistinguishable.

Such generalizations are defied by the reality that the scriptwriters Maria Osten-Sacken and Peter Francke screened no less than four hundred children whose mothers had responded to the call of a "4 to 5 year-old Negro girl sought for film role" in a Munich newspaper, before encountering Fiegert. As Osten-Sacken recalls: "We received so many photos that we literally started seeing black. And once we had narrowed the candidates down to twenty very charming coffee-brown girls, it became clear to us that we still had not found the girl who corresponded to what we had in mind. And then suddenly the real 'Toxi' was at our doorstep just as we had envisioned her" (*Aktuelle Film Nachrichten*, 1 August 1952: 8).

The screenwriter's words confirm the truism that any fictional script works with preconceived imagery and affect during the casting process. It also implies that Fiegert's success as an actress resulted from her fortuitous

hypostatization of particular fantasies of childhood innocence—in conflu-
ence with tropes of the tragic mulatto unable to transcend her blackness
and that of the resilient Sambo who remains "the eternal child, the eternal
dependent, happy though given to unaccountable moods of depression"
(Nederveen-Pieterse 1992: 152). Osten-Sacken's anecdotes are subsumed
under the revealing title, *Wie ich Toxi entdeckte* (How I discovered Toxi),
evincing the extent to which biographical figure and fictional character
had become indistinguishable, forming a singular static entity preclud-
ing character development within either the diegesis or its metonymic
correlative, national history (*Aktuelle Film Nachrichten*, 1 August 1952: 8).
Instead, the monolith of the Afro-German orphan served to fill a certain
place within a historically contingent mise-en-scène, one that I will subsequently outline as interpellating historical spectators into the symbolic
position of democratic citizens within the nascent West German state.

Precarious Status of Afro-German Subjectivity

Questions of agency are also foregrounded in a feature story in the
West German magazine *Der Spiegel*. Apparently, Stemmle had become
particularly adept during his directorial career at using children on the
set and allegedly never even revealed to Fiegert that she was acting in a
film: "In her capacity as lead actress, she never had to memorize a single
line of the very extensive script; she just repeated before the camera
whatever Robert read to her.... 'It's terrible, really, what one does with
such a child,' he admitted. In order not to upset this lively creature of
above-average intelligence, he refrained from telling Toxi [*sic*] that she
was performing in a film. Even on the last day of shooting, she was still
under the impression that she was merely being photographed" (*Der
Spiegel*, 23 July 1952: 27).

Whatever the truth about Fiegert's stage experience, both the various
personnel involved in creating the film and the press responsible for
reflecting upon its significance and reception within the public sphere
appeared reluctant to regard her as an active agent in the process of her
own subject formation. At dispute is the extent to which she was aware
of operating within the scopic field of the camera, of being looked at—a
point absolutely central to Jacques Lacan's account of the mirror stage as
a decisive step in accumulating images around which to coalesce one's
identity (1977: 106). Inherent to this specular relationship is "the gaze of
the Other," not just in this founding moment but upon the occasion of
any number of subsequent self-recognitions. Lacan reworks the Carte-
sian notion of self-consciousness, one in which a mirror could be said to

simply show us ourselves seeing ourselves. But if the gaze is ultimately something exterior to us, as Lacan maintains, then it is impossible to "see" an unmediated image of oneself. That image is always ideologically preorganized and it is in this respect that we can be understood necessarily to see ourselves from the field of the Other. This also means that the constitution of the subject is grounded equally upon voyeurism, that is, looking, as well as upon exhibitionism, that is, being looked at. To deny that Fiegert was aware of her role as an object of the gaze is to disavow her capacity for exhibitionism as a form of agency, insofar as the displayer "captures" and "contains" the attention of the voyeur. Furthermore, if Fiegert is not deemed to be "playacting," then this denies the possibility that her identity is culturally conceived and that the film camera, now metaphorically standing in for the normativizing gaze of West German society, is actively implicated in this process. To bar her from this complex circuit of visual exchanges involved in the film shooting process, and by logical extension, in the constitution of subjectivity, is to relegate her to a place outside of the parameters of cultural conditioning and of history itself.

Having earlier invoked Laplanche and Pontalis's notion of fantasy as the mise-en-scène of desire, I would like to explore in greater detail the question of whose desire is really at stake in Stemmle's film. At first glance, the trope of adoption seems to position the orphaned Toxi as bearing the most compelling petition: for access to food and shelter in the most fundamental sense, for entry into the social configuration of the nuclear family, for participation in the Christian drama of redemption when she "plays" at being a white king in a Christmas pageant, and for a role in the putative ontology of white femininity when she peers thoughtfully at a stocking-clad mannequin's leg in a storefront. But I would argue that Toxi's petition is ultimately compelling because of the resonances it set into motion with regard to the desires and yearnings of historical spectators.

This is perhaps best demonstrated via the example of Elfie Fiegert's adoptive mother, whose own biographical narrative was so frequently invoked by the press. Gertrud Fiegert had lost her own child during the trek from Silesia to Bavaria immediately following the war, and had been told that she could never have children again. As a solution to her ensuing depression a doctor recommended: "What you need is someone to take care of again! Then your depression will subside!" ("Filmstoff und Wirklichkeit: Die Geschichte des Negerkindes Toxi," *Film*, Erbach, June 1952). Another journalist takes this implicit discourse of object relations a step further, framing Gertrud Fiegert's account of adoption in a manner that implies that the experience of trauma and dislocation experienced by many Germans during and immediately following the war finds its specular correspondence in the abjection of orphaned Afro-German children:

> Her home was an orphanage in Upper Bavaria, where seventy white and mulatto children lived. Most of them still live there today. But fate had better things in store for Elfie-Toxi. A couple from Silesia, whose child died while they were fleeing to Bavaria, adopted the little girl in 1948. "When I walked through the sleeping quarters that evening, she was lying there so sadly in the little institutional bed and reached her arms towards me so trustingly," explains Gertrud Fiegert, the new mother. "So I thought, 'Why not a moor child! She surely doesn't have an easy time of it and will need much love and someone to help her.' (*Westfalen-Blatt*, 2 December 1952)

It is significant that the citizen permitted to speak for herself in this excerpt is one presented as a victim of the war (and by implied extension, of Nazi Germany) rather than as a perpetrator or accomplice. The ensuing specularization exemplifies the line of reasoning established by Alexander and Margarethe Mitscherlich in their classic psychological study on postwar German society, *The Inability to Mourn* (1967), where identification with the victim perpetuates a narcissistic pattern and circumvents the painful task of mourning complicity in the losses inflicted under fascism. As Eric Santner later paraphrases this dilemma, "The capacity to feel grief for others and guilt for the suffering one has directly or indirectly caused, depends on the capacity to experience empathy for the other *as other*" (1990: 7). The identification with Afro-German children as indisputably *German* children, irregardless of their paternal ethnic background is precisely what is missing in the misidentification founded upon Afro-German children as *orphans*, which facilitates a form of false mirroring in which both Elfie and her adoptive parents become casualties within a broader postwar context, socially, culturally, and politically displaced persons seeking to recover a sense of stability and adapt to the rapid ideological and economic changes.

A similar crossover of identificatory processes occurs in the lyrics of Jary's theme song "Ich möcht' so gern nach Hause gehen," which was sung by orphan choirs at local premiers of *Toxi* and which appears at various points within the film's diegesis, intoned as an instrumental leitmotif in the sound track and sung by children at the local orphanage where the truculent patriarch Theodor Jenrich first sought to dispatch Toxi. While the title words of the song express the orphaned children's most literal yearning for an adoptive home, the phrase can also be understood to insinuate that the true "ancestral" home for Afro-German children resides in the United States or in the African nations of their patrilineal forbearers. For the phrase "nach Hause" is not an abstract category—it always implies a relationship between person and place that is preestablished and that involves a return to the already familiar. At the same time, within the multiple connotative levels of address, the ensuing second verse, "Die Heimat möcht' ich wiederseh'n. Ay-ay-ay" ("I want to see my home again"), could also be understood as holding particular resonance for Germany's broader national population. Whether the yearning is for the social order represented by the National Socialist era or for another era viewed as retrospectively prelapsarian, prior to the catastrophes of dictatorship, ethnic genocide, and global warfare, the lyrics and the minor key clearly impart a feeling of nostalgia for some earlier spatio temporal realm. I would suggest that these lyrics were moving for postwar German audiences because they gave the most basic expression to prevalent feelings of acute abjection and disorientation. The subtext of national loss of status and esteem within the global community following military defeat, the experience of cultural dislocation and of constricted freedom of movement during Allied occupation, as well as individual self-doubt, guilt, or confusion in relation to the political past can all be retraced in the words: "Who will love me and take me with them? Ay-ay-ay. I'm so forlorn and never hear a kind word, every street is foreign to me. Why can't I leave? Does no one understand my heart?"

Good Object Choices: Symbolic Identification and the German Worthy of Love Again

Here it is necessary to stress that the type of identification with the figure of Toxi that I ascribe to the (implicitly white) West German viewership is not the strictly psychoanalytic notion defined by Laplanche and Pontalis as the "psychological process whereby the subject assimilates an aspect, property or attribute of the other and is transformed, wholly or partially, after the model the other provides" (1967: 205). For the film is not actually intent upon any sort of a profound transformation in racialized perceptions; rather, it solicits a form of identification that necessarily results in a misperception. A sociological study by Klaus Eyferth on the status of Afro-German children attempted to facilitate public understanding of the situation of this particular population on the basis of a similar misidentification. Eyferth wrote in the forward to the study: "Many people will be able to relate to the fate of colored children in Germany quite well because they themselves were ostracized by their fellow citizens or belonged to a maligned minority. I'm thinking of refugees, former prisoners of war, those persecuted under Nazism, National Socialists who were subject to scorn after the war, and many others. We anticipate a particularly sympathetic response from these people as we present the general public with this study about children of mixed heritage" (Eyferth, Brandt, and Hawel 1960: 7).

Eyferth's benevolently motivated remarks establish a degree of contiguity between the experiences of distinct populations on the basis of historically specific forms of abjection. I invoke the term abjection here in the deeply provocative sense cultivated by Julia Kristeva (1982), in which abjection in the broadest sense can be said to be about expulsion in all of its psychic, social, physiological, discursive, and, indeed, even moral manifestations. It might assume the form of repression of the desires of the psyche, the ejection of wastes from the human body, the projection onto others of undesirable moral qualities actually present to oneself, the exclusion of certain ideas from social discourse, or the ostracization of certain members of a society.

In this particular instance, I would want to question the extent to which abjection experienced by Afro-German children on the basis of chromatic difference is really psychologically and historically equitable with other forms of abjection associated with, for example, postwar physical or psychical trauma, or scarcity of material resources. In disputing any claim to coeval status, I do not mean to establish a hierarchy in terms of whose trauma is more compelling or profound. It is quite simply a matter of qualitatively different forms of abjection. The social ostracization experienced by Afro-German children generally functioned to project ahistorical tropes upon them on the basis of an entirely arbitrary corporeal feature, and involves prejudicial biases that predefined the parameters of their identity, isolated them from peers, and in some instances resulted in their rejection or abandonment by parents or extended family. Forms of trauma experienced by, for example, civilian survivors of the war could, in contrast, be said to have often involved quite severe material deprivations, homelessness, malnutrition, personal injury, and loss of family members, accompanied by dysphoria and ideological or political confusion. Yet these experiences could be located within material circumstances bound to historical events; they were not causally linked to features of the corporeal self perceived as ineradicable and irrepressible.

Furthermore, while German citizens enchanted with the screen figure Toxi or with other Afro-German orphans depicted in print media may indeed have experienced a degree of imaginary identification, misrecognizing in the orphan's plight their own sense of dislocation, they arguably would not actually wish to share their fate. It was precisely the fact that this identification was grounded upon misrecognition that made it safe and gratifying. In fact, these children served as ideal objects for identification at a moment in national history in which the category of victimhood was highly politically charged. The eponymous screen character Toxi and the stylized media photos of Afro-German children circulating in journals and newspapers, proffered a nonthreatening point of identification, not only because their young age marked them as untainted by earlier historical realities, but because they occupied a social status with which few Germans had any lived practical experience. A retrospective in 1963 of Fiegert as a child actress offers evidence that a certain iconography coalesced out of the many photographs of Afro-German children circulating in the media at that time—an iconography that I will rhetorically divide into "the abject gaze" and "the adoring gaze." The journalist reminisces: "The charming little occupation child won the hearts of moviegoers back then most especially because 'she looked so sweet and sad'" ("Das ist 'Toxi' heute: Wieder eine Filmrolle für Elfie!" *Das grüne Blatt*, 20). The utilization of paraphrasing clearly implies that Toxi's melancholy (or "abject") gaze had achieved the status of a veritable cliché during the early Federal Republic—a surmise corroborated in further contemporaneous news clippings.

The *Hamburger Abendblatt*, for example, ran a feature story on local Afro-German children because several were utilized as extras for *Toxi*'s orphanage scene shot at Real-Film studios in Wandsbek. Titled "Kein Grund zum Weinen" (No Cause for Tears), the article includes a photo of an Afro-German boy looking soulfully into the camera as tears stream down his face (apparently he thought the photographer was going to take away his toy saxophone). Commenting on this same child, the writer observes: "Even the children in Alstertal can't get enough of looking at the chocolate brown little boy. If someone were to get cross about his skin color, they would surely have to melt at the sight of his pitch black eyes. Christian is happiest when Ihmy takes him for a walk. Ihmy is his foster mother. When he sees her, his eyes are aglow" (*Hamburger Abendblatt*, 24 June 1952).

Christian's tearful face exemplifies what I have termed "the abject gaze," while the accompanying textual description captures "the adoring gaze." In both instances, the axis of vision is clearly upheld as the medium through which identification is solicited, evincing the Lacanian distinction between the respective subject positions of the ideal ego and the ego ideal (Lacan 1977: see especially 144; 244-60). The ideal ego could be crudely described as that subject position or quality of character that displays to us as spectators what we believe or desire to also be present in ourselves. It is a relatively simplistic form of imaginary identification in contradistinction to the degree of symbolic identification inhering in the ego ideal, that virtual realm pertaining to the way in which we perceive or would like to perceive others to regard us. The mutual adoration that the media posits between Afro-German orphans and German citizens establishes imaginary equivalences between their unhappy and misunderstood fate. Symbolic identification, in turn, is evoked through the orphans' adoring gaze metonymically standing in for an anticipated international audience for whom the German citizen wishes to evince a moral conscience and the successful internalization of a democratic syntax in which racist bias has been overcome—in effect, hailing a crucial subject position for members of the Federal Republic that I would coin "the German worthy of love again."

Enjoyment as Political Factor

While the mechanisms of identification that I have just outlined might seem to play themselves out "merely" at the level of fantasy, the Eastern European sociologists Renata Salecl and Slavoj Zizek have elaborated extensively on the structuring role that mechanisms of fantasy play in economic, political, and psycho-national discourses. Salecl points out that "the success of a political discourse depends not on offering us direct images with which to identify but on constructing a symbolic space, a point of view from which we can appear likable to ourselves" (1994: 73). In essence then, there is an inevitable and even necessary gap between the ideological platform of a given political discourse and its unspoken fantasy, that is, the promise of enjoyment that functions as its often illicit surmise. This gap corresponds to Lacan's notion of the inherently split subject, who by definition cannot fully master the unconscious motivations spoken through his speech and actions or, for that matter, anticipate the intersubjective effects these set into motion (see Lacan 1977: 136-48). Salecl subdivides the speech acts of such a subject, who speaks from a place outside the self, that is, from the place of the Other, into three rhetorical elements, namely: the proposition itself, its presupposition (underlying cultural assumptions or empirical knowledge), and its surmise (the underlying motivations for the assertion, which herein correspond to the level of fantasy) (1994: 35).

The sociological study of Afro-German children by Klaus Eyferth and his colleagues performatively evinces this discrepancy between proposition and surmise that pervaded so much of the rhetoric in this significant era of reshuffling of signs and ideological valences. In his epilogue, he wrote:

> There is tremendous political significance bound into Germany's efforts to achieve completely equal rights and full social integration for colored children. After the total destruction of humanist ideals and human reason

under the reign of National Socialism, we can't afford to lose our self-respect and the respect other nations grant us, by disregarding again the ideals and laws we have loudly proclaimed and denying members of our population a rightful place just because they bear the appearance of another race. We would be placing in question our own political maturity and the validity of the humanitarian and Christian corner stones of our society, which would lose all credibility in the eyes of others. (Eyferth, Brandt, and Hawel 1960: 109)

The author identifies racism and discrimination as behaviors violating the presupposed ideals of democracy, humanism, and Christianity, yet at the level of surmise he acknowledges that it is the vigilant gaze of other nations for whom the Federal Republic must exhibit a reformed attitude ("the German worthy of love again") and moreover reinscribes the Afro-German population as "separate but equal" by invoking rigid visual categories of alterity.

Within *Toxi*'s narrative plot, it is the figure of Theodor Jenrich, the owner of a pharmaceutical firm and the father of two small children, who becomes the didactic vehicle for underscoring the necessity for this disparity between ideology and fantasy. The film conveys the sense that the problem with Theodor's racism is that it is too zealous and too literal, too faithfully aligned with earlier versions of fascist rhetoric. When Theodor resists Toxi's presence in the Rose household on the basis of personal sentiment, Grandfather Rose queries: "And your first sentiment is racist?" He encourages a path of reconciliation, pointing out that "We've learned to see things differently," and implying a learned shift in perception without actually calling the very designation of differences into question. As Zizek reasons, "an ideological edifice can be undermined by a too literal identification, which is why its successful functioning requires a minimum of distance towards its explicit rules" (1996: 83). Other figures in the film, such as Theodor's sister-in-law Hertha and her fiancé Robert, as well as Theodor's wife and the children Ilse and Susi, are presented as successfully transforming xenophobia into xenophilia and mastering the distinction between identification at the symbolic/imaginary level and that kernel of the real that can only transpire as a result of distancing one's self from the "official" symbolic. In an absolutely typical strategy for engendering suspense in the melodramatic mode, the audience is poised from the beginning to expect that Theodor must undergo this development "from Saul to Paul," a change of heart toward Toxi that complies with the ongoing reterritorialization of desire within the film mapped along the new coordinates of consumer culture, Christian humanism, and a certain degree of neocolonial nostalgia. In more vernacular terms, we all know that Theodor really does desire Toxi—when will he realize it? The turning point in the film is therefore not the *deux ex machina* arrival of Toxi's American father to take her home, a denouement that ultimately serves as little more than a narratological afterthought. Rather, it takes place when Theodor accepts the same relationship toward Toxi as sustained by the other characters, one in which the silent conviction that Toxi is different is yoked to an accompanying agreement to disavow this publicly, indeed to extend that disavowal beyond the realm of the cinematic story. It is this perception that unites the extended Rose family, the doctor, the detective, and historical spectators into a national community grounded in maintaining solid boundaries against every form of infiltration. To draw upon another Zizekian aphorism: "A shared lie is an incomparably more effective bond for a group than the truth" (1996: 83-84).

The installment of the West German state heralded a new definition of the nation that shifted the terms of membership from the mythical parameters of *Gemeinschaft* or organic community, to those of *Gesellschaft* or inalienable civic rights and a political economy based upon the unhampered circulation of capital. Naturally, there are tremendous ideological contradictions that surface in the effort to conjoin capitalist and democratic discourses with earlier idealized perceptions of community. In the film in question, the illusion of reconciliation could only be staged at the price of a peculiar repression implicating both the fictional Rose family as well as spectators addressed through the film. The Rose family offered a plea for a return to the bonds of *Gemeinschaft*, that is, of a people conjoined through their whiteness and their Christian humanism, rather than by the purely financially driven interdependencies of the newly reconstructed free market economy. Even as *Toxi*'s ideological mission sought to reconcile the tension between *Gemeinschaft* and *Gesellschaft* through a new concept of civil society based upon formal relations of equality regardless of imputed racial origin, what better way to reinforce the impression of secured bonds of white community than through the performance of benevolent acts of inclusion that thereby predetermined targeted groups as exterior to this community? In effect, the fantasy of the adopted Afro-German virtually becomes a conceptual precondition for positing a unified nation. And yet, the narrative ending forecloses even this possibility when Toxi's American father arrives to retrieve her. Toxi, as a child of dual heritage and moreover bearing no direct blood relation to the Rose family, is conveniently removed from the national stage. The sanctity of the white family is restored, effectively achieving what Zizek refers to as "capitalism-*cum-Gemeinschaft*." If citizenship assumes its contours through a particular access to enjoyment, then

Toxi would have stood a slim chance anyway, for as one of the objects around which enjoyment is organized, she could not be integrated into civil society without emptying out that space and completely undermining the way in which community and the fantasy of national identity are organized in this film.

Notes

Unless otherwise noted, all translations are by the author.

Chapter 12

ALLEGORIES OF MANAGEMENT: NORBERT SCHULZE'S SOUND TRACK FOR *DAS MÄDCHEN ROSEMARIE*

Larson Powell

In recent scholarship, *Das Mädchen Rosemarie* (The Girl Rosemarie, 1958) has regained something of its erstwhile status as "the prestige problem film of German cinema" of the 1950s (Seidl 1987: 198), due to its investigation of postwar redefinitions of gender roles. Film in particular is now seen as "an exploration of contradictions between two conflicting bourgeois models: the model of bourgeois family order pitched against postwar visions of mass participation in bourgeois affluence" (Carter 1997: 182). The problematic boundaries of women's consumerism were thematized in melodramas such as *Die Sünderin* (The Story of a Sinner, 1951), where a female "single city dweller threatened to sabotage German reconstruction by renouncing motherhood in favor of selfish pleasure-seeking" (Fehrenbach 1995: 113). Like *Die Sünderin*, and like other West German *Problemfilme* (social problem films) of the period, *Das Mädchen Rosemarie* depicts sexual relations as a social issue of larger concern for a postwar society perceived as unstable and corrupt. Like these other films, too, *Das Mädchen Rosemarie* links this problematic to one of luxury consumption as a political problem for the Germany of the Economic Miracle. Yet the ambiguity and complexity of the film cannot be rendered legible within the historical framework of consumption alone. Below West Germany's postwar surface tensions between a newly individualistic consumer ethos versus more traditional communitarian rhetoric, deeper structural transformations were taking place that could not help implicating film production. Theodor W. Adorno sensed this already in the introduction to his 1956 volume *Dissonanzen. Musik in der verwalteten Welt* (Dissonances: Music in the Managed World): "The articles included in this volume . . . are concerned with what happens to music in the managed world, under the conditions of planning, organizing registration [*Erfassung*], that withdraw the social basis for artistic freedom and spontaneity" (in *Gesammelte Schriften* 1997, Vol.14: 9).

Film, and thus also film music, had been caught up in this Weberian iron cage of administrative rationality from the beginning; it is not surprising that Adorno's collaboration with Hanns Eisler on the aesthetics of film music should have been centrally preoccupied with the aesthetic consequences of management. These consequences have, however, still not been fully worked out, and Adorno's suggestive formula of "the managed world" needs to be unfolded in more specific historical and structural detail.

The following discussion will thus examine the film—most specifically its sound track—in the context of changes in the structure of film production at a very particular moment, namely, the end of the 1950s, when it was made. A closer examination of the relation between sound and image in *Das Mädchen Rosemarie* can offer not only insights into the tensions informing this particular film, but also hint at larger problems in West German film on the eve of the 1962 Oberhausen Manifesto. The status of music in this film will emerge as emblematic for a larger structural transformation in film production, resulting from a decoupling from the once-powerful German state and a reorientation toward a functional differentiation of society (in Niklas Luhmann's sense). The public controversies around films such as *Die Sünderin* or *Das Mädchen Rosemarie* (which was nearly censored itself) can thus be seen as symptoms of a larger shift away from an older model of social structure wherein state and society were seen as nearly identical, and the state had thus to maintain social integration (see Luhmann 2002: 131f.).

On first listening, the sound track to the film indeed contains ironic aspects that were apparently overheard by the original audience, including contemporary critics up to the early 1960s. Most of the newspaper reviews from 1958, when they commented on the sound track at all, concentrated on the cabaret songs, often comparing them unfavorably to Weill (*Badische Zeitung*, 30 August 1958; *Der Mittag*, 26 August 1958); at best, the music was "critical-satirical" (*Hamburger Abendblatt*, 26 August 1958) or "grotesque" (Karena Niehoff, *Tagesspiegel*, 3 September 1958, Friedrich Luft, *Die Welt*, 26 August 1958) or "clever and witty" (Else Goetz, *Stuttgarter Zeitung*, 23 August 1958). Yet the final critical verdict was that the cabaretistic element in the film was too harmless (Gregor and Patalas 1965: 173; Feldvoss 1989). What was largely overlooked until recently was the film's peculiar combination of those cabaret numbers with a montage of abstract electronic sounds that may be seen to function "as a distanciating effect, signifying the artifice of the spectacle on screen" (Baer 2004: n.p.).

In the musical context of the 1950s, those electronic sounds acquire connotations more specific than merely those of "modern life" or the cliché of "machine music." The last few years of the 1950s saw the peak of abstract electronic composition in the studios of Cologne, bound up moreover with a specific media coupling to the *Nordwestdeutscher Rundfunk* (Northwest German Radio) that assured this music prominent public exposure. Although recent cultural studies work on the 1950s, with its populist tendencies, has tended to neglect this branch of music, post-Webernist composition was in fact a central component of the West German government's postwar cultural campaign of international rehabilitation, and a very successful one at that. Edgar Reitz's *Heimat* (1984) and *Zweite Heimat* (The Second Heimat,1992) series have reconstructed to what degree this music was indeed very much in the public's ear at the time; many in the film industry must have envied and wanted to emulate the international renown of the Darmstadt school and of Karlheinz Stockhausen in particular (one may recall Jean-Marie Straub's later evocation of Stockhausen as a model for his own film aesthetic).

In this light, it is noteworthy that the sound track to *Das Mädchen Rosemarie* does not, as have so many other electronic film music scores, make electronic sounds equivalent to mere illustrative or parodistic grotesquerie. Although the use of electronic special effects can be found early on, near the origins of sound film, in the work of Rouben Mamoulian (e.g., the 1931 *Dr. Jekyll and Mr. Hyde*; see Milne 1969: 49n.), such effects were used only sparingly until the age of the synthesizer score in the 1980s. Extensive use of electronics was largely confined to science fiction films such as *Forbidden Planet* (1956) or horror films such as, most famously, *The Birds* (1963), a film we will need to refer to later. In West German 1950s film, a comparable instance of electronics being used to suggest modernism would be Ottomar Domnick's *Jonas* (1957), which, like *Das Mädchen Rosemarie*, combined popular and modernist musical styles, in Domnick's case Duke Ellington and a score by Adorno's favorite contemporary composer, Winfried Zillig. Within mainstream cinema, though, electronic music could connote abnormality, as in the score to Veit Harlan's infamous *Problemfilm* about homosexuality, *Anders als du und ich* (Different from You and Me, 1957). German film musical practice did not significantly differ from Hollywood's, where musical modernist techniques such as atonality made "deepest inroads in suspense, horror and science fiction films" (Neumeyer and Buehler 2001: 23). Like the traditional opposition of major and minor keys, or the opposition of dissonant and consonant, and atonal and tonal, electronic sounds came to be associated with "cultural musical codes" (Gorbman 1987: 3) within the film industry: not only with specific dramaturgical states of "subjective crisis and psychological rupture . . . alienation, incomprehension and absence" (Neumeyer and Buehler 2001: 23), but also with forms of social deviance felt to be threatening to the larger community.

As noted, however, *Das Mädchen Rosemarie* uses its electronic elements rather for ironic distanciation than shock, to produce an aesthetic of dry impassivity or indifference. In addition, beyond mere surface effects, the sound track uses electronics in a specifically structural manner. The opening sequence is a case in point. After the expulsion of Rosemarie from the hotel lobby, and a view of the city skyline, accompanied by electronically distorted scraps of melody, the camera slowly tilts back from street level to show the clean lines of a tall postwar modernist building. (The actual image anticipates the modern apartment building to which Rosemarie will later move and in which she will be murdered, and the camera tilt might remind one of the opening shot of another famous film about sleeping one's way to the top, namely *Baby Face* of 1933.) A little later, the viewer sees Rosemarie in the street, mechanically turning her head with each passing car. As she does so, we hear a sequence of rising electronic intervals suggesting the timbre of car horns within the shot. Although the series of intervals composing this harmonic sequence is not atonal, its very serialism points to the film's later use of ironic repetition, such as the businessmen's identical black cars and their identical striped pajamas in the bedroom scenes with Rosemarie. Could one go further and see this series as an ironic, tongue-in-cheek reference to the contemporary domination of serial music as the aesthetic embodiment of 1950s functionalism? If we were to pursue this analogy, *Das Mädchen Rosemarie* would then emerge as an anticipation of the "composition in parameters" that Noel Burch would put forth some ten years later in a model itself borrowed from Pierre Boulez and Jean Barraqué (1973: 51ff.).

There are a number of good reasons why this comparison rapidly becomes inadequate. To begin with, the upward tilt of the camera over the modernist building is accompanied by a musical shift of style, abandoning the abstraction of the opening to yield to popular dance rhythms with a sly cadence. This is immediately followed by a fade from the modern building to a neighboring ruin that reminds one of the recent historical memories of war that 1950s functionalism sought to elide. (This auditory dissolve from noise to music, diegetic to nondiegetic, is found also in the opening of Rouben Mamoulian's 1932 *Love Me Tonight*.) As this music is in turn replaced by the ironic ballad of Jo Herbst and Mario Adorf, one might suspect that the music is making a comment on a potential dubious political function of serial electronic music—that, as Adorno's biting aphorism from *Minima Moralia* had it, "where it is most brightly illuminated, the fecal secretly rules" (1997, vol. 4: 65). At the very least, the sound track is thereby ironically relativizing its serial quotation within a larger, eclectic context of functional film music that must be subordinate to dramaturgical requirements and not those of an abstract, autonomous musical structure.

Secondly, there is a crucial element of medial nonsimultaneity here, in that the electronic sounds were produced by Oskar Sala on the Trautonium, and not under the more advanced conditions of the Cologne electronic studios. Like the Theremin and the Ondes Martenot, the Trautonium was a peculiar transitional instrument, resembling a keyboard, and only anticipating the peak period of electronic composition in the 1950s (for the history of the instrument, see Ruschkowski 1998). None of these instruments ever succeeded in establishing themselves in the domain of autonomous concert music, with the exception of a few works for the Ondes Martenot by Olivier Messiaen, Edgard Varèse, and Arthur Honegger, and a small number of compositions for the Trautonium by Paul Hindemith.[1] In fact, the entire project of postwar, post-Webernist *electronic* music was defined in part polemically against the merely *electric* music performed on instruments such as the Trautonium (Ruschkowski 1998: 228f.). Even measured against Sala's later and better known score for *The Birds*, the use of the Trautonium seems to be very moderate. We have thus only returned to our point of departure: *Das Mädchen Rosemarie*'s sound track still appears to be vulnerable to the same criticisms made of its images, which Adorno and Eisler formulated a decade earlier in *Komposition für den Film*, namely, of sinking into "a certain tendency to a moderate line . . . the ominous demand to be modern, but not too much," thus becoming "a second, decorative, pseudo-modern routine" (1997: 49). Is *Das Mädchen Rosemarie*'s aural modernism, too, finally only yet another form of postwar consumerism?

The answer to this question cannot be sought in a purely immanent description of the sound track, but only through consideration of those sounds' larger dramaturgical function. It is here, in dramaturgical and genre terms, that the continuing oddness of this sound track emerges most clearly. For *Das Mädchen Rosemarie*'s peculiar mix of musical styles situates it somewhere between the *Problemfilm* (problem film) and the musical or operetta—surely one of the reasons for so many critics' irritation with its presumed lack of "critical" edge. Another peculiarity of the film is the musical profiling—or lack of same—of its heroine. Nadja Tiller's bid for stardom was clearly marked by the type of the femme fatale: a two-page feature on her in *Filmrevue* (1954, vol. 12) termed her precisely that, and director Rolf Thiele, who made something of a specialty of films devoted to deviant or unusual women characters (*Die Halbzarte* [Eva, 1958], with Romy Schneider; *Labyrinth*, 1959, with Tiller), would cast Tiller in the title role in a 1962 remake of Frank Wedekind's *Lulu* plays. The publicity for *Rosemarie* insistently tried to set up Tiller as a modern Nana after the manner of Emile Zola. Yet the sound track to *Das Mädchen Rosemarie* offers Tiller no chance at any strong vocal profiling. As Mario Adorf's Horst informs Rosemarie early on in the film, "Du hast 'ne Stimme wie 'ne Giesskanne" (You have a voice like a watering can), although Tiller herself was the daughter of an Austrian opera singer and a graduate of the Dresden Music and Drama Academy. Even her low-voiced *parlando* delivery during her first back-alley performance for the businessmen seems tame in comparison with more spectacular numbers such as Marlene Dietrich's "Black Market" in *A Foreign Affair* (1948). Like Lina Lamont in *Singin' in the Rain* (1952), whose unmusical voice is deliberately hidden by the film company that employs her, Tiller seems marginalized by the larger musical spectacle or acoustic stage of the film.

This is all the more surprising given the biography of *Das Mädchen Rosemarie*'s composer, Norbert Schultze of "Lili Marleen" fame. Schultze had produced for the Nazis individual numbers such as "Bomben auf Engelland (*sic*)," "Das U-Boot-Lied" and "Das Russlandlied" (for the armed forces), and composed the scores for *Ich klage an* (I Accuse, 1941) and *Kolberg* (1945); his career was not long interrupted by de-Nazification, and he had returned to film music with popular operetta successes including *Käpt'n Bay-Bay* (1953) with Hans Albers. Given that the German film industry, like Hollywood after Dmitri Tiomkin's success with *High Noon* (1952), was ever on the lookout for salable tunes, Schultze's interest in operetta made commercial sense. In his memoirs he would note—with apparently no trace of irony—that *The Threepenny Opera* "had always been my model," and that even after 1945, "the old dream has not been forgotten" (Schultze 1995: 115): the "old dream" of Brecht and Weill here meaning little more than commercial success, with perhaps a stylish seasoning of irony. This explains why certain of the tunes in *Das Mädchen Rosemarie* are so similar to Weill's, especially the refrain "Ja, die Liebe will bewacht sein" from "Die Liebe geht auf Reisen," which is nearly a straight plagiarism of "Mackie Messer." Schultze admitted that he had "unconsciously" plagiarized Kodaly's *Hary Janos* for another score (129). Yet not only does *Das Mädchen Rosemarie* not have any grand stage numbers (in the performative manner of Dietrich in *A Foreign Affair* or Rita Hayworth in *Gilda* [1946]); she also does not have the sort of easily identifiable melodic moniker that the composer David Raksin devised for Otto Preminger's *Laura* (1944) and that—with words by Johnny Mercer—reached "the top of the hit parade in 1944" (Kalinak 1992: 183).

The reasons for this abstinence lay not with any limit on Schultze's talent, but elsewhere: in the larger turn of international film music away from the grand orchestral scores of the 1930s and 1940s, and in a larger historical fading of the femme fatale over the course of the 1950s, which James Harvey has recently documented in the case of Hollywood (2001: 10, 45) but that is applicable to West Germany as well. It was easier for Romy Schneider as Sissi than for the femme fatale to become a star in Adenauer Germany. One might suspect that the enduring associations of the nightclub torch-song singer with "Nazism as femme fatale" (Byg 1997) could also have contributed to impeding any performative musical staging of *Das Mädchen Rosemarie*.

Thus, the film is marked by a permanent ambivalence, since it both frames Rosemarie as a desirable star and as a (visual) fetish, yet does not fill in the contours of that desirability in musical terms. Rosemarie seems to be ambivalently located between the silent impassivity of a Louise Brooks and the knowing conspiratorial look (and voice) of a Dietrich. In place of her voice, we have the frequently misogynistic commentary of the cabaretists Walter and Horst, or the sound of Rosemarie's car horn, which is associated with her almost as a leitmotif. When Rosemarie triumphantly acquires her convertible, paid for by Hartog as a farewell present, she stands on the street in a shot obviously modeled on the famous documentary photographs of the real-life Rosemarie Nitribitt with her black Mercedes Cabrio SL. As if to underline the emblematic quality of this shot, the sound track gives us an abbreviated version of the opening sequence's camera-tilt series, now diegetically localized as a car horn (although it is not Rosemarie's car, since she is standing outside it). Musically, Rosemarie has been displaced by—or reified into—the material symbol of her success.

That we are meant to see Rosemarie herself as a machine is made clear by other aspects of her acoustic representation. When we first see her standing on the street watching the traffic pass, the regular and mechanical turns of her head are accompanied by a mechanical noise.[2] In film musical terminology, this literal synchronization of action and noise is called *mickey-mousing*, "a somewhat pejorative term that recalls the music of cartoons" (Neumeyer and Buehler 2001: 45). It is a technique that had been out of favor for some time, although occasionally used effectively in scenes such as that of Wally's clumsy crashing around in the beach house early on in *Mildred Pierce* (1945), or in the famous clumsy walk of Gypo in *The Informer* (1935), which has been described as an allegory (Neumeyer and Buehler 2001: 48). It is in this respect interesting that Schultze had,

only a few years previously, written the sound track for Wolfgang Liebeneiner's *Das tanzende Herz* (The Dancing Heart, 1953), a retelling of E. T.
A. Hoffmann's famous Sandman story. In his sound track, Schultze has
Hoffmann's mechanical puppet Olimpia accompanied by nothing other
than Sala's Trautonium. As Schultze described it in his memoirs: "In this
film, the 'authentic' coloratura of the engineer's daughter is clearly contrasted with the 'artificial' one of the doll—a good opportunity to deploy
the Trautonium and recall the many hours of practicing I had spent during
the war as a student of Oskar Sala at his instrument, which was always
totally 'out of tune' ten minutes of practicing and had to be electrically
retuned" (1995: 130–31).

It seems likely that Schultze also envisioned Rosemarie as a mechanical
doll; she was certainly perceived as such by critics, including Marli Feldvoss: "she feeds herself like a mechanical doll from the hard currency of the
economic miracle, and her choppy and forced sounding voice reminds one
of a robot" (1989: 176). In addition, she is ultimately defined by her relation to the recording technology of tape recorders that she first serves and
then seeks, fatally, to expropriate for herself. (In most films it is men who
have control over recording technology: one might think of Alan Pakula's
Klute [1971] or Francis Ford Coppola's *The Conversation* [1974].) The electronic noises and pitches to which Rosemarie is ultimately subjected are
often extradiegetic and thus have something of the authority of an inanimate voiceover: if "nondiegetic music . . . always speaks from a position of
discursive authority on a narrative plane" (Neumeyer and Buehler 2001:
52), this must, via extension, hold true of nondiegetic sounds as well. One
begins to wonder just what that inanimate and allegorizing authority might
be. Its historical sources are not hard to trace. That the electronic media
technology thematized in *Das Mädchen Rosemarie* had its origins in "the
abuse of military equipment" (Kittler 1999: 97) is something Schultze himself was well aware of, yet evidently did not think worthy of any particular
reflection. He himself continued to nurture retrograde, nostalgic utopian
fantasies of composing an opera (to be titled *Kayronga*) that would depict
a European island "of intellectual, social, spiritistic-pious musical high culture" (Schultze 1995: 130) opposed to the "Americanized" musical modernity that banished him to an underling's role in the film industry.

One of the most central—and also most overtly allegorical—scenes
of *Das Mädchen Rosemarie* gives us a hint as to what may be behind the
allegorical ambivalences of its main figure and its sound track as a whole.
When Hartog first installs Rosemarie in her new apartment, and arrives
bearing a panoply of consumer products, from a *Starmix-Gerät* (a brand-
name food processor) to a television set, Horst (Mario Adorf) and Walter
(Jo Herbst), who serve as makeshift deliverymen, pause on the landing

to plug in the television, singing their "Kanal" (Canal) march. At this point the shooting script (52) adds: "On the television screen appear the images that comment on the song, also faces, among them Erhard, Ollenhauer, Strauss etc." As they continue upstairs to Rosemarie's apartment, the script notes (53): "Bars from 'Lili Marleen,' while all three men move through the door into Rosemarie's apartment. She stands in the doorway and watches the parade, stupidly astonished (*dumm-fassungslos*)." This last detail is key: dependent on new media herself, Rosemarie can hardly understand them with the sovereign irony of Horst and Walter.

But the kinship to television may be detected throughout the film, most prominently in its valorizing of sound effects, a feature typical of television (Chion 1994: 157–59). The mickey-mousing earlier mentioned has something of a television gag about it; so does the "auditory wipe" or smear made by the sound track when Eduard Manet's *Olympia* appears on the wall of the hotel room where Hartog's sister is staying, and then cuts to Rosemarie herself. ("The use of nondiegetic sound is less common in film than in television, where the nondiegetic effect serves occasionally as a sound bumper distinguishing story threads" [see Neumeyer and Buehler 2001: 52]). Another television-like gag is the punning between horses' neighing and the mechanical laughter of the snobby riding club members. None of this is surprising, given the connection between the production group's links to television (cf. Abich 1989), or Erich Kuby's frequent work as a television writer. The influence of television was to be an accusation in Joe Hembus's *Der deutsche Film kann gar nicht besser sein* (German Film Couldn't Be any Better, 1961). The irony of this is that it would be a revamped and better organized television that would later prove to be one of the chief advocates of the New German Cinema. This reorganization process, however, was not yet completed at the time of *Das Mädchen Rosemarie*, since it lasted at least until the foundation of the ZDF in 1961. Knut Hickethier has described the process as follows: "This restructuring of television took place on several levels, often parallel in time, not always bound together as a conscious process, often driven forward by opposing motives and stamped by non-contemporaneous aspects" (1998: 114).

It is within the matrix of this complex transformation of the *Dispositiv Kino* (*dispositif* cinema), which recoupled film from radio to television, that we can best understand the ambiguities of *Das Mädchen Rosemarie*.[3] The *Isoliermattenkartel* (insulating cartel) whose shady doings the film illustrates, may thus be seen as an allegory for this same process. Cartels were, in fact, an extremely topical theme at the time: under ongoing pressure from the Americans, the Adenauer administration had in 1957 finally passed a law against monopolies, which would, however, prove ineffective in the face of ongoing administrative centralization (on this, see Abelshauser 1987: 56, with the text of the law itself, 148–52; also Guillén 1994: 139). That centralization was connected to a larger shift in West German business toward the world market beginning after 1957 (Guillén 1994: 137); the government's belated recognition of the importance of export markets for film must itself be seen in this context.

We may take the implications of this historical context even further still. Within this refunctionalizing of film, the figure of Rosemarie and her ambivalent musical or sonorous profiling begins to sound like an allegory of the historical position of the film composer in the late 1950s. Adorno and Eisler had already been quite free of illusions as to the status of the film composer in 1944: "The whole domain of musical reproduction bears the social stigma of 'services' for those who can pay. Musicianship has always had about it something of selling oneself—one's immediate service (*Leistung*), not even in its commodity form—with shadings off to the role of the lackey, the clown, or prostitution" (1997: 52).

Schultze, too, was well aware of his subordinate position within the machinery of the film industry, and complained at times about his low wages and uncertain status (1995: 136). Thus, the high-class prostitute Rosemarie is a figure for the composer himself. Film music, in Adorno and Eisler's quotation, is in so subaltern a position that it is not yet even a commodity (*Ware*): indeed, it must struggle to define itself as precisely such a commodity by appearing individual within a managerial apparatus that functionally absorbs it. Schultze, whose repentance for his Nazi past seems not always credible, had in fact done much better at producing such desirable and salable film-musical commodities (e.g., "Lili Marleen") during the period of film's coupling with radio, which just happened to coincide with the period of National Socialism.[4] Thus the misogynistic, suppressed bitterness of Rosemarie's sonorous framing as a voiceless puppet may have sources in Schultze's own resentment, which was both personal and professionally conditioned, about the industrial working conditions of the film composer. During the course of the film, Rosemarie changes management from the thug-like pair of Walter and Horst to the clean, efficient, rational Fribert, played by Peter van Eyck. (Despite their respective coding as imitation Weimar cabaretists and suave Frenchman, the historical context described in this essay would suggest that we read them instead as allegories for Nazism and American-style management.) Yet despite this shift, Rosemarie has not learned to change her expectations accordingly, and brings into her new relation a desire for an older form of erotic power that will prove fatally miscalculated. (Alternately, we may see the new management of Fribert as being still based on the same Mafia-like implicit threat as the old.)

This larger acoustic text of the film moreover helps us to account for why Rosemarie as a figure or character has often seemed so implausible to critics, especially in her desire to be loved by, or at least married to, Hartog. Her lack of psychological motivation or depth may be traced directly and materially to her sonorous profile. Here the insight of Adorno and Eisler that the function of film music is to provide causality is helpful: "The concrete moment of unity of music and film lies in gesture (*Gestik*). It is related not to movement or the 'rhythm' of the film in itself . . . it is far less the purpose of music, to 'express' this movement . . . than to set it going, or more precisely, to justify it" (1997: 77).

Music provides, in other words, the (fictive) inner causality of images, which allows for affective identification. The most effective form of causality will produce the commodity of stardom. Yet the problem with Rosemarie, is that precisely this sort of acoustical motivation was being undercut by specific historical shifts in the *Dispositiv Fernsehen* (*dispositif* television). We may illuminate this shift still further with one final historical reference. At the same time the film was made, and as German business was preparing its shift from the domestic markets of the *Wiederaufbau* (reconstruction) to global ones, there was a shift in management models from the older scientific models that had dominated Germany since the Weimar Republic to a more structural model. (Significantly, Germany in the 1950s largely rejected the "human relations" model then prevalent in the United States, much to the irritation of American business people; it would be interesting to explore the ramifications of this difference for film culture; see Guillén 1994: 126ff.) One of the theorists elaborating this structural model was the younger Luhmann, whose first articles on management and organization theory appeared in the late 1950s, which was thus contemporary with *Das Mädchen Rosemarie*. Parts of a 1958 article by Luhmann on organizational functionalism seem almost too directly applicable to Rosemarie: "Miss A. is irreplaceable. In her function as a steno typist, however, she is replaceable by other girls, or also partially by a dictaphone" (1958: 100). Further sections of the same article characterize, some six years before the appearance of Herbert Marcuse's *One Dimensional Man* (1966), the stereotyping and "strange, one-sided discipline" (Luhmann 1958: 104) to which behavior is subjected by large organizations. In the same year, the young Jürgen Habermas would connect the same collapse of traditional individual character ("Ich-Schwäche") to a growth in managerial control (1963: 40).

Such descriptions were, of course, made popular already during the 1950s through books like William Whyte's *Organization Man* (1956). What is particularly relevant to the context of this essay is Luhmann's insistence that structural functionalism loosens traditional personal or individual attribution of act to actor. In his 1964 *Funktionen und Folgen formaler Organi-sation* (Functions and Consequences of Formal Organization), Luhmann notes that in functional analysis, "[the actor's] action is seen by him in a strange sense, in an expanded horizon, as separable, replaceable, exchange-able; that action appears, as a contribution to the system (*Systembeitrag*), variable" (1964: 19). It is precisely this relation between actor and act that, as Adorno and Eisler intuited, music should establish, and that is so oddly lacking in *Das Mädchen Rosemarie*. The absence of agency can be found also at the level of production, for Sala, the Trautonium performer whose work is so central to the sound track, is not properly acknowledged in the credits; this suppression of his work as mere "service" goes along with a larger lack of what one must term *musical auteurism*.

Instead of that normal musical causal nexus, we have a gap or hiatus, an allegory for management that is alternately witty and uncanny. Adorno and Eisler, again, had suggested that one of the ways in which film music can redeem itself from its functional servitude or prostitution was through discretion (*Vorsicht*) and wit (*Witz*) (1997: 140–41). From Freud we know that one of the sources of wit or jokes lies precisely in the impression of automatism, and that wit is bound up with a suspension of identification between observer and actor (1970). It may finally make more sense to try to understand the sound track to *Das Mädchen Rosemarie* less as a critique than as a peculiar, structural form of wit. This type of wit may also be seen as the ambiguous historical signature of the period in which the film was made. For as Luhmann understood in a comment of which we have still not worked out the full implications, "the age of bureaucracy forms its own rhetoric" (1964: 372).

In conclusion, the term *allegory* frequently used here should be ren-dered more explicit. Johannes von Moltke has analyzed how the peculiar shot of a couple in a car's rearview mirror at the end of *Wenn die Heide blüht* (When the Heath Is in Bloom,1960) "is emblematic of some central generic concerns of the *Heimatfilm*" (2002a: 23), namely, its ambiguous combination of nature with technology, local with global. I would submit that the uncanny disconnection between Rosemarie's visual and aural images is similarly "emblematic" of her split roles as consumer, prostitute, and puppet of international finance. This points to a larger allegorical aspect of German 1950s film in toto. The term *allegory*, however, is so rich with reference that it cannot be used without specification. The "emblem-atic" may remind us of Walter Benjamin's Baroque allegories, with their split between the material of the signifier and an arbitrarily imposed sig-nification; alternately, we might recall Paul de Man's modernist view of allegory as the ultimate inconclusiveness of all signifying and reading processes. Beyond this, however, I would like to propose a new notion of allegory specifically bound to the postwar historical processes discussed in this essay, thus to functional differentiation. Recent literature on the postwar period has not always fully grasped the implications of the word "functional." Functional analysis, as developed by Talcott Parsons and developed further by Luhmann, does not mean a binary model whereby, for instance, "cultural apparatuses . . . produce 'the nation'" (James Donald, cited in Carter 1997: 111); rather it is always multivariable. "Religion solves the problem x, but it does not solve it in the same way that b, c, d etc. solve it. The function thus places the object in direct lighting and side lighting" (Luhmann 1977: 9).[5]

Thus in von Moltke's reading of *Heimatfilme*, these films both suggest a return to idyllic local community *and also* make economic and technological modernization palatable. Similarly, Fehrenbach notes that the *Heimatfilme* succeeded on economic grounds, not due to its "support by state and church officials" (1995: 147). So too *Das Mädchen Rosemarie*, along with its ostensible surface thematics of sexual scandal and a critique of consumerism, is being pulled upon by other forces of modernization at the same time. The result is that *Das Mädchen Rosemarie* ends up being neither a self-consciously modernist film nor a retrospective restoration, but rather an instance of "involuntary modernism" (Koepnick 2002: 258). The hiatus between agent and act that has been analyzed in the case of the film's acoustic motivation of its characters may also be found on the larger level of the film's aesthetics. This is the structural reason why unambiguous and stable signifiers, whether mythical or metaphoric, seem unavailable to *Das Mädchen Rosemarie*. The failure of the film to stabilize itself around the reference of the classical femme fatale (Benjamin's and Baudelaire's allegorical prostitute-as-commodity) is an instance of this. For allegory, in the sense here sketched in, cannot represent any totality of a system for itself (as did the traditional symbol), since it is inseparable from the differentiation, and thus contingency, of function.

Notes

My thanks to Sandra Klefenz for help at the Deutsches Filmmuseum Frankfurt, as also to Hester Baer (2004) and Tim Bergfelder for generously sharing yet unpublished work with me, and to Rick Rentschler for the Schultze documentary. All translations from German are my own.

1. Oskar Sala (1910–2002), who was partly "discovered" in recent years by a small cult of aficionados, recorded a number of these works on CD before his death (*Elektronische Impressionen*. Erdenklang CD 81032). Hindemith's compositions, a set of pieces for three Trautoniums, are completely traditional, even neoclassical, in their musical language

and make no attempt to reflect the new instrumental sonorities of the instrument in structural terms. Sala's own compositions seem derivative imitations of the Darmstadt aesthetic.

2. In Kaja Silverman's terms, this could be seen as an instance of a procedure "whereby female characters are incorporated into an exaggeratedly diegetic locus (1988: 54), and yet that locus is here also overdetermined by its abstract and mechanical associations, being more than merely the "intractable materiality" (61) of the woman's body. As will become evident, the allegorical dimensions of Rosemarie make it difficult to situate her in Silverman's opposition between male voiceover and female diegesis.

3. For a discussion of television as a *dispositif* and its relationship to cinema, see Elsner, Müller, and Spangenberg in Hickethier (1993) as well as Zielinski (1999).

4. The power of radio broadcasting was arguably at its historical zenith during the Nazi period, and the symbiosis of radio and film was embodied in the weekly Sunday afternoon *Wunschkonzert* broadcasts, then made into a film by Eduard von Borsody, *Wunschkonzert* (Request Concert, 1940). The broadcasts featured "performances by Marika Rökk and Heinz Rühmann," among others (Kreimeier 1999: 316). One might also point to the popularity of other Nazi hit films such as *Die grosse Liebe* (The Great Love, 1942), featuring the cabaret singer Zarah Leander (see the discussion in Schulte-Sasse 1996: 288–301). Norbert Frei and Johannes Schmitz (1999) have underlined the domination of music over word in Nazi broadcasting in their history of Nazi media politics.

5. Put differently: functionalist *allegory* cannot be reduced to the two-tiered *metaphoric* model of Louis Althusser's Ideological State Apparatuses, which holds on to the binary opposition of substructure and infrastructure; thus the old notion of "ideology," which in this version "represents the imaginary relationship of individuals to their real conditions of existence" (1971: 162) is insufficiently complex. To see "cultural apparatuses"— whatever they might be—as *solely* functioning "to produce the nation" would be more than a little redolent of Voltaire's Dr. Pangloss, who believed God had created our nose to put glasses on. Another way of historicizing allegory is to see it as tied to periods of transition (cf. Luhmann 1995: 276): the Trautonium, a transitional instrument if ever there was one, thus both allegorizes and embodies a historical shift in musical technology.

Chapter 13

THE RESTRUCTURING OF THE WEST GERMAN FILM INDUSTRY IN THE 1950S

Knut Hickethier

The end of World War II marked the beginning of the Allies' involvement with a state-owned and state-controlled (*reichsmittelbar*) film concern that had owned all large production companies in the Third Reich: the Ufa GmbH. This concern was called "UFI" in order to distinguish it from the still-existent Ufa AG (Universum Film Aktiengesellschaft), which it controlled together with Terra, Tobis, Bavaria, Berlin-Film, and a number of smaller production companies. Like other German industrial monopolies, the UFI was to be liquidated by the Allies after 1945. Their goal was to destroy the state monopoly structure that had defined German filmmaking especially during the war years. Moreover, the Allies hoped to control what they saw as the unhealthy influence of film on the German imagination and to utilize film for the advancement of democratic and, in the western zones, pro-Western ideas. In these zones the "democratization" of film and the restoration of free-market principles were seen as synonymous by the late 1940s, despite the fact that the Allies themselves had practiced a very centralized film politics during the early postwar years.

The Initial Situation

Producing films in Germany after World War II required a license from the occupying forces. On 17 May 1946, the Soviet occupation forces (SMAD) gave a license to the newly founded DEFA, which would eventually become the central film production company for the Soviet occupation zone (Mückenberger and Jordan 1994). On 27 May 1946, the British military government began granting licenses to new film companies, among others Camera-Film and Studio 45-Film; the Americans started licensing in January 1947 (Hauser 1989). Receiving a license required the applicants to go through a process of de-Nazification. However, this did not stop numerous film professionals who had worked before 1945 from becoming active once again in the newly emerging film industry of the Federal Republic. The restructuring of the film industry depended on their experience and knowledge, meaning that "nearly all directors, actors, cameramen, and technicians [working after 1945] had been more or less active members of the NSDAP [before 1945]" (Pleyer 1965: 29).

Decartelization and deconcentration were the maxims of the Western Allies, and their policies aimed at preventing the creation of a new vertically integrated monopoly. No film company was allowed to be active in more than one branch of the industry; the distinction between the three branches of production, distribution, and exhibition sectors had to be maintained. This led to the founding of a number of small production companies by dramaturges, directors, screenwriters, and even actors. Some of the most important and productive companies of the immediate postwar period were located in Hamburg. Headed by the film director Helmut Käutner, the Camera-Film Produktion produced his *In jenen Tagen* (In Those Days, 1947) and Rudolf Jugert's *Film Ohne Titel* (Film Without a Title, 1948). The Junge Film-Union under the management of Rolf Meyer produced *Menschen in Gottes Hand* (People in God's Hand, 1948) and *Wege im Zwielicht* (Paths in Twilight, 1948). Founded by Walter Koppel and Gyula Trebitsch, the Real-Film produced *Arche Nora* (Nora's Ark, 1948) and *Finale* (1948). Berlin had the Studio 45-Film, known for *Sag die Wahrheit* (Speak the Truth, 1946) and *Und finden dereinst wir uns wieder* (And Someday We Shall Find Each Other Again, 1947), and the Berolina-Film led by production veteran Kurt Ulrich, responsible for *Morgen ist alles besser* (Everything Will Be Better Tomorrow, 1948). In Göttingen, Hans Abich and Rolf Thiele started the Filmaufbau in an old airplane hangar where Wolfgang Liebeneiner directed his first postwar film, *Liebe 47* (Love '47, 1948), based on the Wolfgang Borchert drama, *Draußen vor der Tür* of that year.

Close to two hundred film production companies were founded in the early postwar years. All of these newly formed companies suffered from extreme undercapitalization. To remedy this situation, the Allied military offices allocated films from the holdings of the UFI concern that were considered politically harmless and that subsequently appeared in theaters as "reprises." Additionally, some companies were allowed to complete film projects that had been started before 1945. With these so-called *Überläuferfilme* (crossover films), companies like Bavaria, DEFA, and others acquired capital for their new productions; in the Western zones, part of the profit had to be paid into the liquidation fund of the old UFI concern.

The plan to decartelize the UFI concern did not progress smoothly because of conflicting interests among the various parties involved. The Western Allies, in particular the Americans, were less interested in quickly rebuilding the West German film industry than in giving their own film industry the largest possible influence over the West German market. The Deutsche Revisions- und Treuhand AG (German Audit and Trust) realized that they could make money with the UFI assets by renting out studio facilities and by rereleasing old films from the UFI library. The new film producers in turn had no interest in additional competitors, especially those bolstered by having access to the former UFI's assets. At the same time, the West German government had an interest in building a strong domestic film industry and was therefore inclined toward resurrecting the old Ufa studio, but could not say so publicly, since doing so would have brought them into conflict with the Allies' cultural policies. After the end of the licensing period in 1950, the Allied High Commission redefined the process of decartelization in a new law (Gesetz Nr. 32). The West German film industry hoped for a decartalization law that would be more favorable, but had to wait for its passage until 1953. Finally, the Allied regulations concerning the liquidation of UFI were abolished in 1957, despite the fact that full liquidation was not yet achieved.

Film Industry, Film Financing, and the Rise of Genre Cinema

At the beginning of the 1950s, the Federal Republic had a decentralized and highly localized film industry. Essentially, the industry was based around the production facilities that were owned by individual film companies such as Real-Film in Hamburg and Bavaria in Munich, but also used by other producers. Aside from the Ufa Studios in Tempelhof, West Berlin had a new studio complex built in Spandau by Artur Brauner of CCC Film. Then there were three smaller centers: Göttingen (for Filmaufbau), Bendestorf near Hamburg (for Rolf Meyer's Junge Union-Film), and Wiesbaden. This decentralization of film production inhibited filmmaking since it provided few opportunities for synergy effects.

Characteristic for this time is the dominance of many small companies with a small number of employees. Walter Dadek writes about the prevalence of "mom-and-pop businesses (*Zwergbetriebe*) with two to four employees" (1957: 52). For him, filmmaking in the Federal Republic was characterized by an *accidental* rather than a *continual* mode of production. Almost three-quarters of the companies produced only irregularly (i.e., accidentally), barely a fourth produced continually—that is, they had at least a functioning production facility—and only a few companies managed to crossover into *simultaneous* production where several projects were in different stages of planning and completion, the model to be expected in industrial production.

At the same time, this filmic mode of production was characterized by an elaborate division of labor and far-reaching standardization of the various stages in the making of a film. Highly specialized occupations such as producer, production manager, director, screenwriter, cameraman, set designer, technician, and film actor had already developed in the 1920s and resulted in a clearly defined hierarchy on the set where all of those professionals worked together as a team. Only such team work guaranteed the successful completion of a film. The collaborative nature of filmmaking stood, and still stands, in conflict with the various claims to authorship primarily by the director and by the equally important contributions by the screenwriter, cameraman, and leading actors.

From the perspective of financing, the economic theorists of the 1950s saw film production as systemically marked by a "permanent production cost deficit" (Dadek 1957: 108; cf. Schweins 1958; Plschek 1959; Clemens 1959). In order to recoup the average expenditures of DM 800,000, a film had to bring in DM 3.7 million at the box office, something that rarely happened. Dadek assumes that producers had an average loss of 25 percent of their production costs (1957:108), which explains the producers' repeated pleas for state support.

In the 1950s, only Real-Film, Fama-Film (the owners of the Europa-Filmverleih F.A. Mainz), Berolina-Film, Ostermayr-Film, Divina-Film, and Melodie-Film were considered economically "stable." Financing was generally secured through a heavy reliance on hard assets (film studios, technical equipment, and raw materials), which added to the need for high productivity and maximum utilization. The risk for investing directly into individual films was relatively high, given the difficulties of calculating the revenues generated by what was essentially one product. Public reactions, box-office receipts, and profit margins were impossible to predict. In the words of Martin Osterland: "Regardless of the current market conditions, film producers are often forced to release completed films as quickly as possible in order to finance new productions with the returns and thereby to keep working at capacity" (1970: 21). According to Osterland, this resulted in a "chronic oversupply" where individual films competed with each other and contributed to a so-called "deficit-driven production model" (1970: 21). In coming to these conclusions, he relies heavily on Dadek, who formulated this theory of deficit-driven overproduction based on the West German film of the 1950s (see Dadek 1957: 112–13).

The basis for this theory was the conception of a more or less closed economic cycle according to which a film ideally passes through all the stages of production, distribution, and exhibition before reaching the audience. The revenues from theatrical exhibition return by way of the distributors to the producers, who in turn use them to produce a new film. This model of the economic cycle (cf. Gercke's untranslatable notion of "zwischen-betrieblicher Wertumlauf," 1956: 206) is based on the assumption that the resources invested in the making of films are regained in theatrical exhibition and then cycled back into film production. That is how, according to the theory, an economic cycle works.

However, Dadek was well aware of the fact that this model did not apply to 1950s West German film, because the box office receipts that were "returned" to the producers averaged less than the costs of film production, thus creating a permanent "production cost deficit" (1957: 108ff.). In other words, the producers did not work cost-effectively and, over the short or long haul, the majority had to give up their company if they could not find alternative means of financing. Repeatedly evoked as arguments by film journalists at that time, the reasons for this lack of refinancing in film production were due to (1) the oversupply of foreign films; (2) the overproduction of German films; (3) the advent of television, which "stole" audiences and thus reduced profits; and (4) the tax burden, above all, the so-called *Vergnügungssteuer* (entertainment tax), which removed money from this closed cycle. Nevertheless, even taking these problems into account, the model of the closed economic cycle still remained applicable.

Three solutions to the economic situation were debated in the 1950s. The first was an increase in profitability, which could be achieved through lifting the entertainment tax on film that, at the end of the 1940s, amounted to almost 30 percent. Between 1952 and 1956 alone, the state took in a total of over DM 635 million through film exhibition (SPIO 1962: 64). Since these taxes benefited local communities, the federal government was ultimately not responsible for them. Therefore, the entertainment tax remained a bone of contention for the film industry until it was abolished in response to the continuing decline of the movies in the 1960s.

The second solution to be considered was the reduction of economic risk through the identification of films with successful genres. This return to genre in the West German cinema of the 1950s happened without much reflection or calculation; a theoretical model for the genre film did not exist. A genre already established in the 1930s, the *Heimatfilm*, forged the path after the phenomenal success of *Schwarzwaldmädel* (Black Forest Girl, 1950) and *Grün ist die Heide* (Green Is the Heather, 1951). Among the medium-size companies it was above all Berolina-Film that produced many *Heimatfilme*, including these first two hits. The majority were made by smaller companies that produced *Heimatfilme* exclusively or primarily. Aside from the Munich-based Ostermayr-Film with its ten Ganghofer adaptations, including *Schloss Hubertus* (Castle Hubertus, 1954) and *Das Schweigen im Walde* (Silence in the Forest, 1955), it was H.D.-Film (Hans Deppe), Rex-Film, König-Film, and Franz-Seitz-Film that produced most of the *Heimatfilme* (Höfig 1973: 99ff.). Due to its high standardization, *Heimatfilm* production remained at the same levels throughout the 1950s. Other successful genres included war films (in some cases "antiwar films"), family films, as well as *Schlagerfilme* (literally: hit song films), which replaced the operetta and revue films, mostly because they were more cost-effective and appeared more "modern."

The move toward genres was only halfhearted, however, and certainly not pursued with the same self-confidence found in Hollywood. Even the producers, directors, and authors involved approached genre films less as an artistic challenge, something that needed to be mastered, than as a mere commercial undertaking. Ultimately, this lack of self-confidence led to the demise of several genres. By the end of the 1950s, the *Heimatfilm* in particular was aesthetically exhausted and fell out of favor with the general public as a form of popular entertainment.

The third potential solution was the infusion of outside capital through public subsidies for the film industry. Between 1951 and 1955, the government developed two guarantee programs for either individual films or annual productions. The goal of both guarantee programs was to help the film industry with economic consolidation at a time while the liquidation of UFI was still going on and the remaining UFI assets could not yet be utilized by the industry. The guarantees served as a transitional solution until a new Ufa could arise as a "highly capitalized and government-supported [*regierungsnah*] film company" (Berger, Reichmann, and Worschech 1989: 80). The volume of subsidies was relatively small in comparison with the revenues generated through the entertainment tax, which over five years amounted to roughly DM 90 million.

The awarding of guarantees was always based on an assessment of the production plan. An advisory committee of the Deutsche Revisions- und Treuhand AG evaluated the screenplay for its dramaturgical qualities, moral and religious appropriateness, considered casting decisions, choice of director, and initial budget, and occasionally even revised the budget. These assessments were then presented to the Interministerielle Ausschuß der Bundesregierung (Federal Inner-Ministerial Commission), which made its decisions primarily in accordance with political criteria.

Especially scandalous was the refusal of guarantees for the Hamburg-based Real-Film (Trebitsch and Koppel) because Walter Koppel, who was critical of the CDU, the Christian Democratic Party, was suspected of being a communist. Similarly, Wolfgang Staudte was denied a guarantee for *Gift im Zoo* (Poison in the Zoo, 1952). Staudte was asked to first distance himself from DEFA, where he had worked earlier, which he refused to do. As a result, the company had to find another director in order to receive the guarantee. The committee also reserved its right to change the completed film through additional cuts. These requests seem outrageous today because the Basic Law of the Federal Republic guaranteed freedom from censorship. But here a de facto censorship was practiced even the minor matters.

The second round of guarantees was interrupted in 1955 in light of the rebuilding of film companies out of the UFI assets in 1955–56 (Roeber and Jacoby 1973: 549). The government decided not to interfere with the founding of the Ufa and Bavaria studios in the same year by subsidizing other film companies. After all, that year, a new all-time high was reached with an annual output of approximately 125 feature films, most of which had a difficult time being amortized despite the steady rise in movie attendance. The termination of the guarantees had a devastating effect on small- and medium-size producers.

Basically, the guarantees, the evaluation of films through the Freiwillige Selbstkontrolle (Voluntary Self-Control of the Film Industry), the award of *Prädikate* (film ratings), which reduced the amount of the entertainment tax to be paid, and the political control of film imports (in particular from East European countries) established a system of censorship that must be considered largely responsible for the formal and thematic conformity of the West German cinema of the 1950s. Based on an understanding of "popular" culture shared by the experts and bureaucrats of the Deutsche Revisions- und Treuhand AG and the Ministries in Bonn, official film politics strived to support films that were as "conflict-free" and "unobjectionable" as possible.

The Interplay of Film Production, Distribution, and Exhibition

In order to understand the model of the closed economic cycle, it is necessary to outline briefly the dynamic system of production, distribution, and exhibition. The system partially relies on practices from the 1920s and 1930s. The production companies offered the distributors their film projects who, if they were interested in adding the film to their program, offered a distribution guarantee in the amount of 50 to 70 percent of the production costs. With this guarantee the production companies could procure further bank loans; sometimes the distributors financed the productions themselves. The distributors in turn gave these guarantees in late summer, before the beginning of the new movie season on the first of September, but after offering the theater owners their new releases and finalizing the season's lineup of films. Theater owners could only book the entire lineup and thus had to agree to show films destined to become box-office hits together with those expected to be less successful. They booked the films as a "block"; this block-booking also determined the release dates. A season was generally comprised of sixteen films, sometimes over twenty; the Kartellamt (cartel office) later limited the number to six films (Schröder 1995: 75).

On the basis of these release dates, the distributors could then estimate the expected box-office receipts and give the producers a distribution guarantee. At this point, however, the film was often still in production. The cinema owners had to book blindly, solely on the basis of the distributors' advertisements and promises. During the booking phase, the distributors also received an overview of the competing lineups so that they could demand changes to the films in production that would make them more competitive.

The example of a 1957 Gloria-Filmverleih project shows how such changes to a film in production were actually implemented. After announcing the Wega-Film production *Das alte Försterhaus* (The Old Forester House, 1956) as a *Heimatfilm* and making direct references to the successful hit song and music album of the same name, the distributor found out that forty *Heimatfilme* were already in production for the 1956–57 season. As a result, Gloria "reworked" the story into "a modern Theo-Lingen farce" (Kubaschewski 1957: 43). When it became apparent that the season would also see an oversupply of comedies, a third version had to be developed: "The Gloria screenwriters rewrote the calm musical piece as a cheerful musical comedy that was advertised by the distributor with this new tag line: 'Rock 'n' roll and romance, glowing colors and dark figures, tender love and excruciating jealousy, sweet melodies and raging rhythms . . . all are united in the old forester house'" (1957: 43). The film produced under these conditions was regarded as a low point of German entertainment cinema because of its complete lack of coherence.

Because most production companies were undercapitalized, they were dependent on the financing provided by distributors or distribution guarantees and thus had to accept their increased artistic interference. As a rule, the distributors kept the distribution rights for a film for five years, at which point the film returned to the producers if the distributor was not also a coproducer. In most cases, a film was already considered *abgespielt* (literally: played out) at a much earlier point. In their dealings with theater owners, the distributors were in an equally strong position. The owners had to agree to block booking and blind booking if they wanted to receive attractive films for their programs. The distributors gained even more influence through their ability to proscribe the minimum run for individual films. According to the block-booking principle, the theater owners were supposed to share the risks of film distribution, but in fact had no influence in shaping the movie program. If a film fared badly at the box office, they could not change the program, which of course was detrimental to their box-office receipts. The distributors preferred this arrangement, because it allowed them to orchestrate the release of films very carefully. Moreover, they were able to use a limited number of copies for their scheduled releases in different categories of movie theaters (first-run theaters, reprise theaters, etc.).

By asserting their right to interfere in the making of a film, to demand changes in the screenplay, to interfere in casting decisions, and to call for reedited versions of already completed films, distributors sought to minimize the kind of losses that resulted from they saw as "production mistakes." As entrepreneurs guided by economic rather than by artistic interests, the distributors based their criteria for success on past successful films and looked for similar or identical films in order to repeat these successes. The logical result was a preference for genre films with standardized storylines. To achieve this standardization, producers relied on "tried and tested" screenwriters, including Bobby E. Lüthge, who were known for writing box-office hits; "reliable" directors included Wolfgang Liebeneiner, Hans Deppe, Geza von Bolvary, and Josef von Baky. New directors had few opportunities within this system since they represented an economic risk for the producers. As a result, film production was more or less closed off to the younger generation of directors and screenwriters who rebelled against this system at the 1962 Oberhausen Shortfilm Festival in the most spectacular fashion.

The problem of film production did not solely lie in standardization. Standards exist to maintain levels of quality and establish those as a general norm. The problem of the genre film of the 1950s had to do with the steady lowering of these standards over the course of the decade. The absence of the kind of filmic effects achieved through the interplay of camera movement, mise-en-scène, and montage is particularly noticeable. A comparison between Hans Deppe's two films, *Grün ist die Heide*—by no means a cinematographic masterpiece—and *Wenn die Heide blüht* (When the Heath Is in Bloom, 1960), shows how aesthetic impoverishment in the course of the decade affected even films with similar themes.

The Resurrection of Ufa and its Final Collapse

The decartelization law passed by the Bundestag in 1953 essentially adopted the wording of the decartelization law ratified earlier by the Allies, with one small yet decisive difference. The West German law allowed exceptions in the liquidation of the UFI companies "if the decartelization required by law [could] be achieved through the sale of shares" (cited in Hauser 1989: 329). This legal exception became a determining principle in the official approach to the UFI assets. An *Abwicklungsausschuß* (liquidation committee) of the Bundestag decided not to dissolve the legal structure of the UFI companies and to found three new companies instead: the Ufa Theater AG on 5 May 1955, the Bavaria Filmkunst AG on 29 December 1955, and the Universum Film AG on 4 July 1956. A banking consortium carried out the privatization in exchange for 70 percent of the shares. The offers of another banker, Rudolf Münemann, and the remigrant director William Dieterle were rejected because of suspicions that Dieterle's offer was backed by Hollywood interests (Bauer 1976: 260). An offer from a consortium comprised of Mosaik-Film, CCC, and Gloria Filmverleih (Ilse Kubaschewski) was also rejected, and that despite the fact that it had offered DM 14 million, DM 1.5 million more than the banking consortium.

The new Universum Film AG and Bavaria Filmkunst AG were offered the opportunity to acquire 25 percent of Ufa-Theater AG, an offer Bavaria declined. The outcome of this arrangement was that Ufa Film AG and Ufa Theater AG, while operating as separate legal entities, had the same shareholders and the same chairman of the board: "Thus the new Ufa complex attained the character of a conglomerate" (Roeber and Jacoby 1973: 233). In a 1970 report about the handling of the UFI properties, the film journalist Reinhold E. Thiel concluded: "The goal was to keep the corporate group as intact as possible" and the UFI proudly called itself again "the biggest corporation in Europe" (1970: 5).

The new Universum Film AG and the new Bavaria AG had over 60 percent of the country's studio capacity at their disposal. With the Schorcht Filmverleih and the Herzog Filmverleih they owned large distribution companies and could fall back on a large chain of movie theaters. A former accountant and Ufa trustee Arno Hauke became the director of the new Universum Film AG and of the new Ufa Theater AG. However, Hauke possessed little experience in the film industry and had already bankrupted the Capitol Film GmbH and the Prisma Verleih in 1955 (see Dillmann 1992). In 1961, Walter Schmieding described Hauke's production strategy at Ufa as "identical to the one at Capitol." As a result, "Ufa could neither keep nor attract an audience" (Schmieding 1961: 141).

In 1958, the first season brought the following films into the theaters: a family comedy, *Ist Mama nicht fabelhaft?* (Isn't Mama Fabulous?); a comedy about a precocious seventeen-year-old girl, *Stefanie;* and, a "problem-film," *Solange das Herz schlägt* (As Long as the Heart Beats), none of which was very successful. In subsequent years, Ufa tried to develop an ambitious program and to respond to the challenges posed by the rise of television. One strategy was to confront television "with the strengths of the movies" (Worschech 1992a: 488). Thus, Georg Tressler, who at the time was considered a "young talented director" due to his success with *Die Halbstarken* (The Hooligans, 1956) and *Endstation Liebe* (Last Stop Love, 1957), directed a Hollywood-like *Das Totenschiff* (Ship of the Dead, 1959), based on the much-read novel by B. Traven. Hailed by some critics as one of the best German films of the 1950s, the film found neither box-office success nor critical acclaim (Worschech 1992b: 489).

Under Hauke, the new Ufa AG operated without any luck and managed within only a few years to incur losses of nearly DM 30 million. In 1959 alone Ufa created a deficit of DM 5.4 million, and amassed further debts totaling DM 22 million ("Ufa: Rote Zahlen," *Der Spiegel,* no. 32 [1960]: 55). On average, Ufa in 1959–60 lost "DM 350,000 to 450,000 with every film" (Worschech 1992c: 487). That is why Ufa shareholders finally fired Hauke in the mid-1960s. Hauke was succeeded by Theo Osterwind, head of the Deutsche Film Hansa, the fourth largest West German distribution company. He had been relatively successful distributing foreign productions such as Carol Reed's *The Third Man* (1959), Marcel Camus's *Orfeu Negro* (Black Orpheus, 1959), Soviet films such as *Letyat zhuravli* (The Cranes Are Flying, 1957), as well as domestic productions like *Haie und kleine Fische* (Sharks and Small Fish, 1957), *Hunde wollt ihr ewig leben?* (Dogs, Do You Want to Live Forever? 1958), and *Die Brücke* (The Bridge, 1959). Osterwind insisted that Ufa give up their own distribution company, which was actually profitable, and acquire 50 percent of the shares of Film Hansa for DM 2.2 million (cf. "Ufa: Entschwundene Millionen," *Der Spiegel,* no. 26 [1961]: 63–65 and "Ufa: Bei Durchsicht der Bücher," *Der Spiegel,* no. 7 [1962]: 78–75). From then on Film Hansa functioned under the title of Ufa Film Hansa.

The initiated restructuring of Ufa proved unsuccessful, the "strangling" of the old Ufa distribution company (to cite the 1962 *Spiegel* article listed above) cost additional millions, and the remaining Ufa films were not utilized effectively. Osterwind cut back production to sixteen new films for the 1961–62 season, but even these films only added to the company's deficits. Finally, the Ufa board of directors decided in 1962 first to pull out of Ufa Film Hansa and then to give up on Ufa production and exhibition altogether (Roeber and Jacoby 1973: 233ff.). At the end of 1963, the

Deutsche Bank sold the existing assets of Ufa Film AG for DM 11 million to the Bertelsmann publishing group in Gütersloh. The film studios and print labs in West Berlin as well as all of the buildings went to the real estate firm Becker & Kries and to the new Berlin Universal Film Studio (later named Berlin Union Film) (Thiel 1970). When the newly founded Ufa collapsed after only six years, the dream of a strong film industry led by Ufa died once and for all. According to the film critic Heinz Ungureit, this failure was largely "caused by Bonn's provincial film politics"; hence his final conclusion: this was "an obsolete dream factory built on old formulas and controlled by aging professionals that was no longer needed in the age of television" (1964: 15).

Corporate restructuring at the newly founded Bavaria Filmkunst AG proved to be equally unsuccessful. To some extent, Bavaria was able to compensate for its losses by restructuring the company (from an AG to a GmbH in 1961), making the studio facilities a separate entity, and selling 51 percent of its shares to commercial subsidiaries of West German (WDR) and South German Radio (SDR). With the breakup of the company, the creation at Bavaria of a vertically integrated corporation out of the UFI legacies had failed. So had the attempt to prevent the splintering of the film industry after 1945 through a politics of restoration—that is, the creation of large corporations—meant to give the West German film a new economical boost.

What was the cause of this failure? Throughout the 1950s, many had worked hard in resurrecting the UFI concern after its collapse in 1945. By the time this structure had been recreated through the Ufa Film AG and through the Bavaria Filmkunst AG, the underlying model of a corporation focused exclusively on motion pictures had become obsolete. The companies that focused on theaters as the only exhibition venues for films could not survive on film markets fundamentally changed by the rapid rise of television—from one million registered television sets in 1959 to four million in 1960—as well as new leisure time activities. Moreover, the company's directors, who came from a long tradition of administrating the UFI assets, were not aggressive and flexible enough to change their concepts radically. The fixation on Ufa obviously produced a blockage in entrepreneurial spirit, and the banks showed no willingness to invest long-term in the media industry. However, the newly formed companies were not "victims of circumstance" (Roeber and Jacoby 1973: 249). A more aggressive corporate strategy that reassessed film production in relation to television was never developed, or only halfheartedly. Here the example of the U.S. majors, their successful entry into television production, and the coordination of film and television production might have shown a way out of the malaise.

Different Film Markets and
the Open Model of the Film Industry

For the film industry of the 1950s, Dadek differentiates between a "film market," comprised of film producers, distributors, and theater owners, and a "cinema market," which is defined by the relationship between the movies and their audiences (1957: 65–84). His distinction is accurate insofar as the two correspond with each other, while simultaneously functioning as independent markets. Not everything that occurs in the various sectors of the film industry has an impact on the box office. The "film market" has to be further differentiated: there is a market defined by everything pertaining to the technical aspects of the film, including makers of camera equipment, studio facilities, copy labs, film producers, and so forth. In addition, there are markets in which the professionals (directors, screenwriters, cameramen, and, last but not least, actors) enter into business relationships with the producers. Furthermore, there is a market for the producers and distributors where the former want to enter their films into distribution and where the latter want to put together their programs based on the optimal mixture of films. Finally, there is the market where distributors and exhibitors meet.

This differentiation of markets highlights the different interests within the film industry. The rise of television created an additional market for films (the same would later be true for merchandizing and for the video and DVD markets) in which many, though not all sectors participated; these developments brought a new dynamic quality to the film industry. For example, it could be in the interest of the producer to sell films to television stations in order to cover his costs, yet this did not serve the interests of theater owners and distributors. This model, which had been developed for the film industry of the 1950s, shows that the film industry had additional dimensions not accounted for in the closed model.

The theory of oversupply was only valid as long as the movie theater remained the only exhibition venue and as long as films that had completed their theatrical runs had no other uses. In the 1950s, distributors often destroyed film copies after their initial run. The practice of generating revenues from films in different contexts began to gain ground in the 1960s with the *Programmkinos* (art houses), which showed retrospectives and film classics, and that really took off with television and with its growing need for feature films. If the word "reprise" still had a negative aftertaste in the 1950s, the screening of films from the past (now considered film classics) in the 1960s became the hallmark of a unique film culture.

From a practical perspective, a model would have been more productive that already in the 1950s would have used other existing film markets (film clubs, the production of educational films, television, etc.) and other forms of financing (contract work, subventions, etc.), a model similar to the one that would later be introduced in the 1960s. On some level, the film of the 1950s already functioned as a commodity for which new markets had to be opened. But the categorical opposition to television (captured by the slogan "No meter of film for television!") harmed the film industry, not the television stations. Only in the 1960s did it become possible to change economic strategies and to expand the economic cycle in a way that was no longer limited to the motion picture in the narrow sense.

The Production of Film for Nontheatrical Exhibition

The model of a "closed shop" for the film industry was a self-deception already in the 1950s, given the growing presence as coproducers and financiers of two large entities: the state, which exerted influence through the different ministries of the federal government, and public television, which had started in the early 1950s and that steadily gained in influence during the late 1950s. The CDU-led government actively used film as a medium of political indoctrination (e.g., the political educational film). Supported by Inter Nationes, Trans Tel, and the Goethe Institute, the Foreign Ministry published the monthly film magazine *Deutschlandspiegel* in ten languages. The Ministry of the Interior organized countless film screenings for millions of visitors where politically acceptable feature and documentary films were shown (Roeber and Jacoby 1973: 774). Moreover, military films were produced for the Ministry of Defense and the Federal Armed Forces, as were agrarian films for the Ministry of Economics and for numerous educational and instructional films for other ministries.

Of particular importance were the film activities of the Bundesministerium für gesamtdeutsche Fragen (Federal Ministry for German-German Concerns, BMG), which used numerous feature films about the East/West problematic in their work with young people. Aside from the documentaries, feature films in the 1960s regularly emphasized the East-West topic: *Tunnel 28* (Escape from East Berlin, 1962), *Verspätung in Marienborn* (Delay in Marienborn, 1963), *Durchbruch Lok 234* (The Breakthrough, 1963), *Ninotschka und Peer* (also known as *Geliebte Genossin* [Beloved Comrade], 1961), as well as the British production *1984* (1955–56). By 1972, the number of film copies used by the film office of the BMG have increased to 17,350 copies (Roeber and Jacoby 1973: 787). It goes without saying that this particular use of films was very profitable for film producers and distributors.

Other federal ministries also began to use films extensively. Especially noteworthy are the film activities of the Bundesministerium für Vertriebene,

Flüchtlinge und Kriegsgeschädigte (Federal Ministry for Displaced Persons, Expellees, and Veterans, BMVt) during the 1950s. They screened many films about the expellees as part of their film work for associations, at public events, and in schools: from *Wohin die Züge fahren* (Where the Trains Go, 1949) and *Gottes Engel sind überall* (God's Angels Are Everywhere, 1947) to *Kinder, Mütter und ein General* (Children, Mothers, and the General, 1955) and the above-mentioned *Grün ist die Heide*. The film initiatives of the CDU-lead government, too, were considerable. Even without a systematic approach, the government went beyond the standard means of film censorship and film subsidies to influence public life through films. Always looking for ways to maximize profits, film studios liked producing these films because they could be shot in between the big feature film productions.

By commissioning documentaries and feature films, public television emerged as an exhibition venue in competition with the movies, a development that proved profitable for film producers and, to a degree, film distributors but not to theater owners. Television stations commissioned films—from Ufa initially—that were meant to air on television, thereby infusing additional capital into the film industry. Finally, television became part of the film industry as the economically most viable television stations bought large studio facilities and used them for film and television production. In 1959, the Bavaria studios were largely taken over by subsidiaries of South German and West German Radio, whereas the Realfilm studios in Hamburg were taken over by a subsidiary of North German Radio, which would later become Studio Hamburg. As a result, the closed economic cycle of the film industry—if there ever was one—was finally forced open and transformed into a film and television industry.

The End of the 1950s

The year 1962 is considered the end of the 1950s for the West German film. In this year a group of young directors decided to reinvent German film at the Oberhausen Short Film Festival. In reality, the West German film industry had long ago begun to change its structure (see Elsaesser 1994). With new film policies advocated by Alexander Kluge and by other tireless advocates for the Young German Film, an open subsidy system was established and the crisis-ridden sector of feature film production infused with new life. However, the crucial phase of the reorganization began only in 1974 with the Film Television Frame Agreement between television stations and film companies that led to the production of diverse films that could be shown in the cinema as well as on television. Günter Rohrbach, in charge of television plays at WDR and later director of the Bavaria Studios, called these "amphibian films" since they could be used in both media, film and television. However, this is already a later stage of development in the West German film and television industry.

Chapter 14

THE OTHER "GERMAN" CINEMA

Mary Wauchope

No treatment of German cinema in the 1950s would be complete without a discussion of Austrian cinema during this period. Although East and West Germany and Austria were all developing separate film industries at this time, the interconnections between the Austrian and German film systems—including economic dependencies, coproductions, shared personnel, and similar ideological goals—suggest that for some aspects of film study it makes less sense to speak of separate national film traditions for this period than of regional developments in German-language film that ignore national boundaries. Since the beginnings of cinema the German and Austrian film industries have been so closely intertwined both culturally and economically that, as Agnes Bleier-Brody points out, when looking for Austrian film in most film encyclopedias, one finds under the rubric "Austria": "see Germany" (1979: 144).[1] The political and cultural situation of the 1950s makes it particularly limiting to consider German cinema in isolation from Austrian films during this time period.

After 1938, when Austria was annexed to Third Reich Germany, the Austrian film industry functioned as a branch of Third Reich cinema. Although the film studios of Vienna continued to focus during this time on what had become traditional genres and themes of Austrian films, Austrian film personnel worked in close cooperation with those in the rest of the German industry, and much of this interaction continued into the postwar period. After World War II the division of the Third Reich by the Allies into four German and four Austrian occupation zones split the territories into an eastern region within the Soviet sphere and a western region under the influence of the remaining Allies. In 1949 separate East and West German states were founded, while Austria remained under Allied occupation until 1955, when the Second Republic of Austria came into existence. In the decades following World War II the East German, West German, and Austrian film industries were all involved in contributing to the development of three separate cultural identities, as part of the postwar nation building process. Yet it is precisely in this period of postwar development, including the 1950s, that a clear distinction among the industries and products of these three national cinemas is particularly difficult to maintain. Sabine Hake suggests in her history of German national cinema that Cold War divisions have led scholars to underestimate the postwar connections between the East and West German cinemas, including "the many movements across East-West borders and the stylistic and thematic continuities in what will best be described as one German cinema" (2002: 86). The strong connections between Austria and the two German states should also not be underestimated for the postwar period.

While categorization in cinema on the basis of national divisions— based at times on location of the film's production firm, at others on the nationality of a film director, the country of the director's birth, the location of film shooting, or typical national trends—never provides fully discrete categories for film, during the 1950s such national film distinctions are particularly unstable. The designation "German" was often used indiscriminately at that time to indicate origins in West Germany and/or East Germany—but also to origins in German-speaking Austria. And neither film distributors nor the public distinguished consistently between German and Austrian films, due at least in part to the close historical connections between Germany and Austria, but also to the continued interconnections between the Austrian and both East and West German film industries in the 1950s. For example, the Austrian-produced *Die letzte Brücke* (The Last Bridge, 1954), frequently cited as the major postwar Austrian antiwar film, was directed by the (West) German Helmut Käutner, while the antiwar film that was the West German entry for the 1960 Oscar for Best Foreign Film, *Die Brücke* (The Bridge, 1959), was directed by the Viennese-born Bernhard Wicki, who held Swiss citizenship. Likewise, such influential postwar West German films as *Die Sünderin* (The Story of a Sinner, 1951) and *Die Halbstarken* (The Hooligans, 1956) were directed by Austrians, Willi Forst and Georg Tressler respectively. On the other hand, two important films for contributing to the image of postwar Austria were both made by the (West) German director Wolfgang Liebeneiner: *1. April 2000* (1952), a film commissioned by the Austrian provisional government to encourage the granting of sovereignty to Austria, and *Die Trapp-Familie* (The Trapp Family, 1956), the West German film that served as a model for the film that did as much as any other to construct an image for postwar Austria: *The Sound of Music* (1965). And, although the film adaptations of

Bertolt Brecht's *Die Gewehre der Frau Carrar* (Senora Carrar's Rifles, 1953) and *Mutter Courage und ihre Kinder* (Mother Courage and Her Children, 1955) were shot by DEFA in Potsdam, the adaptation of his drama *Herr Puntila und sein Knecht Matti* (Herr Puntila and His Servant Matti, 1955) was made, under the personal supervision of Brecht, at the Soviet-led Rosenhügel studio in eastern Austria.

Austrian film talent had always been drawn to the larger, wealthier film industry of Germany, and in the 1950s—as the number of films produced in West Germany grew—increasing numbers of Austrians again looked elsewhere for work in film, so that many Austrian actors were soon well integrated into the West German film business. Gerhard Bliersbach comments, for example, that "there was little awareness among the West German public that many of our film stars were from Austria: Otto Wilhelm Fischer, Heidemarie Hatheyer, Maria Schell [actually born in Switzerland], Romy Schneider, Dietmar Schönherr" (1985: 76). Several Austrians even numbered among the most popular West German film stars: thus, for example, the Austrian Rudolf Prack became, along with Sonja Ziemann, "the dream pair of German film" (Seidl 1987: 72). Further contributing to the difficulty of making a clear distinction between Austrian and West German cinemas in the 1950s is the fact that many Austrian directors worked primarily in Berlin at that time, while many German filmmakers were active in Vienna. It was not unusual for filmmakers to be working both in Austria and in one of the German states simultaneously during the 1950s. For example, both the Vienna-born director Georg Klaren and the Hamburg-born director Georg Wildhagen made films in both East Berlin and Vienna in the early 1950s, while the Austrian-born Georg Wilhelm Pabst released a film both in Austria—*Der letzte Akt* (The Last Ten Days, 1955)—and in West Germany—*Es geschah am 20. Juli* (It Happened on 20 July, 1955)—in the same year.

The imbalance of financial power and the dependence of Austrian film-makers on the large West German market contributed to a situation where West German films distributed in Austria were generally clearly distinguished as such, while Austrian films often lost their national designation once they were introduced into the German market. While Austrians were intent upon asserting their cultural identity as distinct from that of Germans in order to justify the founding of a separate sovereign state, Germans were not faced with similar concerns with regard to Austria. German film distributors in the 1950s frequently removed mention of the Austrian producer from the credits of an Austrian film after having bought the distribution rights to that film (Fritz 1996: 246).

There was even at times a similar lack of clarity between East German films and the films made under the Soviets in eastern Austria. This

confusion is compounded by the fact that a variety of fictitious production firms—Nova, Akkord, and Projektograph, for example—were
listed in the credits of films produced at the Soviet-run Wien-Film am
Rosenhügel studio (Fibich 2000: 163). The titles of Austrian films were
also frequently changed for release on the German market, which led
at times to the mistaken impression that the films with their "German"
titles were actually German-made films, distinct from the films under
their "Austrian" titles. For example, the Austrian film *Hannerl* (Little
Hanna, 1952) became *Ich tanze mit dir in den Himmel hinein* (I'm Dancing
with You into Heaven) in Germany. The Austrian director Franz Antel
recalled that his film *Zirkuskinder* (Circus Children, 1958) was renamed
Solange die Sterne glüh'n (As Long as the Stars Shine) in West Germany,
where, he says, "at that time the German distributors often even gave
foreign films totally arbitrary titles, as if they were drawing them from
a hat" (2001: 125). Such inconsistency in film labeling further blurred
the distinctions between films made in Austria and in West Germany
and lends weight to complaints on the part of some Austrian film scholars that as far as the postwar Austrian film industry is concerned, "the
Anschluß continued, for better or for worse" (Fritz 1996: 227).

The Austrian connection to the German film industries went beyond
the mere exchange of personnel and films, however. For example, the
financial relationship between Austria and West Germany in the postwar
years led to an increased influence of each country on the other in the
sphere of filmmaking. The economic miracle taking place in West Germany in the 1950s caused an economic discrepancy between the two countries, which exacerbated the financial dependency of the Austrian film
industry on the West German market, leading to ever increasing contact
between the two film industries. In fact, Austrian directors frequently had
to depend on West German financing to get their films produced—even
in Austria. Franz Antel and Christian Winkler comment in their history
of Austrian film on the impact this had on the Austrian film industry: "It
is often difficult to classify a film as Austrian, since in those years it was
mostly German production firms which made use of Austrian actors and
the local landscapes as well as the local film studios. This interweaving of
domestic production and foreign financing and distribution is often difficult to make sense of" (1991: 177–78).

The financial imbalance had an impact on the West German film busi-
ness as well. For example, because the salaries of the Austrian film stars
working in Germany were converted into the weak Austrian schilling,
Austrian actors were getting more purchase power for their pay than were
West German actors. This contributed to a dramatic rise in salaries of West
German stars, who wanted equity with their Austrian counterparts (Fritz

1996: 249). A 1951 article in *Der Spiegel* also reports on complaints of those in the West German film industry that film roles were going increasingly to Austrian actors, and also that—due to the imbalance between the schilling and the mark, the lower taxes in Austria, the lower wages for crews in Austria, and the inexpensive rental fee for the Austrian studios—German films were being shot more and more frequently at Austrian studios ("Filmland Österreich," *Der Spiegel* 31 [1951]). Austria therefore quickly became "a film mecca for German distributors and producers" (Guha 1975: 84), leading many in the German film industry to protest against the "so-called German-Austrian coproductions in Thiersee [Austria]" which were then imported back into Germany ("Filmland Österreich"). For example, the 1951 winner of the German Film Prize for outstanding feature film, *Das doppelte Lottchen* (Two Times Lotte, 1950), was made in Thiersee. The Austrian newspaper *Salzburger Nachrichten* commented tongue in cheek on the making of this film: "Almost half of those involved in making it are Austrians, when one includes the studio employees. This, then, is proof that the Germans make their best films in Austria" (Fritz 1996: 249). Willi Höfig sums up the result of the active commercial interaction between the West German and Austrian film industries thus: "A distinction on the basis of national origin is often impossible to make due to the close financial cooperation between the Austrian and West German film businesses" (1973: 164).

In the area of thematics, the film industries of both Germanies and Austria shared in the development and treatment of many common genres and storylines during the 1950s. They interacted through the frequent production of remakes and sequels of each other's films. For example, three popular film series of the period, which were created around the characters Mariandl, Mikosch, and Graf Bobby, included films made both in West Germany and in Austria. Austria and West Germany also both contributed films to what is referred to as the *Silberwald* series, with no fewer than seven sequels following the popular *Echo der Berge* (Echo of the Mountains, 1954). And two remakes of the pastor from Kirchfeld story came out in one year, 1955, one film in Austria and the other in West Germany. West Germans even contributed to (and adopted as their own) the traditionally Austrian "Viennese film," which—with its sentimental depictions of courtly life, and its light, frequently humorous, themes—had been incorporated into Third Reich filmmaking, where it thrived as, according to Hake, "a variation on, if not alternative to, true Germanness" (2001: 156).

In the 1950s, Austrian filmmakers contributed to the development of such popular West German genres as the nobility film, including the popular *Sissi* (1955)—the trilogy of *Sissi* films was released in a shortened, one-film version in the U.S. under the title *Forever, My Love*—dance or ice skating revue films, some featuring the famous ice skating troupe, the *Wiener Eisrevue*, youth/street films, including *Unter 18* (Under 18, 1957) and *Geständnisse einer Sechzehnjährigen* (Confessions of a Sixteen-Year-Old, 1960) (both by the Austrian director of *Die Halbstarken*), and historical biographies, including films on the lives of Mozart, Schubert, and Beethoven. This cooperation makes it difficult to treat many film genres and themes of the 1950s as national developments.

The *Heimatfilm* genre is just such a regional development, concentrated in the western German-speaking area.[2] Considered by many to be particularly representative of popular West German cinema of the 1950s, it is frequently referred to as "the German genre." However, Gertraud Steiner writes that after 1945 the *Heimatfilm* "became the typical product of the Austrian film industry" (1987: 45). This, then, is one postwar film genre that surely benefits from treatment as a joint project of the postwar West German and Austrian film industries and imaginations. And indeed the vast majority of 1950s *Heimatfilme* were made in western Austria and West Germany, where the two film industries developed together the prototypical themes, plots and characters of the 1950s *Heimatfilm*. (This regional East-West distinction is maintained within the typical *Heimatfilm* itself: a frequently occurring character of this genre is the refugee from the East, an outsider who finds a new home in the West.) While the West German *Grün ist die Heide* (Green is the Heather, 1951) set the standards for the postwar *Heimatfilm*, it was the 1954 Austrian film *Echo der Berge*—also known as *Der Förster vom Silberwald* (The Forester of Silberwald)—which is credited with starting the *Heimatfilm* boom of the mid 1950s and that became the most successful *Heimatfilm* of the postwar period (Buchschwentner 1996: 264–65).

A number of features surely contributed to the appeal of this regional genre for filmmakers and audiences in both West Germany and Austria in this time period.[3] The postwar *Heimatfilm* may have provided a reassuring continuity to earlier examples of this genre (and in some cases to the popular *Bergfilm* genre), and it provided a more "German" option to the American films flooding the postwar European market. Much of the appeal of the postwar *Heimatfilm* must also have lain in the contrast of the genre's typical settings—beautiful landscapes, sentimentally depicted villages, and the world of nature—to the reality of rubble-strewn postwar cities. But *Heimatfilme* did not merely offer their audiences retreat to a countryside untouched by the devastations of war. Although they generally avoided the overtly political, *Heimatfilme* nonetheless provided the means for dealing with issues of specific importance to both West Germans and Austrians as they faced the challenges of dealing with their joint Third Reich past and their postwar attempts at nation building. Georg

Seeßlen suggests that, "at least for our cultural area" (1990: 347–48), the *Heimatfilm* offers an imaginary space for reconciling the old with the new and provides, in particular, onscreen resolutions for the postwar tensions arising from the modernization and changes in lifestyle taking place in the provinces and from the postwar repression of the Nazi past (see also von Moltke 2002a, 2002b; Boa and Palfreymann 2000).

Becoming ever more spatially localized, the setting of the *Heimatfilm* came to be situated more and more in the southern German-speaking area. The most common locations for *Heimatfilme* are found south of the Main River, in Upper Bavaria, in the Salzkammer region or in Tyrol (Bessen 1989: 241). This location had the advantage of being visually as different as possible from the contested regions of the northeast, including the city of Berlin, with their "specter of Prussianism" (Applegate 1990: 243). The North-South distinction is frequently illustrated in the *Heimatfilme* themselves by contrasting (often with humor) Northern German characters, particularly those from Berlin, with Southern Germans or Austrians. According to Celia Applegate (1990: 228–46) the regional differentiation typical of the *Heimatfilm* reflects a general postwar tendency in West Germany to privilege the local or regional over the national. She argues convincingly that the postwar *Heimat* trend in West Germany stemmed at least in part from a general West German loss of confidence in the nation, which led many to undertake "the recovery of that distinctively German, locally rooted patriotism that Nazism had discouraged" (Applegate 1990: 244). In Austria as well, according to Gerald Stourz, the *Länder* or states "were the most stabile element" during the early postwar period: "with the return of the structure of the *Länder* which had existed before the *Anschluß* (annexation), the year 1945 brought a rediscovery of what was lost, that of which one had been robbed" (cited in Schachinger 1993: 115). The particular appeal of the *Heimatfilm*'s increased localization in the Alps benefited, then, from the strong sense of regional identity projected by Southern Germans and Austrians, where a cultural identity was nourished which cut across national borders and where people prided themselves on well-preserved local traditions. For both Austrians and West Germans, then, one appeal of the *Heimatfilm* appears to have been that it constructed onscreen general regional identities rather than what would have to have been very problematic postwar national identities.

While the *Heimatfilm* provides one example of interaction among the German and Austrian film industries in the west, a look at cooperation and similarities between the two eastern regions for German and Austrian film in the 1950s points to further advantages to treating German film of this period as regional, rather than strictly national, cinemas. Although the interaction between East Germany and the eastern zone of Austria was not as widespread as it was in the west, the Soviet occupation of the two postwar eastern zones and continued influence on eastern Austrian and German film in the 1950s did lead to parallels and cooperation between these two industries, at least until the Soviet withdrawal from Austria in 1955.

It is difficult to trace broad common trends in the films of eastern Austria and East Germany, since the studio-commissioned production in eastern Vienna lasted only five years, from 1950 to 1955, and resulted in only sixteen films (two of which were not completed until after the departure of the Soviets).[4] Yet films made at the Wien-Film am Rosenhügel studio in the eastern zone of Austria during this period did exhibit many ideological and thematic parallels to films made at the DEFA studios in East Germany. Early on, the Soviets recognized the political potential for filmmaking in East Germany for, as the Soviet film adviser Sergei Tulpanov put it, it was "wrestling for the education of the German people" (cited in Schittly 2002: 27). By the time of the founding of the GDR in 1949, DEFA was subject to an increasingly ideological—although erratically applied—agenda, functioning under the watchful eye of the East German Socialist Unity Party (see Allan 1999; Gersch 1993; Hake 2002; Mückenberger 1994). In the eastern zone of Austria, on the other hand, the Soviets initially dismantled much of the Rosenhügel film studio and confiscated its film equipment, much of which was sent back to the Soviet Union as partial payment of German war reparations. While film production in East Berlin was managed primarily by Germans, some of whom had returned from exile or from concentration camps, the eastern Austrian studio remained under tight control of its Soviet managers. Although Stalin made it known that he wanted the eastern zone of Austria to have a film industry, the initial goal there was to bring in badly needed foreign currency to the Soviet Union by renting out the studios to production firms from both east and west (Steiner 1997; see also, Fibich 2000; Guha 1975; Pruha 1996; Rathkolb 1988). So it was not until the 1950s, when the Rosenhügel Studio was finally commissioned to produce its own films, that significant similarities in the functioning of the two eastern studios can be seen and thematic and ideological parallels between films made in East Berlin and eastern Vienna begin to exhibit similar patterns.

The ideologically driven films common among postwar DEFA productions were not typical of early postwar filmmaking in eastern Austria. In occupied Austria, where the political leaders were struggling to find a sense of national identity that could justify the creation of a new sovereign Austrian state, the internationalism of communism caused many to see a contradiction in the terms *communist* and *Austrian* (Moser 2002: 39–40). In addition, the tradition of communism had always been weaker in Austria than it had been in Germany. While the Soviets were able to rely on long-time members of the German Communist Party or on recent converts to the goals of a socialist Germany to offer contributions to the development of a film industry in East Berlin, in Austria there was a much smaller group of artists committed to a socialist agenda who became active in filmmaking at the Rosenhügel studio, most notably Karl Paryla, Ruth von Mayenburg, and Peter Loos. The majority of the filmmakers directing films under the Soviets in Austria were not overtly sympathetic to socialism (e.g., Jacoby, Kolm-Veltee, Steinboeck, von Borsody and Hübler-Kahla). Due to these differences between the situations in postwar Germany and in postwar Austria, most early films commissioned by the Soviets in Vienna had only a very mild socialist message and made few direct references to communism or the Soviet Union.

Both East Berlin and eastern Vienna continued well into the 1950s to make entertainment films, albeit frequently tinged with Soviet ideology, in hopes of appealing to audiences in both east and west while at the same time carrying out their goal of educating the public about socialism. And both East German and eastern Austrian filmmakers made contributions to the development of genres typical of 1950s German film such as the literary adaptation, the genius or biographical film, and the music film. While the DEFA studios took up figures like Ernst Thälmann, a German socialist hero, as the subject of a two-part biographical film, in Austria a milder form of Austro-communism, which aimed to promote socialist ideals within the local Austrian setting, was encouraged in an effort to combat strong anticommunist and anti-Soviet sentiment in postwar Austria (Moser 2002: 40). The major film biographies at the Rosenhügel studio therefore focused on cultural figures from the Austrian past: the composer Franz Schubert and the Viennese comic actor Alexander Girardi.

Where the Rosenhügel studio made its strongest contribution to film, however, was in its production of genres that developed out of Austria's longtime music traditions: the revue film or musical and the opera or operetta film. In 1950 Leonid Leonov, a film expert and choreographer from Moscow whose primary interest lay in the production of entertainment films, was brought in to direct the Wien-Film am Rosenhügel studio. Unlike the DEFA studio, which had become the single official film studio of the German Democratic Republic and had begun to close its doors to filmmakers living in the west, the Rosenhügel studio, in an Austria that was still under joint occupation by the four Allies until 1955, had to compete directly with Western studios for personnel and with Western distributors (including the Americans) for market shares. By releasing primarily entertainment films, the Rosenhügel studio had a chance of remaining competitive.

The first film produced by the Soviets in Austria, *Das Kind der Donau* (Marika, 1951), was a musical revue, starring none other than the Third Reich star Marika Rökk and directed by her husband, Georg Jacoby. Premiered in East Berlin, the film centers on a theater troupe that must work together to find a way to put on their show after their theater has burned down. In spite of the film's subtle socialist slant, with its "motif of solidarity" and "elements of socialist realism" (Pruha 1996: 64), its entertainment value predominated, so that it was popular not only throughout eastern Europe, but throughout Western Europe as well—and was even sold to the United States.

Other early revue films and musicals with an understated ideological message include *Frühling auf dem Eis* (Springtime on Ice, 1951), *Abenteuer im Schloß* (Adventure in the Castle, 1952), *Seesterne* (Starfish, 1952), and *Verlorene Melodie* (Vanished Melody, 1952). The revue film lent itself particularly well to presenting, in an easily digestible fashion, themes of socialist solidarity and anticapitalism through a familiar "the-show-must-go-on" plot. All of the Rosenhügel studio-produced films, with the possible exception of *Gasparone* (1956), were shown in East Germany.[5] But these early Austrian entertainment films were not always well received critically there. The film *Seesterne*, for example, was sharply criticized in East Berlin as "such abstruse nonsense squeezed out of the tortured brains and minds of Viennese film producers led astray by the box office" (Pruha 1996: 70)—which may have contributed to the fact that *Seesterne*, released in 1952, was the last musical or revue film to be produced on the Rosenhügel.

The next director of the Rosenhügel film studio was Andrej Andreijewski, former director of production at Eisenstein Films in Moscow, who had an interest in producing films of serious musical interest in Austria. One advantage of producing films based on operas and operettas was the relative ease with which they were likely to get past Soviet censors compared to original film scripts. In addition, their lack of obvious socialist message gave such films broad appeal to Austrian and German audiences in both east and west. Andreijewski's primary goal lay in producing music films in Vienna with high cultural standards (Pruha 1996: 70). Known for its excellent sound studio (Steiner 1997: 62), the Rosenhügel studio was particularly well-suited for taping high quality sound tracks for the several films based on operas or operettas that the new studio director put into production: *Die Regimentstochter* (Daughter of the Regiment, 1953), *Eine Nacht in Venedig* (A Night in Venice, 1953), *Gasparone*, and *Fidelio* (1955). Under the head dramaturg Ruth von Mayenburg, those active at the Rosenhügel studio saw a potential during these years "to create film operas which would become a model for the music film" (Pruha 1996: 72).

Filmmakers at DEFA, where big-budget opera films like *Die lustigen Weiber von Windsor* (The Merry Wives of Windsor, 1950) and *Zar und Zimmermann* (The Tsar and the Carpenter, 1956) had been produced, began to interact with the Rosenhügel studio in the development of the opera and operetta film genres. Some East German filmmakers even served as directors for some of the Austrian films. For example, the Vienna-born Georg Klaren, who had been director of DEFA, came to Wien-Film am Rosenhügel in 1953 to codirect the first operetta film produced there, *Die Regimentstochter*. Georg Wildhagen, a native of Hamburg who had studied music in Salzburg, also directed opera films in East Germany, including *Figaros Hochzeit* (The Marriage of Figaro, 1949) and *Die lustigen Weiber von Windsor*, before coming to eastern Vienna to direct *Eine Nacht in Venedig* in 1953. The Viennese-born Walter Felsenstein was active after the war in the music circles of East Berlin, where he became director of the Komische Oper. In 1955 he was brought to Vienna to direct the opera film *Fidelio*. And the composer Hanns Eisler, who had moved to East Berlin after the war and wrote the music for several DEFA films there, also composed or arranged the scores for several Rosenhügel studio films: *Gasparone, Herr Puntila und sein Knecht Matti, Bel Ami* (1957), *Schicksal am Lenkrad* (Destiny at the Steering Wheel, 1954), and *Fidelio*.

Though fewer Austrians were active at DEFA than were East Germans at Rosenhügel, the critically acclaimed Austrian actor Karl Paryla worked for both studios in the early 1950s. Paryla, who had made his name as an actor in the Soviet-sponsored *Neues Theater an der Scala* in Vienna, also acted in the DEFA films *Semmelweis—Retter der Mütter* (Dr. Semmelweis, 1950) and *Die Unbesiegbaren* (The Inconquerable, 1953). In 1954 he then directed two films at the Rosenhügel studio, *Der Komödiant von Wien* (The Comedian of Vienna, 1954) and *Gasparone*. The ties, then, in filmmaking during these years were stronger with regard to goals and ideology—and to a lesser extent personnel—between eastern Austria and East Germany than they were between eastern and western Austria.

In the final years of filmmaking on the Rosenhügel, there was a turn away from the entertainment and music film in favor of more ideologically committed films, a change that paralleled developments at DEFA in the mid 1950s. However, rather than turn to Austrian filmmakers for these films, the Rosenhügel studio looked outside the country for its directors. This may be due in part to a scarcity of Austrian filmmakers prepared to make these films, either because they were not committed to the new strictly socialist filmmaking agenda or because they were boycotting the Rosenhügel studio for fear that they might be blacklisted by the more lucrative Western studios. At any rate, this period of more politically engaged filmmaking at Rosenhügel did provide new filmmaking opportunities for international directors who had shown a commitment to socialism. The Italian director Aldo Vergano was brought in 1954 to film *Schicksal am Lenkrad*, a sociocritical film in neorealistic style, while the French director Louis Daquin was hired in 1955 to direct *Bel Ami*, a film that was said to have represented the most obvious form of "the political demagogy of the Rosenhügel studio" (Pruha 1996: 74). The East German author Bertolt Brecht agreed to have his drama *Herr Puntila und sein Knecht Matti* (begun in 1955 but not completed until 1960, after the withdrawal of the Soviets) directed at the Rosenhügel studio by Alberto Cavalcanti, who had been blacklisted as a communist in his home country of Brazil and worked in London during the war.

This new agenda of socialist filmmaking was cut short when the Soviets withdrew from Austria in 1955. After a short five years of Soviet-commissioned film production at the Rosenhügel studio, which had provided an alternative forum in Austria for filmmaking to that of the Western studios, the last Soviet director of Wien-Film am Rosenhügel, Vladimir Lichatschov, turned the studio over to the Austrian government. After making significant contributions to the music and opera film, and for a short time providing a home for the making of socialist films by international filmmakers, the Rosenhügel studio was integrated in 1955 into the new, Western-oriented Wien-Film company of Austria's Second Republic. The division between east and west in Austria's film industry ended, then, with the withdrawal of the Soviets, and with that the brief period of intense cooperation between the eastern German and eastern Austrian film industries also came to an end.

After the departure of the Soviets in 1955 many in the Austrian film industry continued to blacklist those who had worked at Rosenhügel. While some filmmakers who had been active under the Soviets in Vienna nonetheless managed to continue to make films in Austria after 1955, others chose to move to East Germany and continue with their careers at DEFA. Felsenstein, the director of *Fidelio*, returned to East Berlin to become vice president of the *Deutsche Akademie der Künste* there. And Karl Paryla, the committed Austrian socialist who had already been active at both the Rosenhügel and DEFA studios, moved to East Germany, where he directed the DEFA film *Mich dürstet* (I'm Thirsty) in 1956. Austrian actor Wolfgang Heinz, who had had roles in the Rosenhügel films *Der Komödiant von Wien* and *Gasparone*, also moved to East Berlin, where he acted in *Geschwader Fledermaus* (Bat Squadron, 1958) and in *Professor Mamlock* (1961).

The many examples of close collaboration and interaction between film studios and personnel in Austria and in the two Germanys—whether through shared personnel, financial interdependence, common political goals, competition for the same German-speaking audience, or joint development of genres like the *Heimatfilm* and the opera film—indicate that studies of German film in both east and west are without doubt enriched by consideration of the contributions of the Austrian film industry. While East Germany, West Germany, and Austria were all in the process of developing their own national film characteristics in the formative years of the 1950s, such developments took place against a backdrop of continuing film traditions and regional trends. Continuities from the longtime association of Austrian film to its German counterpart, including its actual integration into the German film system under the Third Reich, contributed to the development of common features for all three national cinemas in the postwar period. In addition, the similar political situations of the three states during the postwar decades of transition contributed greatly to the development of common trends in German and Austrian film both in the east and in the west. The Cold War challenges to the development of new cultural and national identities for, on the one hand, the eastern regions of Austria and Germany and, on the other hand, their counterparts in the West, had decisive regional impacts on the development of German and Austrian cinema in the postwar decades. Research, then, that takes into account the influence of Austrian cinema on German cinema and looks at regional trends which function in conjunction with national tendencies, has the advantage of being able to present more complete, albeit more complex, treatments of many aspects of German film in the 1950s.

Notes

1. Translations are the author's own, unless otherwise indicated.
2. In his 1973 volume on the *Heimatfilm*, Willi Höfig gives the following features for the genre: "simple content, beautiful landscape, the happy love story, interest concentrated on the private world, poor aesthetics, as well as a simplified portrayal of mankind's rootedness in the surroundings, as indicated through folk costumes and easily comprehended cultural customs" (as summarized by Steiner 1987: 46).
3. According to Silberman the popularity of the *Heimatfilm* "reached a high point in 1955 when one-third of the film production consisted of *Heimat* features, and the genre accounted for nearly 25 percent of all releases during the 1950s" (1995:115).
4. *Abenteuer im Schloß* (Adventure in the Castle, 1952), *Bel ami* (1957), *Don Juan* (1955), *Fidelio* (1955), *Franz Schubert—Ein Leben in zwei Sätzen* (1953), *Frühling auf dem Eis* (Springtime on Ice, 1951), *Gasparone* (1955), *Herr Puntila and sein Knecht Matti* (1955), *Das Herz einer Frau* (The Heart of a Woman, 1951), *Das Kind der Donau* (Marika, 1951), *Der Komödiant von Wien* (The Comedian of Vienna, 1954), *Eine Nacht in Venedig* (A Night in Venice, 1953), *Die Regimentstochter* (Daughter of the Regiment, 1953), *Schicksal am Lenkrad* (Destiny at the Steering Wheel, 1954), *Seesterne* (Starfish, 1952), and *Verlorene Melodie* (Vanished Melody, 1952).
5. According to e-mail communication from Birgit Scholz, Film Museum Potsdam, 11 June 2003.

WORKS CITED

Abelshauser, Werner. 1987. *Die langen fünfziger Jahre*. Düsseldorf: Schwann.

Abich, Hans. 1989. "Die Göttinger Produktionen in dem Film der 50er Jahre. Eine Ortsbeschreibung." In *Zwischen gestern und morgen*, eds. Hilmar Hoffmann and Walter Schobert. Frankfurt am Main: Deutsches Filmmuseum.

Adorno, Theodor W. 1997. *Gesammelte Schriften*. Frankfurt am Main: Suhrkamp.

Adorno, Theodor W. and Hanns Eisler. 1997. *Komposition für den Film*. Vol. 15, Adorno's *Gesammelte Schriften*. Frankfurt am Main: Suhrkamp.

Allan, Sean. 1999. "DEFA: An Historical Overview." In *DEFA: East German Cinema, 1946–1992*, eds. Sean Allan and John Sandford. New York and Oxford: Berghahn.

Althusser, Louis. 1971. *Lenin and Philosophy*. Trans. Ben Brewster. New York: Monthly Review Press.

Antel, Franz. 2001. *Verdreht, verliebt, mein Leben*. Written by Peter Orthofer from the notes of the author. Vienna and Munich: Almathea.

Antel, Franz and Christian F. Winkler. 1991. *Hollywoood an der Donau: Geschichte der Wien Film in Sievering*. Vienna: Österreichische Staatsdruckerei.

Applegate, Celia. 1990. *A Nation of Provincials: The German Idea of Heimat*. Berkeley: University of California Press.

Arendt, Hannah and Karl Jaspers. 1992. *Hannah Arendt Karl Jaspers: Correspondence, 1926–29*, eds. Lotte Kohler and Hans Saner. Trans. Robert and Rita Kimber. New York: Harcourt Brace Jovanovich.

Aurich, Rolf, Wolfgang Jacobson, and Cornelius Schnauber, eds. 2001. *Fritz Lang: Leben und Werk. Bilder und Dokumente*. Berlin: jovis.

Baer, Hester. 2003. "Negotiating the Popular and the Avant Garde: The Failure of Herbert Vesely's *The Bread of Those Early Years* (1962)." In *Light Motives: German Popular Film in Perspective*, eds. Randall Halle and Margaret McCarthy. Detroit: Wayne State University Press.

———. 2004. "Sound Money. Aural Strategies in Rolf Thiele's *A Call Girl Named Rosemarie*." In *Sound Matters: Essays on the Acoustics of Modern German Culture*, eds. Nora Alter and Lutz Koepnick. New York: Berghahn.

Bänsch, Dieter. 1985. *Die 50er Jahre: Beiträge zur Politik und Kultur*. Tübingen: Narr.

Barthel, Manfred. 1986. *Der deutsche Nachkriegsfilm*. Munich: Herbig.

———. 1991. *Als Opas Kino jung war. Der deutsche Nachkriegsfilm*. Frankfurt am Main: Ullstein.

Basinger, Jeanine. 2003. *The World War Two Combat Film: Anatomy of a Genre*. Middletown, Conn.: Wesleyan University Press.

Bathrick, David. 1995. *The Powers of Speech: The Politics of Culture in the GDR*. Lincoln and London: University of Nebraska Press.

Baudry, Jean-Louis. 1975. "The Apparatus: Metaphysical Approaches to the Impression of Reality in Cinema." In *Narrative, Apparatus, Ideology*, ed. Philip Rosen. New York: Columbia University Press.

Bauer, Alfred. 1976. *Deutscher Spielfilm-Almanach 1929–1950*. Reprint, Berlin 1950. Munich: Winterberg.

———. 1981. *Deutscher Spielfilmalmanach Band 2: 1946–55*. Munich: Winterberg.

Becker, Wolfgang and Norbert Schöll. 1995. *In jenen Tagen: Wie der deutsche Nachkriegsfilm die Vergangenheit bewältigte*. With Heide Becker, Ruth Kayser, and Peter Nowotny. Opladen: Leske + Budrich.

Berger, Jürgen, Hans-Peter Reichmann, and Rudolf Worschech, eds. 1989. *Zwischen Gestern und Morgen. Westdeutscher Nachkriegsfilm 1946–1962*. Frankfurt am Main: Deutsches Filmmuseum.

Bergfelder, Tim. "Lola's Hidden Past: Fassbinder, Film History, and the West German Cinema of the 1950s." Unpublished manuscript.

———. 2003. "Extraterritorial Fantasies: Edgar Wallace and the German Crime Film." In *The German Cinema Book*, eds. Tim Bergfelder, Erica Carter, and Deniz Göktürk. London: BFI.

———. 2004. *International Adventures: Popular German Cinema and European Co-Productions in the 1960s*. Oxford and New York: Berghahn.

Bergfelder, Tim, Erica Carter, and Deniz Göktürk, eds. 2003. *German National Cinema*. London: BFI.

Bessen, Ursula. 1989. *Trümmer und Träume: Nachkriegszeit und fünfziger Jahre auf Zelluloid: Deutsche Spielfilme als Zeugnisse ihrer Zeit: Eine Dokumentation*. Bochum: Studienverlag Dr. N. Brockmeyer.

Bessy, Maurice and Raymond Chirat. 1987. *Histoire du cinéma français: Encyclopédie des films*. Vol. 2. Paris : Pygmalion.

Bettelheim, Bruno. 1976. *The Uses of Enchantment: The Meaning and Importance of Fairy Tales*. New York: Knopf.

Biess, Frank. 2001. "Survivors of Totalitarianism: Returning POWs and the Reconstruction of Masculine Citizenship in West Germany, 1945–55." In *The Miracle Years: A Cultural History of West Germany, 1949–1968*, ed. Hanna Schissler. Princeton: Princeton University Press.

Bleier-Brody, Agnes. 1979. "Österreich in der ausländischen Filmliteratur." *Österreichische Zeitschrift für Soziologie* 3–4: 136–49.

Bletschacher, R.S. 1953. "Geballte Ladung." In "So kritisieren unsere Leser: Der Kinofreund soll selbst zu Filmen Stellung nehmen." *Abendpost*, 10 October.

Bliersbach, Gerhard. 1985. *So grün war die Heide: Der deutsche Nachkriegsfilm in neuer Sicht*. Weinheim und Basel: Beltz.

Blum-Reid, Sylvie. 2003. *East-West Encounters: Franco-Asian Cinema and Literature*. London: Wallflower Press.

Boa, Elizabeth and Rachel Palfreymann, eds. 2000. *Heimat: A German Dream. Regional Loyalties and National Identity in German Culture 1890–1990*. New York and Oxford: Oxford University Press.

Bodensieck, Heinrich. 1992. "Blickrichtung Westen. Die britisch-amerikanische Wochenschau *Welt im Film* als Instrument der Umerziehung." In *Unsere Medien, unsere Republik 2. Deutsche Selbst- und Fremdbilder in den Medien von BRD und DDR*. Vol. 1. Marl: Adolf Grimm Institut

Bogdanovich, Peter. 1967. *Fritz Lang in America*. London: Studio Vista.

Bongartz, Barbara. 1992. *Von Caligari zu Hitler—von Hitler zu Dr. Mabuse?: Eine psychologische Geschichte des deutschen Films von 1946 bis 1960*. Münster: MAkS.

Borchert, Wolfgang. 1947. "Draussen vor der Tür." *Der Ruf*. 1 December.

Borgelt, H. 1959. "Bei den Aufnahmen zu *Rommel ruft Kairo*." *Abendpost*, 10–11 January.

Brady, Martin. 1999. "Discussion with Kurt Maetzig." In *DEFA: East German Cinema, 1946–1992*, eds. Seán Allen and John Sanford. New York: Berghahn.

Brandlmeier, Thomas. 1997. "Et ego fui in Arcadia: Die exotischen Spielfilme der 20er Jahre." In *Triviale Tropen: Exotische Reise- und Abenteuerfilme aus Deutschland 1919–1939*, ed. Jörg Schöning. Munich: edition text + kritik.

Brauerhoch, Annette. 1983. "Moral in Golddruck: Die Illustrierte *Film und Frau*." *Frauen und Film* 35: 48–57.

————. 1997. "'Mohrenkopf'": Schwarzes Kind und Weiße Nachkriegsgesellschaft in *Toxi.*" *Frauen und Film* 60 (October): 106–30.

Bredel Papers. Stiftung Archiv der Akademie der Künste. Berlin, Federal Republic of Germany.

Brink, Cornelia. 1998. *Ikonen der Vernichtung: Öffentlicher Gebrauch von Fotografien aus nationalsozialistischen Konzentrationslagern nach 1945.* Berlin: Akademie Verlag.

Browne, Nick. 1989. "Orientalism as an Ideological Form: American Film Theory in the Silent Period." *Wide Angle,* no. 4: 23–31.

Buchschwentner, Robert. 1996. "Ruf der Berge—Echo des Fremdenverkehrs. Der Heimatfilm: Ein österreichischer Konjunkturritt." In *Ohne Untertitel,* eds. Ruth Beckermann and Christa Blümlinger. Vienna: Sonderzahl.

Buchwald, Frank A. 1992. "Kontrastprogramm. Die Berlinaktion des Bundespresseamtes von 1959." In *Unsere Medien, unsere Republik 2* Vol. 3. Marl: Adolf Grimm Institut.

Burch, Noel. 1973. *Theory of Film Practice.* Trans. Helen R. Lane. New York: Praeger.

Burghardt, Kirsten.1996. "Moralische Aufrüstung im frühen deutschen Nachkriegsfilm." Discurs Film 8: 241–76.

Byg, Barton. 1997. "Nazism as Femme Fatale: Recuperations of Cinematic Masculinity in Postwar Berlin." In *Gender and Germanness: Cultural Productions of Nation,* eds. Patricia Herminghouse and Magda Mueller. Providence: Berg.

Carter, Erica. 1997. *How German Is She? Postwar West German Reconstruction and the Consuming Woman.* Ann Arbor: University of Michigan Press.

Chandler, Raymond. 1946. "The Simple Art of Murder." *The Art of the Mystery Story,* ed. Howard Haycraft. New York: Simon & Schuster.

Chion, Michel. 1994. *Audio Vision.* Trans. Claudia Gorbman. New York: Columbia University Press.

Clemens, Rudolf. 1959. "Staat and Filmwirtschaft." Ph.D. diss., University of Wuerzburg.

Confino, Alon. 1997. *The Nation as Local Metaphor: Württemberg, Imperial Germany, and National Memory, 1871–1918.* Chapel Hill: University of North Carolina Press.

Cook, David. 1981. *A History of Narrative Film.* New York: Norton.

Copjec, Joan, ed. 1993. *Shades of Noir.* London: Verso.

Cowie, Elizabeth. 1984. "Fantasia." *m/f* 9: 70–105.

Czernitzki, Ursula. 1995. "Leben und Werk von Joe May unter besonderer Berücksichtigung der 'Filmstadt' Woltersdorf und des dort gedrehten Filmes *Das Indische Grabmal* (1921)." M.A. thesis, Free University of Berlin.

Dadek, Walter. 1957. *Die Filmwirtschaft. Grundiss einer Theorie der Filmökonomik.* Freiburg: Herder.

Davidson, John E. 1999. *Deterritorializing the New German Cinema.* Minneapolis: University of Minnesota Press.

Demonsablon, Philippe. 1959. "Le Tigre d'Argol," *Cahiers du Cinéma,* no. 98: 58–59.

Dietrich, Gerd. 1993. *Politik und Kultur in der SBZ 1945–1949.* Berne: Peter Lang.

Dillmann, Claudia. 1992. "Schurkenstücke: Entflechtung und Lex UFI." In *Das Ufa—Buch. Kunst und Krisen, Stars und Regisseure, Wirtschaft und Politik,* eds. Hans-Michael Bock and Michael Töteberg. Frankfurt am Main: Zweitausendeins.

Doane, Mary Ann. 1984. "The 'Woman's Film': Possession and Address." In *Re-vision: Essays in Feminist Film Criticism,* eds. Mary Ann Doane, Patricia Mellencamp, and Linda Williams. Frederick, Maryland: The American Film Institute.

————. 1987. *The Desire to Desire: The Woman's Film of the 1940s.* Bloomington: Indiana University Press.

Dombrowski, I. 1965. "Kein Hang zur Bühne." *Hamburger Abendblatt.* 12 June.

Donzelot, Jacques. 1979. *Policing Families.* New York: Random House.

Dorpalen, Andreas. 1988. *German History in Marxist Perspective: The East German Approach.* Detroit: Wayne State University Press.

DR1. Kulturministerium. Stiftung Archiv der Parteien und Massenorganisationen der ehemaligen DDR im Bundesarchiv. Berlin, Federal Republic of Germany.

Duras, Marguerite. 1965. *Le Vice-consul*. Paris: Gallimard.

———. 1973. *India song. Texte, Théâtre, Film*. Paris: Gallimard.

Eisner, Lotte. 1976. *Fritz Lang*. New York: Da Capo.

———. 1988. *Ich hatte einst ein schönes Vaterland.* Munich: dtv.

Elsaesser, Thomas. 1987. "Tales of Sound and Fury: Observations on the Family Melodrama." In *Home Is Where the Heart Is: Studies in Melodrama and the Women's Film*, ed. Christine Gledhill. London: BFI. .

———. 1994. *Der neue deutsche Film: von den Anfängen bis zu den neunziger Jahren*. Munich: Wilhelm Heyne Verlag.

———. 2000. *Weimar Cinema and After. Germany's Historical Imaginary*. London: Routledge.

Elsner, Monika, Thomas Müller, and Peter Spangenberg. 1993. "Zur Entstehungsgeschichte des Dispositivs Fernsehen in der Bundesrepublik Deutschland der 50er Jahre." In *Geschichte des Fernsehens in der BRD*, ed. Knut Hickethier. Vol. 1. Munich: Fink.

Eyferth, Klaus, Ursula Brandt, and Wolfgang Hawel. 1960. *Farbige Kinder in Deutschland: Die Situation der Mischlingskinder und die Aufgaben ihrer Eingliederung*. Munich: Juventa.

Fehrenbach, Heide. 1995. *Cinema in Democratizing Germany: Reconstructing National Identity after Hitler*. Chapel Hill: University of North Carolina Press.

———. 1998. "Rehabilitating Fatherland: Race and German Remasculinization." *Signs*, no. 24: 107–28.

———. 2001. "Of German Mothers and 'Negermischlingskinder': Race, Sex, and the Postwar Nation." In *The Miracle Years: A Cultural History of West Germany*, ed. Hanna Schissler. Princeton: Princeton University Press.

Feinstein, Joshua. 2002. *The Triumph of the Ordinary: Depictions of Daily Life in East German Cinema, 1949–1989*. Chapel Hill: University of North Carolina Press.

Feldvoss, Marli. 1989. "Wer hat Angst vor Rosemarie Nitribitt? Eine Chronik von Mord, Sitte und Kunst aus den fünfziger Jahren." In *Zwischen gestern und morgen*, eds. Hilmar Hoffmann and Walter Schobert. Frankfurt am Main: Deutsches Filmmuseum.

Fibich, Bettina. 2000. "Das Projekt 'Filmstadt Wien': Die historische Entwicklung der Wiener Rosenhügel-Ateliers (1919–1999)." Ph.D. diss., University of Vienna.

Film und Frau. 1949–1966. Hamburg: Verlag "Stimme der Frau."

Filmstadt Babelsberg: DEFA Spielfilme. Berlin: Henschel Verlag. 50–157.

Fischer, Hanns and Jürgen Eckl, eds. 1964. *Retrospektive Fritz Lang. Dokumentation, Teil 2: Amerikanische Filme*. Bad Ems: Verband der Deutschen Filmclubs e.V.

Fischer, Joschka. 2003. "Was haben wir uns angetan? Ein ZEIT-Interview mit Außenminister Joschka Fischer über ein Zentrum gegen Vertreibungen und über das Geschichtsbild der Deutschen." *Die Zeit*, no. 36.

Fisher, Jaimey. 2001. "Who's Watching the Rubble-Kids? Youth, Pedagogy and Politics in Early DEFA Films." *New German Critique*, no. 82: 91–125.

———. 2004. "Kinder der Sterne: Jugend und der Wiederaufbau im frühen westdeutschen Nachkriegskino." *Zeitschrift für Germanistik*, no.1: 83–101.

Foucault, Michel. 1978. *History of Sexuality: An Introduction*. Vol.1. Trans. Robert Hurley. New York: Random.

Franzen, K. Erik, ed. 2001. *Die Vertriebenen: Hitlers letzte Opfer*. Berlin: Propyläen.

———. 2003. "Aus dem Geist von 1950: Die Debatte um ein 'Zentrum gegen Vertreibungen.'" *Frankfurter Rundschau*, 18 July.

Frei, Norbert and Johannes Schmitz. 1999. *Journalismus im 3. Reich*. Munich: Beck.

Freud, Sigmund. 1919; rpt. and trans. 1956. "'A Child Is Being Beaten': A Contribution to the Origin of Sexual Perversions." In *Collected Papers*. Vol. 2. Trans. Joan Rivière. London: Hogarth Press.

———. 1970. *Der Witz und seine Beziehung zum Unbewussten. Studienausgabe*. Vol. 4. Frankfurt am Main: Fischer.

Fritz, Walter. 1996. *Im Kino erlebe ich die Welt: 100 Jahre Kino und Film in Österreich*. Vienna and Munich: Verlag Christian Brandstätter.

Gabelmann, Thilo. 1996. *Thälmann ist niemals gefallen? Eine Legende stirbt*. Berlin: Verlag das neue Berlin.

Gad, Urban. 1920. *Der Film: Seine Mittel, seine Ziele*. Berlin: Schuster & Löffler.

Gansera, Rainer. 1989. "'Krieg und Geilheit, die bleiben immer in Mode' (Shakespeare)." In *Kino und Krieg: Von der Faszination eines tödlichen Genres*, vol. 6 *Arnoldshainer Filmgespräche*, ed. Ernst Karpf. Frankfurt am Main: Gemeinschaftswerk der Evangelischen Publizistik.

Garncarz, Joseph. 1992. *Filmfassungen: Eine Theorie signifikanter Filmvariation*. Frankfurt am Main: Peter Lang.

Garsault, Alain. 1994. "*Le Tigre du Bengale, Le Tombeau hindou:* Une manière absolue devoir les choses."*Positif*, no.405: 89–92.

Gates, Lisa. 1998. "Of Seeing and Otherness: Leni Riefenstahl's African Photographs." In *The Imperialist Imagination: German Colonialism and Its Legacy*, eds. Sara Friedrichsmeyer, Sara Lennox, and Susanne Zantop. Ann Arbor: University of Michigan Press.

Gehler, Fred. 1983. "Die Umsiedler kommen . . . Erinnerung an *Die Brücke* (1949)." *Film und Fernsehen* 10: 18–19.

Gercke, Ekhardt. 1956. *Notwendigkeit, Ziel und Weg einer spezifischen Betriebswirtschaftslehre des Films*. Munich: Pohl.

Gerlof, Kathrin. 1999. *Gerhard Löwenthal—Karl-Eduard von Schnitzler*. (Reihe "Gegenspieler") Frankfurt am Main: Fischer.

Gersch, Wolfgang. 1993. "Film in der DDR: Die verlorene Alternative." In *Geschichte des deutschen Films*, eds. Wolfgang Jacobsen, Anton Kaes and Hans Helmut Prinzler. Stuttgart: Metzler.

Giera, Joachim. 1982. "Tradition und Kontinuität: Tendenzen und Entwicklungen im DEFA-Kinderspielfilm von 1970 bis 1980." Ph.D. diss., Humboldt University of Berlin.

Glaser, Hermann. 1986. *The Rubble Years: The Cultural Roots of Postwar Germany, 1945–1948*. New York: Paragon House.

Gorbman, Claudia. 1987. *Unheard Melodies*. Bloomington: University of Indiana Press.

Grass, Günter. 2002. *Im Krebsgang: eine Novelle*. Göttingen: Steidl.

Gregor, Ulrich and Enno Patalas. 1965. *Geschichte des modernen Films*. Gütersloh: S. Mohn.

Gries, Rainer. 1994. "Virtuelle Zeithorizonte. Deutsch-deutsche Geschichtsbilder und Zukunfts-visionen Ende der fünfziger Jahre." In *"Die Heimat hat sich schön gemacht . . ." 1959: Fallstudien zur deutsch-deutschen Propagandageschichte*, eds. M. Gibas and D. Schindelbeck. Leipzig: Leipziger Universitätsverlag.

Grob, Norbert. 1993. "Film der sechziger Jahre. Abschied von den Eltern." *Geschichte des deutschen Films*, eds. Wolfgang Jacobsen, Anton Kaes, and Hans Helmut Prihzler. Stuttgart: Metzler.

Grunenberg, Antonia. 1993. *Antifaschismus–ein deutscher Mythos*. Reinbek: Rowohlt.

Guha, Wilhelm. 1975. "Die Geschichte eines österreichischen Filmunternehmens: Von der Sascha-Film-Fabrik Pfraumberg in Böhmen zur Wien-Film." Ph.D. diss., University of Vienna.

Guillén, Mauro. 1994. *Models of Management*. Chicago: University of Chicago Press.

Gunning, Tom. 2000. *The Films of Fritz Lang: Allegories of Vision and Modernity*. London: BFI. .

Ha, Marie-Paule. 2000. *Figuring the East: Segalen, Malraux, Duras, and Barthes*. Albany: State University of New York Press.

Habermas, Jürgen. 1963. *Kultur und Kritik*. Frankfurt am Main: Suhrkamp.

Hahn, Brigitte J. 1997. *Umerziehung durch Dokumentarfilm? Ein Instrument amerikanischer Kulturpolitik im Nachkriegsdeutschland (1945–1953)*. Münster: LIT Verlag.

Hake, Sabine. 1990. "Architectural Hi/stories: Fritz Lang and *The Nibelungs*." *Wide Angle*, no. 3: 38–57.

———. 2001. *Popular Cinema of the Third Reich*. Austin: University of Texas Press.

———. 2002. *German National Cinema*. London and New York: Routledge.

———. 2004. *Film in Deutschland: Geschichte and Geschichten seit 1895*. Reinbek by Hamburg: Rowolt.

Halle, Randall and Margaret McCarthy, eds. 2002. *Light Motives: German Popular Film in Perspective*. Detroit: Wayne State University Press.

Häntzsche, Hellmuth. 1980. *Der Spiel- und Trickfilm für Kinder in der DDR*. Berlin: Der Kinderbuchverlag.

Harvey, James. 2001. *Movie Love in the Fifties*. New York: Knopf.

Hattendorf, Manfred. 1999. *Dokumentarfilm und Authentizität. Ästhetik und Pragmatik einer Gattung*. 2nd ed. Constance: UVK.

Hauser, Johannes. 1989. *Neuaufbau der westdeutschen Filmwirtschaft 1945—1955 und der Einfluß der US-amerikanischen Filmpolitik*. Pfaffenweiler: Centaurus-Verlagsgesellschaft.

Hay, Gerhard et al., eds. 1973. *Als der Krieg zu Ende war: Literarisch-politische Publizistik, 1945–50*. Stuttgart: Schiller-Nationalmuseum.

Hedinger, Vinzenz and Meenakshi Shedde. 2005. "Import Export: Kulturtransfers zwischen Indien und Österreich, Deutschland. Filmreihe, Symposium, Installationen, Musik." Press Information, Künstlerhaus. <http://www.kuenstlerhaus.at/presse/text/import_export_wien_chapter.pdf>

Heidtmann, Horst. 1992. *Kindermedien*. Stuttgart: Metzler.

Heimann, Thomas. 1997. "'Lehren aus der deutschen Geschichte': Wahrheitstreue und Propaganda im DEFA-Dokumentarfilm *Du und mancher Kamerad*." In *Verwaltete Vergangenheit. Geschichtskultur und Herrschaftslegitimation in der DDR*, ed. M. Sabrow. Leipzig: Akademische Verlagsanstalt.

———. 2000. "Deutsche Brüder und Schwestern im Kalten Krieg der Medien. Beobachtungen zum deutsch-deutschen Dokumentarfilm nach 1945." In *Der geteilte Himmel. Arbeit, Alltag und Geschichte im ost- und westdeutschen Film*, eds. Gebhard Moldenhauer and Peter Zimmermann. Constance: UVK.

Heller, Heinz-B. 2001. "Dokumentarfilm als transitorisches Genre." In *Die Einübung des dokumentarischen Blicks. Fiction Film und Non Fiction Film zwischen Wahrheitsanspruch und expressiver Sachlichkeit 1895–1945*, eds. U.v. Keitz and K. Hoffmann. Marburg: Schüren.

Hembus, Joe. 1961. *Der deutsche Film kann gar nicht besser sein*. Bremen: Schünemann.

Herlinghaus, Hermann. 1969. "Annelie und Andrew Thorndike." In *Filmdokumentaristen der DDR*, eds. R. Liebmann et al. Berlin: Henschelverlag.

Hermand, Jost. 1986. *Kultur im Wiederaufbau: Die Bundesrepublik Deutschland, 1945–1965*. Munich: Nymphenberger.

Hickethier, Knut. 1991. "Ilse Obrig und *das Klingende Haus der Sonntagskinder*: Die Anfänge des deutschen Kinderfernsehens." In *Geschichte des Kinderfernsehens in der Bundesrepublik Deutschland: Entwicklungsprozesse und Trends*, eds. Hans Dieter Erlinger and Dirk Ulf Stötzel. Berlin: Spiess.

———. 1998. *Geschichte des deutschen Fernsehens*. Stuttgart: J. B. Metzler.

Hillier, Jim, ed. 1985. *Cahiers du Cinéma. The 1950s: Neo-Realism, Hollywood, New Wave*. Cambridge: Harvard University Press, 1985.

Hinz, Ottmar. 1989. *Wilhelm Hauff mit Selbstzeugnissen und Bilddokumenten*. Reinbek: Rowohlt.

Höfig, Willi. 1973. *Der deutsche Heimatfilm 1947–1960*. Stuttgart: Ferdinand Enke.

Hofmann, Gunter. 2003. "Unsere Opfer, ihre Opfer: Erinnern an die Vertreibungen—national oder europäisch?" *Die Zeit*, no. 30.

Höhn, Maria. 2002. *GIs and Fräuleins: The German-American Encounter in 1950s West Germany*. Chapel Hill: University of North Carolina Press.

Hortzschansky, Günter, et al. 1985. *Ernst Thälmann: Eine Biographie*. Berlin: Dietz Verlag.

Hoveyda, Fereydoun. 1959. "Les Indes fabulées." *Cahiers du Cinéma*, no. 99: 56–58.

Huyssen, Andreas. 1981. "The Vamp and the Machine: Technology and Sexuality in Fritz Lang's *Metropolis.*" *New German Critique*, no. 25: 221–37.

Irwin, John. 1994. *The Mystery to a Solution: Poe, Borges, and the Analytical Detective Story*. Baltimore: Johns Hopkins University Press.

Jary, Micaela. 1993. *Traumfabriken made in Germany: Die Geschichte des deutschen Nachkriegsfilms 1945–1960*. Berlin: edition q.

Jirgl, Reinhard. 2003. *Die Unvollendeten*. Munich: C. Hanser.

Jordan, Günter. 1996a. "Die frühen Jahre. 1946 bis 1952." In *Schwarzweiß und Farbe. DEFA-Dokumentarfilme 1946–92,* eds. Günter Jordan and Ralf Schenk. Potsdam: jovis.

———. 1996b. "Der Augenzeuge." In *Schwarzweiß und Farbe. DEFA-Dokumentarfilme 1946–92,* eds. Günter Jordan and Ralf Schenk. Potsdam: jovis.

Jungeblodt. Werner. 1960. *Kriegsfilme—noch und noch. Beträge zur Begegnung von Kirche und Welt.* Vol. 47. Rottenburg: Akademie der Diözese Rottenburg.

Kalbus, Oskar. 1956. *Die Situation des deutschen Filmes*. Wiesbaden.

Kalinak, Kathryn. 1992. *Settling the Score: Music and the Classical Hollywood Film*. Madison: University of Wisconsin Press.

Kannapin, Detlef. 2000. "Ernst Thälmann und der DDR-Antifaschismus im Film der fünziger Jahre." In *Ernst Thälmann: Mensch und Mythos,* ed. Peter Monteath. Amsterdam: Rodopi.

———. 2005. *Dialektik der Bilder: Der Nationalsozialismus in deutschen Film. Ein Ost-West Vergleich.* Berlin: Karl Dietz.

Kaplan, Ann E. 1981. *Fritz Lang: A Guide to References and Resources*. Boston: G. K. Hall.

Keiner, Reinhold. 1984. *Thea von Harbou und der deutsche Film bis 1933.* Hildesheim: Georg Olms.

Kelly, Stuart. 2002. *The Hunt for Zerzura: The Lost Oasis and the Desert War*. London: John Murray.

Kempowski, Walter and D. Hempel. 1999. *Das Echolot: Fuga furiosa—ein kollektives Tagebuch, Winter 1945*. Munich: A. Knaus.

Kittler, Friedrich. 1999. *Gramophone Film Typewriter*. Trans. Geoffrey Winthrop-Young and Michael Wutz. Stanford: Stanford University Press.

Klemperer, Viktor. 1975 (1946). *LTI. Notizbuch eines Philologen*. Leipzig: Reclam.

Kleßmann, Christoph. 1997. *Zwei Staaten, eine Nation. Deutsche Geschichte 1955–1970*. 2nd ed. Bonn: Bundeszentrale für politische Bildung.

Knopp, Guido. 2001. *Die große Flucht: Das Schicksal der Vertriebenen*. Munich: Econ.

Koch, Thilo. 1995: "Die rote Optik." In *Blicke in die Welt. Reportagen und Magazine des nordwestdeutschen Fernsehens in den 50er und 60er Jahren,* eds. H.-B. Heller and P. Zimmermann. Constance: UVK-Medien/Ölschläger.

Koebner, Thomas, Rolf-Peter Janz, and Frank Trommler, eds. 1985. *"Mit uns zieht die neue Zeit": Der Mythos Jugend*. Frankfurt am Main: Suhrkamp.

Koepnick, Lutz. 2002. *The Dark Mirror*. Berkeley: University of California Press.

Kolle, O. 1953. "Das Glück hat keine Chance: *Lohn der Angst*: Clouzot's filmisches Meisterwerk." *Frankfurter Nachtausgabe*. 30 September.

König, Ingelore et al eds. 1996. *Zwischen Marx und Muck: DEFA-Filme für Kinder*. Berlin: Henschel.

Konsalik, Heinz G. 1956. *Der Arzt von Stalingrad*. Munich: Kindler.

Krebs, Helmut, ed. 1996. *DEFA Dokumentarfilme und Wochenschau in Deutschland Ost und Deutschland West*. Oberhausen: Verlag Karl Maria Laufen.

Kreimeier, Klaus. 1985. "Der westdeutsche Film in den fünfziger Jahren." *Die fünfziger Jahre*, ed. Dieter Bänsch. Tübingen: Narr.

———. 1999. *The UFA Story*. Trans. Robert Kimber and Rita Kimber. Berkeley: University of California Press.

Kristeva, Julia. 1982. *Powers of Horror: An Essay on Abjection*. New York: Columbia University Press.

Krzeminski, Adam and Adam Michnik. 2002. "Wo Geschichte europäisch wird: Das 'Zentrum gegen Vertreibungen' gehört nach Breslau." *Die Zeit*, no. 26.

Kubaschewski, Ilse. 1957. "Det greift ans Herz," *Der Spiegel*, no. 4: 43.

Lacan, Jacques. 1977. *Four Fundamental Concepts of Psychoanalysis*. Trans. Alan Sheridan. New York: Norton.

Lang, Fritz. 1959. "Drehvermerke." Cinema and Television Library Archive. The University of Southern California. Fritz Lang Collection Box 18: 3: n. p.

Lange, Peter. 2000. "Vor 50 Jahren: der Bundestag plädiert für den Abschluss der Entnazifizierung." Berlin: Deutschland Radio. 16 December.

Laplanche, Jean, and Jean-Betrand Pontalis. 1967. *The Language of Psychoanalysis*, trans. D. Nicholson-Smith. London: Hogarth Press.

Lemke, Michael. 1995. "Instrumentalisierter Antifaschismus und SED-Kampagnenpolitik 1960–1968." In *Die geteilte Vergangenheit. Zum Umgang mit Nationalsozialismus und Widerstand in beiden deutschen Staaten*, ed. Jürgen Danyel. Berlin: Akademie Verlag.

Leyda, Jay. 1967. *Filme aus Filmen—Eine Studie über den Kompilationsfilm*. Berlin: Henschelverlag.

Luhmann, Niklas. 1958. "Der Funktionsbegriff in der Verwaltungswissenschaft." *Verwaltungsarchiv*, no. 2: 97–105.

———. 1962. "Funktion und Kausalität." *Kölner Zeitschrift für Soziologie und Sozialpsychologie*, no.14: 617–44.

———. 1964. *Funktionen und Folgen formaler Organisation*. Berlin: Duncker und Humblot.

———. 1977. *Funktion der Religion*. Frankfurt am Main: Suhrkamp.

———. 1995. *Die Kunst der Gesellschaft*. Frankfurt am Main: Suhrkamp.

———. 2002. *Die Politik der Gesellschaft*. Frankfurt am Main: Suhrkamp.

Lungstrum, Janet. 1997. "Metropolis and the Technosexual Woman of German Modernity." In *Women in the Metropolis: Gender and Modernity in Weimar Culture*, ed. Katharina von Ankum. Berkeley: University of California Press.

Lüthge, Bobby. 1951. "Remaking." *Filmblätter*, nos. 51–52: 1065–66.

Maase, Kaspar. 2000. *BRAVO Amerika: Erkundungen zur Jugendkultur der Bundesrepublik in den fünfziger Jahren*. Hamburg: Junius.

———. 2001. "Establishing Cultural Democracy: Youth, Americanization, and the Irresistible Rise of Popular Culture." In *Miracle Years: A Cultural History of West Germany, 1949–1968*, ed. Hanna Schissler. Princeton: Princeton University Press.

Maetzig Papers. Stiftung Archiv der Akademie der Künste. Berlin, Federal Republic of Germany.

Maltin, Leonard. 1994. *Leonard Maltin's Movie Encyclopedia*. New York: Harper Collins.

Mannheim, Karl. 1945. "Die Rolle der Universitäten: Aus einer deutschen Sendung der Londoner Rundfunks." *Neue Auslese*, no. 4: 50.

Marcuse, Herbert. 1966. *One Dimensional Man: Studies in the Ideology of Advanced Industrial Society*. Boston: Beacon Press.

May, Joe. 1922. "Ist die Ausstattung beim Film die Hauptsache, oder ist es das Spiel?" *Der Kinemat*.

Mayer, Mathias and Jens Tismar. 1997. *Kunstmärchen*. 3rd ed. Stuttgart: Metzler.

Mayne, Judith. 1993. *Cinema and Spectatorship*. New York: Routledge.

Mazdon, Lucy. 2000. *Encore Hollywood: Remaking French Cinema*. London: BFI.

McClintock, Anne. 1995. *Imperial Leather: Race, Gender and Sexuality in Colonial Conquest*. New York: Routledge.

McGilligan, Patrick. 1997. *Fritz Lang: The Nature of the Beast*. New York: St. Martin's Press.

McNeece, Lucy Stone. 1996. *Art and Politics in Duras' "India Cycle."* Gainesville: University of Florida Press.

Mennel, Barbara. 2003. "White Law and the Missing Black Body in Fritz Lang's *Fury* (1936)." *Quarterly Review of Film and Video*, no. 3: 203–23.

Menter, Leo. 1948. "Der neue Film." *Weltbühne*, no. 50, 14 December.

Merivale, Patricia, and Susan E. Sweeney, eds. 1999. *Detecting Texts. The Metaphysical Detective Story from Poe to Postmodernism.* Philadelphia: University of Pennsylvania Press.

Merkelbach, Bernhard and Dirk Ulf Stötzel. 1990. "Das Kinderfernsehen der ARD in den 50er Jahren." In *Fernsehen für Kinder. Vom Experiment zum Konzept*, eds. Hans Dieter Erlinger et al. Siegen: Arbeitsheft Bildschirmmedien 16.

Metz, Christian. 1975. *The Imaginary Signifier: Psychoanalysis and the Cinema.* Trans. Celia Britton, Annwyl Williams, Ben Brewster, and Alfred Guzzetti. Bloomington: Indiana University Press.

Meurer, Hans Joachim. 2000. *Cinema and National Identity in a Divided Germany,1979–1989.* Lewiston: Edwin Mellen Press.

Milne, Tom. 1969. *Mamoulian.* Bloomington: University of Illinois Press.

Mitscherlich, Alexander and Margarethe Mitscherlich. 1975 (1967). *The Inability to Mourn: Principles of Collective Behavior.* Trans. Beverley R. Placzek. New York: Grove Press.

Moeller, Robert G. 2001. *War Stories: The Search for a Usable Past in the Federal Republic of Germany.* Berkeley: University of California Press.

———. 2003. "Sinking Ships, the Lost *Heimat* and Broken Taboos: Günter Grass and the Politics of Memory in Contemporary Germany." *Contemporary European History*, no. 2: 147–81.

Moser, Karin. 2002. "Propaganda und Gegenpropaganda: Das 'kalte' Wechselspiel während der alliierten Besatzung in Österreich." *medien & zeit*, no.1: 27–42.

Mosse, George. 1985. *Nationalism and Sexuality.* Madison: University of Wisconsin Press.

Mückenberger, Christiane. 1994. "1945–1960 Aufbruch und Stagnation." In *Filmstadt Babelsberg: Zur Geschichte des Studios und seiner Filme.* Potsdam: Filmmuseum and Berlin: Nikolai.

———. 1997. "DEFA und 'Kalter Krieg.' Der Blick nach Westen." *Die Bundesrepublik Deutschland im Spiegel der DDR-Medien.* 2nd ed. Bonn: Bundeszentrale für politische Bildung.

———. 2000. "Auseinandersetzung im DEFA-Dokumentarfilm mit dem deutschen Faschismus unter besonderer Berücksichtigung der fünfziger Jahre." In *Der geteilte Himmel. Arbeit, Alltag und Geschichte im ost- und westdeutschen Film*, eds. Gebhard Moldenhauer and Peter Zimmermann. Constance: UVK.

Mückenberger, Christine and Günther Jordan. 1994. *"Sie sehen selbst, Sie hören selbst . . .": Die DEFA von ihren Anfängen bis 1949.* Marburg: Hitzeroth.

Mulvey, Laura. 1988. "Visual Pleasure and Narrative Cinema." In *Feminism and Film Theory*, ed. Constance Penley. New York: Routledge.

Murray, Bruce. 1990. *Film and the German Left in the Weimar Republic: From "Caligari" to "Kuhle Wampe."* Austin: University of Texas Press.

Naimark, Norman. 1995. *The Russians in Germany: A History of the Soviet Zone of Occupation, 1945–49.* Cambridge: Harvard University Press.

Nederveen-Pieterse, Jan. 1992. *White on Black: Images of Africa and Blacks in Western Popular Culture.* New Haven: Yale University Press.

Neue Filmverleih GmbH-Zentralpresseabteilung. 1958. "Stets der Überlegene: Peter van Eyck." *Das Mädchen Rosemarie* (press promotion brochure).

Neues Deutschland. 5 January 1954.

Neumeyer, David and James Buehler. 2001. "Analytical and Interpretive Approaches to Film Music (ii): Analysing the Music." In *Film Music: Critical Approaches*, ed. K. J. Donnelly. New York: Continuum.

Nolte, Ernst. 1985. *Deutschland und der kalte Krieg.* 2nd ed. Stuttgart: Klett-Cotta.

NY4003. Nachlasse Ernst Thälmann. Stiftung Archiv der Parteien und Massenorganisationen der ehemaligen DDR im Bundesarchiv. Berlin, Federal Republic of Germany.

NY4036. Nachlasse Wilhelm Pieck. Stiftung Archiv der Parteien und Massenorganisationen der ehemaligen DDR im Bundesarchiv. Berlin, Federal Republic of Germany.

NY4182. Nachlasse Walter Ulbricht. Stiftung Archiv der Parteien und Massenorganisationen der ehemaligen DDR im Bundesarchiv. Berlin, Federal Republic of Germany.

NY4219. Nachlasse Michael Tschesno-Hell. Stiftung Archiv der Parteien und Massenorganisationen der ehemaligen DDR im Bundesarchiv. Berlin, Federal Republic of Germany.

Odenwald, Ulrike. 2001. "Aufbruch zur Kontinuität: Die frühe DEFA-Kinderfilmproduktion." In *Apropos: Film 2001. Das Jahrbuch der DEFA-Stiftung.* Berlin: Das Neue Berlin.

Odin, Roger. 2000. *De la fiction.* Brussels: De Boeck Université.

Opgenoorth, Ernst. 1984. *Volksdemokratie im Kino. Propagandistische Selbstdarstellung der SED im DEFA-Dokumentarfilm 1946–1957.* Köln: Verlag Wissenschaft und Politik.

Orbanz, Eva, ed. 1977. *Wolfgang Staudte.* Berlin: Spiess.

Osterland, Martin. 1970. *Gesellschaftsbilder in Filmen. Eine soziologische Untersuchung des filmangebots der Jahre 1949–1964.* Stuttgart: Enke.

Penley, Constance. 1985. "Feminism, Film Theory, and the Bachelor Machines." *m/f* 10: 39–59.

Petro, Patrice. 1989. *Joyless Streets: Women and Melodramatic Representation in Wemar Germany.* Princeton: Princeton University Press.

Pfeil, E. 1948. *Der Flüchtling: Gestalt einer Zeitenwende.* Hamburg: H. von Hugo.

Pike, David. 1992. *The Politics of Culture in Soviet-Occupied Germany, 1945–49.* Stanford: Stanford University Press.

Pleyer, Peter. 1965. *Deutscher Nachkriegsfilm 1946–1948.* Studien zur Publizistik, Münsterische Reihe. Vol. 4. Münster: C. J. Fahle.

Plschek, Hans-Peter. 1959. "Die Finanzierung der westdeutschen Filmproduktion nach dem zweiten deutschen Weltkrieg." Ph.D. diss., University of Munich.

Podehl, Peter. 1953. "Zur Geschichte des Films vom *Kleinen Muck.*" *Neue Filmwelt,* no.5: 16–17.

Poiger, Ute. 2000. *Jazz, Rock, and Rebels: Cold War Politics and American Culture in a Divided Germany.* Berkeley: University of California Press.

Prinzler, Hans Helmut. 1995. *Chronik des deutschen Films 1895–1994.* Stuttgart: Metzler.

Pruha, Martin. 1996. "Agfacolor und Kalter Krieg: Die Geschichte der Wien-Film am Rosenhügel 1946–1955." In *Ohne Untertitel,* eds. Ruth Beckermann and Christa Blümlinger. Vienna: Sonderzahl.

Rathkolb, Oliver. 1988. "Die 'Wien-Film'-Produktion am Rosenhügel: Österreichische Filmproduktion und Kalter Krieg." In *Medienkultur in Österreich, Film, Photographie, Fernsehen und Video in der 2. Republik,* eds. H. H. Fabris and K. Luger. Vienna: Kulturstudien 11.

Reichmann, Hans-Peter und Walter Schobert. 1991 *Abschied von gestern: Bundesdeutscher Film der sechziger und siebziger Jahre.* Frankfurt am Main: Deutsches Filmmuseum.

Renov, Michael, ed. 1993. *Theorizing Documentary.* New York and London: Routledge.

Richter-de Vroe, Klaus. 1990. "Zwischen Wirklichkeit und Ideal." In *77 Märchenfilme: Ein Filmführer für jung und alt,* eds. Eberhard Berger und Joachim Giera. Berlin: Henschel.

Riedel, Heide, ed. 1993. *Mit uns zieht die neue Zeit . . . 40 Jahre DDR-Medien.* Berlin: Vistas.

Roeber, Georges and Gerhard Jacoby. 1973. *Handbuch der filmwirtschaftlichen Medienbereiche; die wirtschaftlichen Erscheinungsformen des Films auf den Geieten der Unterhaltung, der Werbung, der Bildung und des Fernsehens.* Pullach near Munich: Verlag Dokumentation.

Ross, Kristin. 1995. *Fast Cars, Clean Bodies: Decolonization and the Reordering of French Culture.* Cambridge: MIT University Press.

Rülicke-Weiler, Käthe. 1979. *Film- und Fernsehkunst der DDR. Traditionen—Beispiele—Tendenzen.* Berlin: Henschelverlag.

Ruschkowski, André. 1998. *Elektronische Klänge und musikalische Entdeckungen.* Stuttgart: Reclam.

Sagar, D. J. 1991. *Major Political Events in Indo-China 1945–1990.* Oxford: Facts on File.

Said, Edward W. 1978. *Orientalism.* New York: Vintage Books.

Salecl, Renata. 1994. *The Spoils of Freedom: Feminism and Psychoanalysis after the Fall of Socialism.* New York: Routledge.

Santner, Eric. 1990. *Stranded Objects: Mourning, Memory, and Film in Postwar Germany.* Ithaca: Cornell University Press.

Schachinger, Sonja. 1993. "Der österreichische Heimatfilm als Konstruktionsprinzip nationaler Identität in Österreich nach 1945." Ph.D. diss., University of Vienna.

Schelsky, Helmut. 1953. *Wandlungen der deutschen Familie in der Gegenwart: Darstellung und Deutung einer empirisch-soziologischen Tatbestandsaufnahme.* Dortmund: Ardey.

Schenk, Ralf. 1994. "Mitten im Kalten Krieg." In *Das Zweite Leben der Filmstadt Babelsberg: DEFA-Spielfilme, 1946–1992,* ed. Ralf Schenk. Potsdam: Henschl.

Schieder, Theodor. 1954. *Die Vertreibung der deutschen Bevölkerung aus den Gebieten östlich der Oder-Neisse.* Bonn: Bundesministerium für Vertriebene.

Schittly, Dagmar. 2002. *Zwischen Regie und Regime. Die Filmpolitik der SED im Spiegel der DEFA-Produktionen.* Berlin: Christoph Links Verlag.

Schmieding, Walter. 1961. *Kunst oder Kasse. Der Ärger mit dem deutschen Film.* Hamburg: Rütten & Loening.

Schröder, Nicolaus. 1995. *Filmindustrie.* Reinbek by Hamburg: Rowolt.

Schulte-Sasse, Linda. 1996. *Entertaining the Third Reich.* Durham: Duke University Press.

Schultze, Norbert. 1995. *Mit dir, Lili Marleen.* Zürich: Atlantis.

Schulze, Brigitte. 1997. "Land des Grauens und der Wunder: Indien im deutschen Kino." In *Triviale Tropen: Exotische Reise-und Abenteuerfilme aus Deutschland 1919–1939,* ed. Jörg Schöning. Munich: edition text + kritik.

Schuster, Andrea. 1999. *Zerfall oder Wandel der Kultur? Eine kultur-soziologische Interpretation des deutschen Films.* Wiesbaden: Deutscher Universitätsverlag.

Schwarz, Ingelene. 1956. "Wesenszüge der modernen deutschen Frauenzeitschrift," Ph.D. diss., Freie Universität Berlin.

Schwarz, Uta. 2002. *Wochenschau, westdeutsche Identität und Geschlecht in den fünfziger Jahren.* Frankfurt am Main and New York: Campus Verlag.

Schweins, Annemarie. 1958. *Die Entwicklung der deutschen Filmwirtschaft.* Nuremberg: n.p.

Seeßlen, Georg. 1990. "Der Heimatfilm. Zur Mythologie eines Genres." In *Sprung im Spiegel: Filmisches Wahrnehmen zwischen Fiktion und Wirklichkeit.* Vienna: Sonderzahl.

Seidl, Claudius. 1987. *Der deutsche Film der fünfziger Jahre.* Munich: Wilhelm Heyne.

Seiffert, Rachel. 2001. *The Dark Room.* London: Heinemann.

Shandley, Robert. 2001. *Rubble Films : German Cinema in the Shadow of the Third Reich.* Philadelphia: Temple University Press.

Shaw, Tony. 2001. *British Cinema and the Cold War. The State, Propaganda and Consensus.* London and New York: I. B. Tauris.

Shohat, Ella. 1997. "Gender and Culture of Empire: Toward a Feminist Ethnography of the Cinema." In *Visions of the East: Orientalism in Film,* eds. Matthew Bernstein and Gaylyn Studlar. New Brunswick: Rutgers University Press.

Silberman, Marc. 1995. *German Cinema: Texts in Context.* Detroit: Wayne State University Press.

———. 2005. "Hauff-Verfilmungen der fünfziger Jahre: Märchen und postfaschistischer Medienwandel." In *Wilhelm Hauff oder die Virtuosität der Einbildungskraft,* eds. Ernst Osterkamp, Andrea Polaschegg and Erhard Schütz. Göttingen: Wallstein.

Silverman, Kaja. 1988. *The Acoustic Mirror: The Female Voice in Psychoanalysis and Cinema.* Bloomington: Indiana University Press.

Spazier, Ingrun and Michael Wedel. 1984. "Richard Eichberg." *CineGraph.* Munich: edition text + kritik.

SPIO. 1962. *Statistisches Bericht.* Wiesbaden: Spitzenorganisation der Filmwirtschaft.

Stacey, Jackie. 1989. "Reception Studies: The Death of the Reader." In *The Cinematic Text: Methods and Approaches,* ed. R. B. Palmer New York: AMS Press.

———. *Star Gazing: Hollywood Cinema and Female Spectatorship.* London and New York: Routledge.

Staiger, Janet. 1992. *Interpreting Films: Studies in the Historical Reception of American Cinema.* Princeton: Princeton University Press.

Steiner, Gertraud. 1987. *Die Heimat-macher: Kino in Österreich 1946–1966.* Vienna: Verlag für Gesellschaftskritik.

———. 1997. *Traumfabrik Rosenhügel.* Vienna: Compress Verlag.

Steinhauer. 1948. "Inge von Wangenheim." *Die neue Filmwelt,* no. 2: 25.

Steinle, Matthias. 2003. "Vom Feindbild zum Fremdbild." *Die gegenseitige Darstellung von BRD und DDR im Dokumentarfilm.* (Close Up, Bd. 18) Constance: UVK.

Tägliche Rundschau. 28 March 1954.

Tent, James. 1982. "Chapter 1 Planning for Reeducation." *Mission on the Rhine: Reeducation and Denazification in American-Occupied Germany.* Chicago: University of Chicago Press.

Thiel, Reinhold E. 1970. "Was wurde aus Goebbels' Ufa?" *Film Aktuell,* no. 2.

Töteberg, Michael. 1985. *Fritz Lang.* Hamburg: Rowohlt.

Traven, B. 1926. *Das Totenschiff.* Leipzig: Büchergilde Gutenberg.

Trimborn, Jürgen. 1998. *Der deutsche Heimatfilm der fünfziger Jahre: Motive, Symbole und Handlungsmuster.* Cologne: Teiresias.

Trumpener, Katie. *Divided Screens: Postwar Cinema in East and West.* Princeton: Princeton University Press (forthcoming).

U.N. 1966. "Der Spion, der aus der Kälte kam." *Filmkritik,* no. 4.

Ungureit, Heinz. 1964. "Filmpolitik in der Bundesrepublik." *Filmkritik* 8.1: 9–20.

Varsori, Antonio. 1994. "The Western Powers and the Geneva Summit Conference (1955)." In *Europe 1945–1990s: The End of an Era?* ed. Antonio Varsori. New York: Palgrave.

Vogel, Amos. 1974. *Film as a Subversive Art.* New York: Random House.

von Harbou, Thea. 1922. (1917) *Das indische Grabmal.* Berlin: Ullstein.

von Moltke, Johannes. 2002a. "Evergreens: The *Heimat* Genre." In *The German Cinema Book,* eds. Tim Bergfelder, Erica Carter, and Deniz Göktürk. London: BFI.

———. 2002b. "*Heimat* and History: *Viehjud Levi.*" *New German Critique,* no. 87: 83–105.

———. 2005. *No Place like Home: Locations of Heimat in German Cinema.* Berkeley: University of California Press.

von Steffens, Hans. 1959. "Rommel ruft Kairo—Eine grobe Film-Lüge." *Der Stahlhelm.* June.

von Thüna, Ulrich. 1989. "Filmzeitschriften der fünfziger Jahre." In *Zwischen gestern und morgen. Westdeutscher Nachkriegsfilm 1946–1962,* eds. Hilmar Hoffmann and Walter Schobert. Frankfurt am Main: Filmmuseum.

Weinberger-Thomas, Catherine. 1987. "Fritz Lang: Le Tigre mis au Tombeau." *Revue du Cinéma,* no. 433: 75–88.

Westermann, Bärbel. 1990. *Nationale Identität im Spielfilm der fünfziger Jahre.* Frankfurt am Main: Peter Lang.

Whyte, William Hollingsworth. 1956. *The Organization Man.* New York: Simon & Schuster.

Wiedemann, Dieter. 1998. "'Es war einmal . . .'—Reise ins DEFA-Märchenland." In *Märchen: Arbeiten mit DEFA-Kinderfilmen,* eds. Ingelore König, Dieter Wiedemann, and Lothar Wolf. Munich: KoPäd Verlag.

Wiener, Susan. 2001. *Enfants Terribles: Youth and Femininity in the Mass Media in France, 1945–68.* Baltimore: Johns Hopkins University Press.

Winston, Jane Bradley. 2001. *Postcolonial Duras: Cultural Memory in Postwar France.* New York: Palgrave.

Wolff, Willi. 1922. "Filmreisen oder Kunstbauten?" *Film-Kurier* 8: 2–3.

Wollenberg, Erich. 2000. "Thälmann—Film und Wirklichkeit." In *Ernst Thälmann: Mensch und Mythos,* ed. Peter Monteath. Amsterdam: Rodopi.

Worschech, Rudolf. 1992a. "Ein schwaches Remake: Arno Hauke und die Ufa der 50er Jahre." In *Das Ufa–Buch. Kunst und Krisen, Stars und Regisseure, Wirtschaft und Politik,* eds. Hans-Michael Bock and Michael Töteberg. Frankfurt am Main: Zweitausendeins.

———. 1992b. "Rauhe Wasser: Georg Tresslers *Das Totenschiff.*" In *Das Ufa–Buch. Kunst und Krisen, Stars und Regisseure, Wirtschaft und Politik,* eds. Hans-Michael Bock and Michael Töteberg. Frankfurt am Main: Zweitausendeins.

———. 1992c. "Ausverkauft: Die Ufa schlingert." In *Das Ufa–Buch. Kunst und Krisen, Stars und Regisseure, Wirtschaft und Politik,* eds. Hans-Michael Bock and Michael Töteberg. Frankfurt am Main: Zweitausendeins.

Wortig, Kurt. 1961. *Ihre Hoheit Lieschen Müller. Hof- und Hinterhofgespräche um Film und Fernsehen.* Munich: Kreisselmeier.

Zantop, Susanne. 1997. *Colonial Fantasies: Conquest, Family, and Nation in Precolonial Germany, 1770–1870.* Durham: Duke University Press.

Zentral-Presse- und Werbeabteilung der Herzog-Film GmbH, Munich. 1949. *Hallo Fräulein!* (promotional brochure).

Zielinski, Siegfried. 1999. *Audiovisions.* Trans. Gloria Constance. Amsterdam: Amsterdam University Press.

Zimmermann, Peter. 1998. "Frères et sœurs ennemis dans la guerre froide des médias. Le film documentaire et la télévision des deux Allemagnes pendant les années 50." In *L'âge d'or du documentaire. Europe: Années cinquantes,* ed. Roger Odin . Vol. 1. Paris: L'Harmattan.

Zimmermann, Peter. 2002. "Stereotypen: dominant. Deutsche Zeitgeschichte in dokumentarischen Programmen." *epd medien,* no. 97: 21–7.

Zizek, Slavoj. 1994. *The Metastases of Enjoyment.* London: Verso.

———. 1996. "Fantasy as Political Category: A Lacanian Approach." *Journal for the Psychoanalysis of Culture and Society* 1.1 (Fall 1996): 77–85.

FILM TITLES

08/15 J. May (1954–55)

1. April 2000 Wolfgang Liebeneiner (1952)

1-2-3 Corona Hans Müller (1948)

1984 Michael Anderson (1956)

Abenteuer im Schloß Rudolf Steinböck (Adventure in the Castle, 1952)

Abschied von den Wolken Gottfried Reinhardt (Rebel Flight to Cuba, 1959)

African Queen, The John Huston (1951)

Agenten im Schatten einer Partei Joachim Hadaschik (Agents in the Shadow of a Party, 1957)

Aktion J Walter Heynowski (Action J, 1961)

Alarm Herbert B. Fredersdorf (1941)

alte Försterhaus, Das Harald Philipp (The Old Forester House, 1956)

Am Tag, als der Regen kam Gerd Oswald (The Day It Rained, 1959)

Ami Go Home Ella Ensink and Karl Gass (1952)

Anders als du und ich Veit Harlan (Different from You and Me, 1957)

Arche Nora Werner Klingler (Nora's Ark, 1948)

Archive sagen aus (The Archives Speak, series)

Armee der SED, Die ND. (The Army of the SED, 1957)

Arzt von Staligrad, Der Geza von Radvanyi (The Doctor of Stalingrad, 1958)

Attack R. Aldrich (1956)

Attentat auf die Freiheit—Berliner Dokumente ND. (Assault on Freedom—Berlin Documents, 1959)

Augenzeuge, Der (The Eyewitness, series)

Baby Face Alfred E. Green (1933)

Bel Ami Louis Daquin (1957)

Berlin kommt wieder Hans Fritz Köllner (Berlin is Coming Back, 1951)

Berlin produziert Hanno Jahn (Berlin Produces, 1950)

Berlin—Ecke Schönhauser Gerhard Klein (Berlin—Corner Schoenhauser, 1957)

Berlin—Stadt der Freiheit A. W. Uhlig (Berlin—City of Freedom, 1959)

Beyond a Reasonable Doubt Fritz Lang (1956)

Bilder aus der Sowjetzone 1955/56 ND (Images from the Soviet Zone 1955/56, 1956)

Birds, The Alfred Hitchcock (1963)

Blick hinter den Eisernen Vorhang ND (A Look behind the Iron Curtain, 1952)

Brot der frühen Jahre, Das Herbert Vesely (The Bread of those Early Years, 1962)

Brücke zur Zukunft Ludwig Lober (Bridge to the Future, 1947)

Brücke, Die Arthur Pohl (The Bridge, 1949)

Brücke, Die Bernhard Wicki (The Bridge, 1959)

Canaris Alfred Weidenmann (Canaris: Master Spy, 1954)

Casablanca Michael Curtiz (1942)

Cendrillon Georges Méliès (Cinderella, 1899)

Conversation, The Francis Ford Coppola (1974)

Cornet, Der Walter Reisch (*The Cornet*, 1955)

D III 88 Herbert Maisch (1939)

Detektive Rudolf Thome (Detectives, 1968)

Deutschlandspiegel (German Monthly Mirror, series)

Doktor Mabuse, der Spieler Fritz Lang (Dr. Mabuse, The Gambler, 1922)

Don Juan Walter Kohn-Veltée (1955)

Donne senza nome Geza von Radvanyi (Women Without Names, 1949)

doppelte Lottchen, Das Josef von Baky (Two Times Lotte, 1950)

Double Indemnity Billy Wilder (1944)

Dr. Crippen an Bord Erich Engels (Dr. Crippen Onboard, 1942)

Dr. Crippen lebt Erich Engels (Dr. Crippen Lives, 1958)

Dr. Jekyll and Mr. Hyde Rouben Mamoulian (1931)

Du und mancher Kamerad Andrew Thorndike and Annelie Thorndike (You and a Few Comrades, 1956)

Durchbruch Lok 234 Frank Wisbar (The Breakthrough, 1963)

Echo der Berge Alfons Stummer (Echo of the Mountains, 1954; alternate title: *Der Förster vom Silberwald*)

Ein Alibi zerbricht Alfred Vohrer (An Alibi for Death, 1963)

Ein Tagebuch für Anne Frank Joachim Hellwig (A Diary for Anne Frank, 1959)

Ein Weg—ein Ziel Bruno Kleberg (One Path—One Purpose, 1948)

Eine Nacht in Venedig Georg Wildhagen (A Night in Venice, 1953; alternate title: *Komm in die Gondel*)

Einmal ist keinmal Konrad Wolf (Once Is Never, 1955)

Emil und die Detektive Gerhard Lamprecht (Emil and the Detectives, 1931)

Endstation Liebe Georg Tressler (Last Stop Love, 1957)

English Patient, The Anthony Minghella (1996)

Epilog: Das Geheimnis der Orplid Helmut Käutner (Epilogue: The Orplid Mystery, 1950)

Ernst Thälmann —Führer seiner Klasse Kurt Maetzig (Ernst Thälmann—Leader of His Class, 1955)

Ernst Thälmann—Sohn seiner Klasse Kurt Maetzig (Ernst Thälmann—Son of His Class, 1954)

Es geschah am 20. Juli Georg Wilhelm Pabst (It Happened on 20 July, 1955; alternate title: *Jackboot Mutiny*)

Es geschah am hellichten Tag Ladislao Vajda (It Happened in Broad Daylight, 1958)

Fabrik der Offiziere Bernhard Wicki (The Officer Factory, 1960)

Fall Dr. Wagner, Der. Harald Mannl (The Case of Dr. Wagner, 1954)

Fall Rabanser, Der Kurt Hoffmann (The Rabanser Case, 1950)

Feinde des Friedens Helmut Schneider (Enemies of Peace, 1954)

feu aux poudres, Le Henri Decoin (Burning Fuse, 1957)

Feuerzeug, Das Siegfried Hartmann (The Tinder Box, 1959)

Fidelio Walter Felsenstein (1955)

Figaros Hochzeit Georg Wildhagen (The Marriage of Figaro, 1949)

Film ohne Titel Rudolf Jugert (Film Without a Name, 1948)

Finale Ulrich Urfurth (1948)

Five Graves to Cairo Billy Wilder (1943)

Flucht ins Dunkel Arthur Maria Rabenalt (Flight into Darkness, 1939)

Foolish Wives Erich von Stroheim (1922)

Forbidden Planet Fred M. Wilcox (1956)

Foreign Affair, A Billy Wilder (1948)

Förster vom Silberwald, Der Alfons Stummer (Forester of Silberwald 1955; alternate title: *Echo der Berge*)

Foxhole in Cairo John Llewellyn Moxey (1961)

Franz Schubert —Ein Leben in zwei Sätzen Walter Kolm-Veltèe (Franz Schubert, 1953)

Frühling auf dem Eis Georg Jacoby (Springtime on Ice, 1951)

Fury Fritz Lang (1936)

Gasparone Karl Paryla (1956)

Geheimaktion Schwarze Kapelle Ralph Habib (The Black Chapel, 1959)

Geliebte Genossin Joachim Mock (Beloved Comrade, 1961; alternate title: *Ninotschka und Peer*)

Germania anno zero Roberto Rosselini (Germany Year Zero, 1947)

Geschichte vom armen Hassan, Die Gerhard Klein (The Story of Poor Hassan, 1958)

Geschichte vom kleinen Muck, Die Wolfgang Staudte (The Story of Little Mook, 1953)

Geschwader Fledermaus Erich Engel (Bat Squandron, 1958)

Geständnisse einer Sechzehnjährigen GeorgTressler (Confessions of a Sixteen-Year-Old, 1960)

Gesucht wird Majora Hermann Pfeiffer (Search for Majora, 1949)

Gewehre der Frau Carrar, Die Egon Monk (Senora Carrar's Rifles, 1953)

Gift im Zoo Hans Müller (Poison in the Zoo, 1952)

Gilda Charles Vidor (1946)

gläserne Turm, Der Harald Braun (The Glass Tower, 1957)

Götter der Pest Rainer Werner Fassbinder (Gods of the Plague, 1970)

Gottes Engel sind überall Hans Thimig (God's Angels Are Everywhere, 1947)

Grand Jeu, Le Robert Siodmak (Flesh and the Woman, 1954)

grosse Liebe, Die Rolf Hansen (The Great Love, 1942)

Grün ist die Heide Hans Behrendt (Green Is the Heather, 1932)

Grün ist die Heide Hans Deppe (Green Is the Heather, 1951)

Haie und kleine Fische Frank Wisbar (Sharks and Small Fish, 1957)

Halbstarken, Die Georg Tressler (The Hooligans, 1956)

Halbzarte, Die Rolf Thiele (Eva, 1958)

Hallo Fräulein! Rudolf Jugert (Hello Fraulein!, 1949)

Hangmen Also Die Fritz Lang (1943)

Hannerl Ernst Marischka (Little Hanna, 1952; alternate title: *Ich tanze mit dir in den Himmel hinein*)

Heimat, Deine Lieder Paul May (Heimat, Your Songs, 1959)

Heimat, eine deutsche Chronik Edgar Reitz (Heimat, 1984)

Herr Puntila und sein Knecht Matti Alberto Cavalcanti (Herr Puntila and His Servant Matti, 1955)

Herz einer Frau, Das Georg Jacoby (The Heart of a Woman, 1951)

High Noon Fred Zinnemann (1952)

Hitlerjunge Quex Hans Steinhoff (Hitler Youth Quex, 1933)

Hunde, wollt ihr ewig leben? Frank Wisbar (Dogs, Do You Want to Live Forever?, 1958)

Ich klage an Wolfgang Liebeneiner (I Accuse, 1941)

In jenen Tagen Helmut Käutner (In Those Days, 1947)

indische Grabmal, Das Fritz Lang (The Indian Tomb, 1959)

indische Grabmal, Das Rudolf Eichberg (The Indian Tomb, 1937)

indische Grabmal, Das: Der Tiger von Eschnapur Joe May (The Tiger of Bengal, 1921)

indische Grabmal, Das: Die Sendung des Yoghi Joe May (The Mission of the Yogi, 1921)

Indische Rache Richard Eichberg (Indian Revenge, 1952)

Informer, The John Ford (1935)

Irgendwo in Berlin Gerhard Lamprecht (Somewhere in Berlin, 1946)

Ist Mama nicht fabelhaft? Peter Beauvais (Isn't Mama Fabulous? 1958)

Jonas Ottomar Domnick (1957)

Junge Adler Alfred Weidenmann (Young Eagles, 1944)

Jungen vom Kranichsee, Die Arthur Pohl (The Boys of Crane Lake, 1950)

kalte Herz, Das Paul Verhoeven (The Cold Heart, 1950)

Kamennyy tsvetok Alelsandr Ptushko (Die steinerne Blume, The Stone Flower, 1946)

Kampfgeschwader Lützow Hans Bertram (Lutzow Bomber Squadron, 1941)

Käpt'n Bay-Bay Helmut Käutner (1953)

KgU—Kampfgruppe der Unmenschlichkeit Joachim Hadaschik (KgU—Brigade of Inhumanity, 1956)

Kind der Donau, Das Georg Jacoby (Marika, 1951)

Kinder, Mütter und ein General Laszlo Benedek (Children, Mothers, and the General, 1955)

Kleine Hofkonzert, Das Paul Verhoeven (The Small Court Concert, 1945)

Klute Alan Pakula (1971)

Kolberg Veit Harlan (1945)

Komödiant von Wien, Der Karl Paryla and Karl Stanzl (The Comedian of Vienna, 1954; alternate title: *Girardi*)

Königskinder Helmut Käutner (Royal Children, 1950)

Kuckucks, Die Hans Deppe (The Cuckoo Family, 1949)

Labyrinth Rolf Thiele (1959: alternate title: *Labyrinth der Leidenschaften*)

Laura Otto Preminger (1944)

Letyat zhuravli Mikheil Kalatozishvili (Wenn die Kraniche ziehen, The Cranes Are Flying, 1957)

letzte Akt, Der Georg Wilhelm Pabst (*The Last Ten Days*, 1955; alternate titles: *Last Ten Days of Adolph Hitler; Ten Days to Die*)

letzte Brücke, Die Helmut Käutner (The Last Bridge, 1954)

Liebe 47 Wolfgang Liebeneiner (Love 47, 1948)

Liebling der Götter Gottfried Reinhardt (Sweetheart of the Gods, 1960)

Lifeboat Alfred Hitchcock (1944)

Love Me Tonight Rouben Mamoulian (1932)

lustigen Weiber von Windsor, Die Georg Wildhagen (The Merry Wives of Windsor, 1950)

Luther-Erinnerungsstätten Günther Lincke (Luther Memorials, 1956)

M Fritz Lang (1931)

Mädchen in Uniform Geza von Radvanyi (Girls in Uniform, 1958)

Mädchen Rosemarie, Das Rolf Thiele (The Girl Rosemarie, 1958)

Maltese Falcon, The John Huston (1941)

Mann, der sich selber sucht, Der Geza von Cziffra (The Man in Search of Himself, 1950)

Mein Vater, der Schauspieler Robert Siodmak (My Father, the Actor 1956)

Menschen in Gottes Hand Rolf Meyer (People in God's Hand, 1948)

Mépris, Le Jean-Luc Godard (Contempt, 1963)

Messer im Kopf Reinhard Hauff (Knife in the Head, 1978)

Metropolis Fritz Lang (1927)

Mich dürstet Karl Paryla (I'm Thirsty, 1956)

Mildred Pierce Michael Curtiz (1945)

Mitteldeutsches Tagebuch (Diary from Middle Germany, series)

Mord in Lwow Walter Heynowski (Murder in Lwow, 1959)

Mord und Totschlag Volker Schlöndorff (A Degree of Murder, 1967)

Mörder sind unter uns, Die Wolfgang Staudte (The Murderers Are among Us, 1946)

Morgen ist alles besser Arthur Maria Rabenalt (Everything Will Be Better Tomorrow, 1948)

Morgenrot Gustav Ucicky (Dawn, 1933)

Mr. Arkadin Orson Welles (1955; alternate title: *Confidential Report*)

Mutter Courage und ihre Kinder Wolfgang Staudte (Mother Courage and Her Children, 1955)

Nacht der Zwölf, Die Hans Schweikart (Night of the Twelve, 1945)

Nacht fiel über Gotenhafen Frank Wisbar (Darkness Fell on Gotenhafen, 1959)

Nacht vor der Premiere, Die Georg Jacoby (The Night before the Premiere, 1959)

Nachts, wenn der Teufel kam Robert Siodmak (The Devil Came at Night, 1957)

Neue deutsche Wochenschau (New German Weekly News, series)

neue Kapitel, Das (The New Chapter, 1954)

Niagara Henry Hathaway (1953)

Nibelungen: Siegfried and *Krimhield's Rache* Fritz Lang (The Nibelungs, 1922 and 1924)

Ninotschka und Peer Joachim Mock (Ninitschka and Peer, 1961; alternate title: *Geliebte Genossin*)

Orfeu Negro Marcel Camus (Black Orpheus, 1959)

Pickup on South Street Samuel Fuller (1953)

Pour le Mérite Karl Ritter (Badge of Honor, 1938)

Professor Mamlock Konrad Wolf (1961)

Protokoll Westberlin Helmut Schneider (Film Proceedings West Berlin,1959)

Razzia Werner Klingler (Police Raid, 1947)

Regimentstochter, Die Günther Hänel and Georg C. Klaren (Daughter of the Regiment, 1953)

Rest ist Schweigen, Der Helmut Käutner (The Rest Is Silence, 1959)

Rommel ruft Kairo Wolfgang Schleif (Rommel Calls Cairo, 1959)

Rose Bernd Alfred Halm (1919)

Rose Bernd Wolfgang Staudte (1957)

Rotation Wolfgang Staudte (1949)

Rote Optik, Die Thilo Koch (The Red Lens, series)

Ruf an das Gewissen, Der Karl Anton (The Appeal to Conscience, 1945)

Ruf, Der Josef von Baky (The Last Illusion, 1949)

Run for the Sun Roy Boulting (1956)

Sag die Wahrheit Helmut Weiss (Speak the Truth, 1946)

Salaire de la Peur, Le Henri-Georges Clouzot (Der Lohn der Angst, The Wages of Fear, 1953)

Saure Wochen—Frohe Feste Wolfgang Schleif (Hard Days—Happy Days, 1950)

Schicksal am Lenkrad Aldo Vergano (Destiny at the Steering Wheel, 1954)

Schloss Hubertus Helmut Weiss (Castle Hubertus, 1954)

Schlösser und Katen Kurt Maetzig (Palaces and Huts, 1957)

Schmutziger Engel Alfred Vohrer (Dirty Angel, 1958)

schwarze Kanal, Der (The Black Channel, series)

Schwarzer Kies Helmut Käutner (Black Gravel, 1960)

Schwarzwaldmädel Hans Deppe (Black Forest Girl, 1950)

Schweigen im Walde, Das Helmut Weiss (Silence in the Forest, 1955)

Seesterne Johannes Alexander Hübler-Kahla (Starfish, 1952)

Semmelweis—Retter der Mütter Georg C. Klaren (Dr. Semmelweis, 1950)

Sieben vom Rhein, Die Andrew and Annelie Thorndike (The Seven from the Rhine, 1954)

singende, klingende Bäumchen, Das Francesco Stefani (The Singing, Ringing Tree, 1957)

Singin' in the Rain Stanley Donen and Gene Kelly (1952)

Single-Handed Roy Boulting (1953)

Sissi Ernst Marischka (1955; adapted version released in the U.S. as *Forever My Love*)

Snorkel, The Guy Green (1958)

So macht man Kanzler Joachim Hellwig (That's How Chancellors are Made, 1961)

Solange das Herz schlägt Alfred Weidenmann (As Long as the Heart Beats, 1958)

Sound of Music, The Robert Wise (1965)

Sowjetzone ohne Zensur Erhard Fitze (Soviet Zone Uncensored, 1954)

Spy Who Came in from the Cold, The Martin Ritt (1965)

Stefanie Josef von Baky (1958)

Stern von Afrika, Der Alfred Weidenmann (The Star of Africa, 1957)

Strafbataillon 999 Harald Philipp (Punishment Battalion 999, 1959)

Sünderin, Die Willi Forst (The Story of a Sinner, 1951)

Sunset Boulevard Billy Wilder (1950)

tanzende Herz, Das Wolfgang Liebeneiner (The Dancing Heart, 1953)

tapfere Schneiderlein, Das Helmut Spiess (The Valiant Tailor, 1956)

tausend Augen des Dr. Mabuse, Die Fritz Lang (The Thousand Eyes of Dr. Mabuse, 1960)

Testament des Dr. Mabuse, Das Fritz Lang (The Testament of Dr. Mabuse, 1933)

Teufel vom Mühlenberg, Der Herbert Ballmann (The Devil from Mill Mountain, 1955)

Teufels General, Des Helmut Käutner (The Devil's General, 1955)

Third Man, The Carol Reed (1959)

Tiger von Eschnapur, Der Fritz Lang (The Tiger of Eschnapur, 1959)

Tiger von Eschnapur, Der Richard Eichberg (The Tiger of Eschnapur, 1937)

Tigre du Bengale, Le Richard Eichberg (The Tiger of Bengal, 1938)

Tombeau hindou, Le Richard Eichberg (The Indian Tomb, 1938)

Totenschiff, Das Georg Tressler (Ship of the Dead, 1959)

Toxi Robert A. Stemmle (1952)

Trapp-Familie, Die Wolfgang Liebeneiner (The Trapp Family, 1956)

Tunnel 28 Robert Siodmak (Escape from East Berlin, 1962)

Two-Faced Woman George Cukor (1941)

Unbesiegbaren, Die Arthur Pohl (The Inconquerable, 1953)

Und finden dereinst wir uns wieder Hans Müller (And Someday We Shall Find Each Other Again, 1947)

Und über uns der Himmel Josef von Baky (And the Sky above Us, 1947)

Und wenn's nur einer wär Wolfgang Schleif (And If Only It Were So, 1949)

Und wieder 48! Gustav von Wagenheim ('48 All Over Again! 1948)

Unter 18 Georg Tressler (Under 18, 1957, alternate title: *Noch minderjährig*)

Unter den Brücken Helmut Käutner (Under the Bridges, 1944)

Urlaub auf Sylt Andrew Thorndike and Annelie Thorndike (Vacation on Sylt, 1957)

Valahol Európában Geza von Radvanyi (It Happened In Europe, 1947)

Verlorene Melodie Ernst von Borsody (Vanished Melody, 1952)

Verlorene, Der Peter Lorre (The Lost One, 1951)

Verspätung in Marienborn Rolf Hädrich (Delay in Marienborn, 1963)

verurteilte Dorf, Das Martin Hellwig (The Condemned Village, 1952)

Von Hamburg bis Stralsund Andrew Thorndike (From Hamburg to Stralsund, 1950)

Waldwinter Fritz Peter Buch (Forest Winter, 1936)

Waldwinter Wolfgang Liebeneiner (Forest Winter; alternate title: *Glocken der Heimat*, 1956)

Weg nach oben, Der Karl Gass and Andrew Thorndike (The Ascending Path, 1950)

Wege im Zwielicht Gustav Fröhlich (Paths in Twilight, 1948)

Welt im Film (The World in Film, series)

Wenn am Sonntagabend die Dorfmusik spielt Charles Klein (When The Village Music Plays on Sunday Nights, 1933)

Wenn am Sonntagabend die Dorfmusik spielt Rudolf Schündler (When The Village Music Plays on Sunday Nights, 1953)

Wenn die Heide blüht Hans Deppe (When the Heath Is in Blossom, 1960)

Wer fuhr den grauen Ford? Otto Wernicke (Who Drove the Gray Ford? 1950)

Wohin die Züge fahren Boleslaw Barlog (Where the Trains Go, 1949)

Wunder des Fliegens: der Film eines deutschen Fliegers Heinz Paul (Miracle of Flight: The Film of a German Pilot, 1935)

Wunschkonzert Eduard von Borsody (Request Concert, 1940)

You and Me Fritz Lang (1938)

You Only Live Once Fritz Lang (1937)

Zar und Zimmermann Hans Müller (The Tsar and the Carpenter, 1956)

Zaubermännchen, Das Christoph Engel (Rumpelstiltskin, 1960)

Zirkuskinder Franz Antel (Circus Children, 1958; alternate title: *Solang' die Sterne glüh'n*)

Zonengrenze Kurt Stefan (Zone Border, 1959)

Zwei Städte Stuart Schulberg (Two Cities, 1949)

Zweite Heimat, Die: Chronik einer Jugend Edgar Reitz (The Second Heimat, 1992)

NOTES ON CONTRIBUTORS

Hester Baer is Assistant Professor of German, and of Film and Video Studies, at the University of Oklahoma. Her research focuses on gender and popular culture in postwar and postunification Germany. She is currently completing a book about female spectators and West German cinema in the 1950s.

Tim Bergfelder is Professor of Film Studies at the University of Southampton/United Kingdom. He is the author of *International Adventures: Popular German Cinema and European Co-Productions in the 1960s* (2005). Other publications include *The German Cinema Book* (2002), coedited with Erica Carter and Deniz Göktürk, and *The Titanic in Myth and Memory: Representations in Visual and Literary Culture* (2004), coedited with Sarah Street.

John E. Davidson is Associate Professor of Germanic Languages and Literatures, and Director of Film Studies at Ohio State University, where he teaches film, literature, and cultural theory. He is the author of *Deterritorializing the New German Cinema* (1999) and serves on the editorial board for *Studies in European Cinema*. He is currently at work on a book exploring the life and art of Ottomar Domnick, as well as a collection of essays on the politics of cinematic space in the New German Cinema and beyond.

Angelica Fenner is cross-appointed Assistant Professor in Germanic Languages and Literatures and in the Cinema Studies Program at the University of Toronto. She is co-editor with historian Eric Weitz of *Fascism and Neofascism: Critical Writings on the Radical Right in Europe* (2004), and has pubished articles and reviews on European cinema in several film anthologies as well as in *Camera Obscura, Film Quarterly, The Journal of Film Music, Quarterly Review of Film and Video*, and *German Studies Review.*

Jamey Fisher is Associate Professor of German at the University of California, Davis. He is the author of *Disciplining Germany: Youth, Reeducation, Reconstruction after the Second World War* (Wayne State, 2007) and co-editor, with Peter Uwe Hohendahl, of *Critical Theory: Current State and Future Prospects* (Berghahn, 2001). He is currently co-editing with Brad Prager, a volume in politics in recent German cinema and working on a project on globalization in German media culture since 1989.

Sabine Hake is Texas Chair of German Literature and Culture in the Department of Germanic Studies at the University of Texas at Austin. Her main research areas are Weimar culture and German film history. Her comprehensive history of German film, *German National Cinema* (2002), was published in an expanded and revised German translation as *Film in Deutschland* (2004) in the rowohlts enzyklopädie series. She is currently working on a book on modern architecture and mass society in Weimar Berlin.

Knut Hickethier is Professor of Media Studies and Dean of Language, Literary, and Media Studies at the University of Hamburg, with previous appointments at the Free University of Berlin and guest professorships in Bremen, Gießen, Siegen, Tübingen, and Marburg. From 1989 to 1994, he was a participant and codirector of the DFG-Sonderforschungsbereich "Screen Media." He has written numerous publications on the history of German film and television, including *Geschichte des deutschen Fernsehens* (1998).

Yogini Joglekar is academic director of the Mountbatten Programme in New York City. She received a Ph.D. from the Ohio State University in 2002 for her dissertation work on West German detective cinema and has taught literature and film studies. Her current research interests include German cinema and Indian cinema produced in Bollywood.

Jennifer M. Kapczynski is Assistant Professor at Washington University in St. Louis in the Department of Germanic Languages and Literatures, where she teaches courses in German and film studies. Her current book project addresses the relationship between illness and guilt in post-World War II German discourses of recovery and reconstruction.

Russel Lemmons is Professor of History and Jacksonville State University. He is the author of *Goebbels and "Der Angriff"* (1994) and is currently working on a book to be titled "Germany's Eternal Son: the Ernst Thälmann Myth, 1925–1989."

Barbara Mennel is Assistant Professor in the Department of German and Slavic Studies and in Film and Media Studies at the University of Florida, Gainesville. She is author of *The Representations of Masochism and Queer Desire* *in Film and Literature* (2007) and *Cities and Cinemas* (forthcoming 2007). Her essays on cinema have been published in *Cinema Obscura, Germanic Review, New German Critique, Quarterly Review of Film and Video, Studies in Twentieth Century Literature,* and *Women in German Yearbook.*

Johannes von Moltke teaches German and Film/Video Studies at the University of Michigan. He is the author of *No Place Like Home: Locations of Heimat in German* Cinema (2005). His work on German film and popular culture has appeared in *New German Critique, German Studies Review, Cinema Journal,* and *Screen.*

Larson Powell is Assistant Professor of German at the University of Missouri, Kansas City. He has published and presented lectures on Adorno, Lacan, Luhmann, Freud, Bachmann, Döblin, Rilke, Loerke, and Kraus, and others. His work focuses on music aesthetics (Boulez, Cage, Carter, Stockhausen, and Wolpe), comparative modernism (French, German, and Russian), and film and media theory. He recently completed a book on the technological unconscious, which examines the persistence of nature in twentieth-century German literature. A second book on music aesthetics is near completion.

Marc Silberman is Professor of German and Affiliate Professor of Theatre/ Drama and Communication Arts at the University of Wisconsin, Madison. His research focuses on the history of German cinema, GDR culture, and political theater in Germany. He edited the "Brecht Yearbook" (International Brecht Society, 1990–95), edited and translated *Brecht on Film and Radio* (2000), and authored *German Cinema: Texts in Context* (1995).

Matthias Steinle is Assistant Scholar in the Department of Media Sciences at Marburg Philipps-University. Having studied cinema, German, and history in Marburg and Paris, he received a Ph.D. in 2002. His fields of research are film and television history, media archives, documentary, and DEFA. He is the author of *Vom Feindbild zum Fremdbild. Die gegenseitige Darstellung von BRD und DDR im Dokumentarfilm* (2003).

Mary Wauchope is Associate Professor of German Studies in the Department of European Studies at San Diego State University. Her research interests include the image of Austria in film and feature films about the Holocaust. She has published articles on postwar German and Austrian film.

INDEX OF NAMES